# An Angel Called My Name

# An Angel Called My Name

*A Story of a Transformational Energy
That Lives in the Body*

By

Jyoti

*Preface by Claudio Naranjo*

DharmaGaia
Prague 1998

DharmaGaia Publishing
Uhelný trh 1
110 00 Prague 1
Czech Republic

Artistic coordinator Margaret Lindsey
Cover layout by Michal Nusko
Layout and typesetting by Bohumil Bednář
Lithographs by Calamarus
Printed by BBS, Vimperk

*Published in the Czech Republic*

Cataloging-in-Publication Data
National Library of Czech Republic

Jyoti
An Angel Called My Name: A Story of
a Transformational Energy That Lives in the Body /
by Jyoti. — Prague: DharmaGaia, 1998
ISBN 80−85905−45−0

294 * 165 * 159.9
■ spiritual knowledge — way
■ kundalini yoga — biography

# Contents

*Preface*　　xi

*Outline of Chapters*　　xvii

*Introduction*　　xxiii

1. Death As Awakening　　1

2. The Seduction　　9

3. Jumping Into the Void　　27

4. The Induction　　43

5. The Marriage of Self　　63

6. Dark Night of the Soul　　85

7. Entering the Heart　　109

8. Pregnant With God　　131

9. Circles Closing　　163

# About the style

This manuscript is written in a style that moves the reader from the right side of the brain to the left. Visionary experience occurs and the synchronicity of events directs the study so that a deeper integration of the experience can take place. It is my hope that this style can model an integrative way one can walk through an archetypal field. Though this manuscript was written some six years ago, the story is still unfolding. This style of working with the archetypes continues to provide an effective method of integration.

# About the art

*Cover art and all illustrations © 1998 by Gina Rose Halpern*

Cover Art     "Emerging Lotus", 1989, Bodhgaya, India

Chapter 1     Healing Touch "Integration", from *A Rainbow Path, Art for Meditation and Healing*, © 1987, published by Healing Through Arts

Chapter 2     (detail) "Healing Vision—Spirit Gateway", 1992, vision quest—Cascade Washington, U.S.A.

Chapter 3     (detail) "They Fed Her With Spiritual Food", 1995

Chapter 4, 5     (details) "Transformation—Accepting the Mantle", 1997

Chapter 6     "Dancing With the Shadow", 1992

Chapter 7     (detail) "Journey to the Land of Release and Rebirth", 1998 (in progress)

Chapter 8     (detail) "Journey to Muktinath", vision quest—Nepal, 1992 (from the collection of Deborah Rose)

Chapter 9     "A Rainbow Path", from *A Rainbow Path, Art for Meditation and Healing*, © 1987, published by Healing Through Arts

# Dedication

This book is dedicated to the Mother's wish for the next 7 generations. May Grace flow into their lives.

# Aknowledgements

My gratitude for the impeccable teachers who have come to guide and validate my walk, as the Mother has transformed my life into a prayer.

I want to thank Michael and Zora Vančura for their tireless hours of translation, Karla Billups, whose editing gave shape to the book, Margaret Lindsey who assisted in facilitating the arts and graphics, which revealed the story's heart, and Lumír Kolíbal, whose faith in it brought vision into form.

# *Preface*

A SHAMAN IS, BEFORE PERHAPS ALL ELSE, an inwardly guided person, and the way of the shaman—particularly when compared to that prescribed by the classical religions—is the most individual of ways.  It is obvious that the account that Jyoti gives of her story is that of a guided and original process at every step.

Though it is well known that a shaman frequently plunges into the path through an encounter with death, it has not been equally pointed out that not only personal near-death experiences can be the stimulus to spiritual awakening, but also the death of our beloved ones. Jyoti is more instance of this than I know.

Not only is visionary experience a pervasive aspect of shamanic experience, but the visionary transformation of the everyday world—which becomes a medium of transcendental meanings and in which synchronicities that are perhaps always in the structure of events become perceptible.  It can surely be said that the path of the sorcerer's apprentice traverses an enchanted world in which the seeker at every turn is in touch with the providential.

Surely the possession of a good "inner cinematographic system" is a talent that supports the shamanic phenomenon and eventually proves to be an important tool in the trade. It is not enough.  Only through sustained and inquiring attention to mental imagery does the observation of fantasy turn into a deepening of oniric content to a level rich in archetypal and intuitive content. It is clear that was the case of Jyoti at the beginning of her inner journey. There came a time for her when she had before her a beautiful being enveloped in golden light. From the time of this vision there arose first physical manifestations that are usually associated to the "Kundalini"—such as the feeling of movement towards the crown of the head. Jyoti appropriately refers to this experience as an "inner initiation," for she can see in retrospect, that it was not merely a passing experience, but one after which she experienced new things: contact with other entities—as is frequently the case in the life of shamans. Whether we interpret Jyoti's "Hooded Ones" to be truly spirits outside her or personifications of an otherwise inaccessible depth of her own mind is of secondary matter in practice: there is reason to believe that the more those inwardly manifesting spontaneous guides are treated as real, the more productive is the teaching experience that derives from the encounter.

Just as Jyoti has known the out-of-the-body experiences that are so much a part of shamanism, she has also known that painful journey "through the under world" that is even more characteristic of a shaman's way. Her story echoes the traditional pattern of ascent and descent: an ecstatic beginning that is a prelude to difficult times. She describes a sickness that even today, nine years after its onset, has not ended. It is possible to feel, however, how inseparable the sickness has been from a deep healing process. This is dramatically shown in the evolution of the first of her "strange" symptoms—the excruciating pain in an arm that turned out to be the first manifestation of a process that was to culminate weeks later (approximately in LeBoyer's presence) in a sense of being in labor and in the experience of her body as a light filled lightening rod. This is one of such experiences that may be called "archetypal"—for it lies in the structure in our organism and in that of the process of human metamorphosis.

Writing in the sixties (in the *One Quest*) I printed out that this is a time when the tasks of growth, healing and enlightment—that have been the separate province of education, medicine and religion—converge toward a system comparable to that before their differentiation, in shamanism, and have ever since been talking about our shamanistic zeitgeist structure...

Sometime in the seventies—on occasion of the Berkeley meeting of the Association for the Humanistic Psychology—I coined the expressions "New Age Shamanism" and "New Shamanism," the use of which has now become widespread in view of a vestibule explosion of the Psycho-cultural phenomenon. In spite of her Cherokee ancestry, Jyoti mostly embodies this contemporary expression of shamanism, not tied to traditional forms, and appreciative of the resources of modern psychology. (It may be parenthetically remarked that one of the unusual features in Jyoti's life is that her calling did not manifest as a withdrawal from the world, but in the desire to seek in an established institution professional training such as could be congruent with her experiences and would enable her to better assist others in the future.) Since I anticipate that the new shamans will prove to be an initial resource in our critical times of collective metamorphosis, I imagine that we will be hearing again from this gifted sorcerer's apprentice. Since Jyoti came to me in search of a magic plant seen in one of her dreams, I have come to know her as a delightfully gentle and spontaneous person with a down to earth ability for management that made her the backbone of the *Spiritual Emergence Network*. A common peculiarity of undergoing rare and dramatic physical manifestations undoubtedly connected to a spiritual process has contributed to our mutual sense of kinship.

I think that Jyoti's writing may provide some validation for people who experience strange things and may, without documents such as this, get unnecessarily frightened at their "craziness." Hopefully it may contribute in shifting a generalized attitude in our society to the "strange" so that it becomes closer to that of traditional societies in which shamanism flourishes, where psychosis and psychological suffering are seen as spiritual opportunity.

Dr. Claudio Naranjo

Berkeley
June 6, 1991

Whatever wisdom or notion I espied on my travels to odd places and unusual people, I learned to shelter, for sometimes old father Academe, like Chronos, still has an inclination to eat the children before they can become either curative or astonishing. That sort of overintellectualization obscures the patterns of the Wild Woman and the instinctual nature of women.

So, to further our kinship relationship with the instinctual nature, it assists greatly if we understand stories as though we are inside them, rather than as though they are outside of us. We enter into a story; through the door of inner hearing...

Ancient dissectionists spoke of the auditory nerve being divided into three or more pathways deep in the brain. They surmised that the ear was meant, therefore, to hear at three different levels. One pathway was said to hear the mundane conversations of the world. A second pathway apprehended learning and art. And the third pathway existed so the soul itself might hear guidance and gain knowledge while here on earth.

Listen then with soul-hearing now, for that is the mission of story.[1]

Clarissa Pinkola Estes
*Women Who Run With the Wolves*

---

[1] Estes, Clarissa Pinkola, *Women Who Run with the Wolves*, Ballantine Books, New York, 1992, pp. 25–26.

# Outline of Chapters

CHAPTER ONE

## DEATH AS AWAKENING

THIS IS A DESCRIPTION OF THE INCIDENTS surrounding my father's death. I had not yet read the reports of clinical near death experiences and was surprised to discover much later that these reports had within them much of what my personal experience had shown me. This event served as the catalyst for my spiritual awakening. I did not discuss this account with anyone until eight years later. It was at that time that the process of Kundalini—a physical, energetic phenomena—would begin to teach me at a deeper, more intense level.

CHAPTER TWO

## THE SEDUCTION

My opening to this energy, Kundalini, is a story about reclaiming a relationship with myself; of learning to trust an inner knowing and to follow it into new dimensions. This experience is not limited to a psychological change, but a physical one as well. Kundalini is seen as the personal manifestation of the active energy of Shakti, the Great Mother. Each stage of development initiates a more intimate knowing of her, and therefore of oneself. This chapter reports a time when love is new. A visionary time when a glimpse of new vistas was revealed to me. This time was full of excitement, nourishing my soul and awakening my personality to a new way of experiencing the world. Psychic phenomena (lucid dreaming, visions, parapsychological occurrences) became a daily happening—filling me with awe and great anticipation.

CHAPTER THREE

## JUMPING INTO THE VOID

As my inner relationship flourished, a time of commitment arose. My dreams and visions became emphatic. A great change would be required in my work and my stand in life. As reported by others, such a step required no less than a turning away from my old world in order to meet the new. In my case, I applied to graduate school at the Jung Institute in Switzerland and was accepted. My family and I sold our home, many of our possessions and moved to another country for the next three years. Everything synchronistically supported such a step. Little did I know how profoundly this step would come to change my life in ways I could not have imagined.

CHAPTER FOUR

## THE INDUCTION

After arriving in Switzerland I had been led, through a chain of synchronicities, to two wonderful women analysts, one of whom had studied with Jung himself. These women would be most influential in my healing process. Though I felt I was going crazy much of the time, they continued to reassure me. My visual experiences began to take on a new dimension. The honeymoon was over, and the real work had begun. My body seemed to be rebuilding, causing me considerable pain. Though I sought out medical assistance, none of the doctors could explain the phenomenon going on. The shamans speak of this process as dismemberment; a time when the body is completely pulled apart and "constituted anew by the god at the anvil" as stated by Nevill Drury in his book *The Shaman and The Magician*. At the end of that year, then and only then, did one of my analysts hand me a book by Gopi Krishna on Kundalini.

CHAPTER FIVE

## THE MARRIAGE OF SELF

There comes a time in any relationship when faith turns into commitment. I was invited to accompany some friends to Yugoslavia where the Madonna was said to be appearing to six young people in a small village called Medjugorje. It would be my great privilege to be allowed into the room with the children as Divine Mother overshadowed us all. This would be the beginning of a year of ceremony and pilgrimage. There had been no conscious intent to seek out initiation, but I certainly found myself in it. During the winter months I would be led to do my first vision quest. It would be a time of deep contemplation and active visionary experience—one which ended with a deep voice bellowing, "And now you are the ravaged bride." Several months later I was invited to the Sun Dance by a native American Indian friend of mine, Tigre, who was a Sun Dancer. The Sun Dance is a four day Indian ceremony in which each participant is physically pierced according to his vision. As I came to discover, Tigre was to pierce in the physical and I in the subtle. I had encountered archetypal energy before, but *never* with the intensity experienced that day.

CHAPTER SIX

## DARK NIGHT OF THE SOUL

Many of the mystics speak of this stage along one's spiritual path. It was a time for me when all I loved began to leave. My schooling abruptly ended, my husband of eight years sought a divorce, and my sons were angry and hurt. Worse yet, my dreams, visions and closeness to God seemed to disappear. It was a time when I could hear my soul scream endlessly with a pain that seemed to tear through the very core of my Being. Would I go crazy? Would I die? Could I die? My issues with abandonment leaped out of the world at me. My anger with God loomed darkly as I came to understand what Jesus meant when he said, "Father, why have you forsaken me?" It is in such times when one faces one's demons, that Love is forged; a Love that once forged proves unshakeable later on.

CHAPTER SEVEN

## ENTERING THE HEART

Having reached a place of deep surrender, Kundalini entered my heart chamber. I was rushed to the hospital with a possible heart attack. For the next nine hours I danced with Death. In India they speak of the chakra system—a subtle, complex system of body energy. The lower chakras are called the hell zones, and the upper chakras starting with the heart, the heavens. It was through my near death experience that I was catapulted into the upper regions. Within one month of this experience, I was to leave Texas, lose my business (a private residential program for abused girls) and move to California where I would begin my work with the Spiritual Emergence Network. In addition, my boys would decide to remain in Texas leaving me on my own alone for the first time in my life.

In other words, my entire identity would shift! No sooner do such shifts occur than the new begins to appear. In his book, *The Shaman And the Magician*, Nevill Drury writes, "The shaman's gift of magical sight and communication are born of heaven and not of earth. Occasionally, in fact, the shaman demonstrates his ongoing relationship with the heavenly domain by taking spirit wives from that dimension. The Buryats believe that the offspring born by such unions are semi-divine." In Irina Tweedie's book, *Daughter of Fire*, her Teacher says, "Man, do prepare yourself for the last journey; Do prepare yourself in time. When your Beloved will call you, will there be time to prepare? When your Beloved comes to fetch you, you cannot stay; You cannot say: wait till I am ready..." And so in this chapter I speak of that relationship with my Beloved. Through these encounters my visions showed a body of Light standing up inside me. The physical manifestations were at times difficult, with bodily convulsions, headaches and extreme fatigue a constant companion. My bodyworker said it was like working on moving sand. My body had gone through a complete restructuring once again. I was later to understand that all this too was preparation for the journey to come.

CHAPTER EIGHT

## PREGNANT WITH GOD

In August of 1988 I was led through my dreams to take a trip to Peru. My intention was to treat this journey as a vision quest— a time of inner reflection and rite of passage into a new phase of one's life. A few days after returning to my home, I went through an intense infusion of energy that lasted four hours. At the end of that time, my belly had extended, making me look five to six months pregnant. This chapter will discuss psyche's map that is being revealed in correlation with a deep inner healing process. I have been led to some eastern literature which describes this process as kumbhaka—a gathering of prana in ones center, or hara. In the beginning my fears ran rampant. My doubts and shadow pieces screamed, "Enough!!!" I later moved into a period of experiencing a Zen stillness—a quieting of the mind. At that point the Mind begins to be absorbed into the Heart. For in the end the Mind must die and this too is a process. Having moved into a period of celibacy, the process continued to unfold. I seemed to be learning the art of holding the formless and the uncertainty of the unknown.

CHAPTER NINE

## CIRCLES CLOSING

Stages of samadhi began to unfold, forcing deeper layers of surrender. At this time deep changes in my physiology seemed to occur effecting the nervous system, neurological system and immune system. Each step led to a more intimate relationship with the Intelligence involved in evolutionary processes and a quieting of the system. Consciousness began to reveal itself in an ever expanding manner. As the sixth chakra cleared and began to stabilize, the seventh began to feel movement. I traveled to India with my teacher Anandi Ma to study with Dhyanyogi, a 115 year old saint and sage, a sat guru of the Kundalini Maha Yoga path. The lessons there brought closure to one part of the process and announced events to come as it initiated me into yet another level of this unfoldment.

# Introduction

## THE KUNDALINI ENERGY

IN THE PREFACE TO SWAMI MUKTANANDA'S BOOK, *Kundalini, The Secret of Life*, Swami Prajnananda presents a significant story to help in our quest to understand the Kundalini energy:

Before creation of the world only God existed. He got bored being alone. So with His power He created the world from Himself, so that He could play and have some fun. But the beings He created knew who they were and how to merge back into their source. So, not being interested in the works, they all returned to God in heaven who, therefore, was not able to enjoy His game. Finally, He called a meeting of the other gods whom He had created to help Him run His creation. They suggested that the gates of heaven be closed and the key be hidden. The idea was excellent, but they were uncertain where to hide the key. There were many suggestions but none of them seemed very good, as human beings were very clever and were sure to find the key. Someone suggested the bottom of the Pacific Ocean, another the top of the Himalaya mountain, and a third suggested the moon, a very distant place that men could not possibly reach. Everyone became excited and God sat in meditation to see the future. He shook His head and said, "None of our plans will work. I see men exploring every nook and corner of the universe. Not only will they conquer the Himalayas and swim to the bottom of the ocean, but they will also land on the moon, take a close look at the planets and try to go to other universes through black holes."

Everyone became silent. Then, suddenly, God said, "I've got it! I know one place where man will never look for the key to heaven. And that place is within his own self, right in the center of his body. He will go millions of miles into space, but he will never go two steps within himself to explore his own inner being." This seemed so true that the gods unanimously agreed to it. And God has had great fun watching man's search for happiness ever since.

Certainly inherent in the human condition is a deep yearning to find the key to our selves.

Muktananda found this key to happiness. From his own experience he says that what is outside is also inside. The whole universe, all knowledge, the answers to the mysteries of human existence and true happiness all lie inside man and become available to him by the awakening of Kundalini, the divine Mother.[2]

Kundalini is described by Gopi Krishna as the mechanism in the body that brings about the transmutation of the species.[3] Russell Park in his dissertation on Spiritual Emergencies describes Kundalini in the following way:

The translation of the East Indian word *kundalini* which comes from the Sanskrit *kundala*, means "coiled" (Rama in White, 1979, p. 27), "life force" (Madhusudandasji, 1975, p. 1), or "she who is coiled" (Sannella, 1987, p. 8) and is often spoken of in conjunction with the concept and term *shakti*, from the root word *shak*, "to have power or to be able" (Rama, 1979, p. 27). Shakti is the feminine force, the great mother, the creative, dynamic aspect of the two primary polarities in the universe. Shakti is responsible for all manifest form; physical matter, mind, and life itself. The other primary polarity, the masculine pole is called Shiva. Shiva's domain is the unmanifest, static quality of consciousness which

---

[2] Muktananda, *Kundalini, The Secret Of Life*, SYDA Bookstore, Box 605, South Fallsburg, N. Y. 12779, pp. 9–10.

[3] Krishna, Gopi, *The Awakening of Kundalini*, E. P. Dutton, New York, 1975, p. 110.

contains the potential of matter and energy, both of which arise from consciousness (p. 54).

Kundalini is said to be consciousness itself, and will move up the spinal column, awakening the chakras and removing blockages and impurities within the physical and psychological make up of an individual. It is this movement of consciousness and the resulting interactions with "impurities" that results in the physical, emotional, or mental symptoms. Upon "awakening" the Kundalini, symptoms are typically very individualized... (p. 18)[4]

In East Indian mythology, Shakti is depicted as a serpent coiled 3 1/2 times at the base of the spine. In every one of us this energy sits dormant until our consciousness evolves to the stage of awakening to the reality of our Eternal Being. At this point, the Kundalini becomes active beginning a journey that presents many tests and initiations. Her final goal is to be reunited with the masculine side of her nature, her Beloved, Shiva. Shakti must be able to pierce the veil of Maya, of illusion, in order for this sacred union, the divine marriage to take place.

In our Christian mythology, many of our saints underwent bodily transformations with manifestations similar to those described in the Hindu tradition in the discussion of Kundalini energy. Saint Theresa of Avila, for example, describes some of this process in her autobiography.[5] She underwent periods of paralysis, visions, ecstatic rapture, levitation, trance states, psychological upheavals, and a time when she was pronounced dead only to be revived several days later.

We in the West need to explore how other cultures explain the phenomena associated with Kundalini. In the Spring of 1990, the Spiritual Emergence Network, held a conference in California to do just that. Over forty presenters discussed how transformative energies or Kundalini-like phenomena were defined by their

---

[4] Park, Russell D., *Spiritual Emergencies: A Quantitative and Descriptive Examination with an Emphasis on Kundalini and the Role of Ego*, Institute of Transpersonal Psychology, Menlo Park, Ca., 1991.

[5] St. Teresa, *The Life of Teresa of Jesus*, The Autobiography of St. Teresa of Avila, Doubleday, New York, 1960.

cultures or in their mythologies. Presentors included American Indians, Hindus, Buddhists, Hawaiian kahunas, and people from many other cultural traditions. Over 500 people from all walks of life—housewives, doctors, judges, psychologists, journalists, artists, bodyworkers and others—came from around the globe. Gopi Krishna said that we would experience a collective Kundalini awakening toward the end of this millennium. I believe that *this* is what the conference participants had begun to witness, and many of us through actual experience. Ken Carey's most recent book, *Starseed, The Third Millennium* speaks to such an awakening: "For you inhabiting the last days of the human species' infancy, awakening is proceeding by stages, subsequent layers of illusion falling away one after another like the peeling layers of an onion. The awakening that is most immediate and that will link you to the multiple levels of Eternal Being occurs now as you feel interconnectivity with the earth and the life force that engenders her biology."[6]

Muktananda mentions several ways in which the Kundalini can be awakened.

> She can be aroused through intense devotion to God, through repetition of mantra, or an aspirant can even experience a spontaneous awakening due to the merit accumulated from sadhana [*spiritual path*] performed in past births. Different modes of awakening the Kundalini have been described in the scriptures. However, the easiest and best method is through Shaktipat from the Guru, when the Guru directly transmits his/her own divine Shakti into the disciple.[7]

## THE JOURNEY BEGINS

My own personal Kundalini awakening was spontaneous. When I look back over my life, I remember times Shakti moved within

---

[6] Karey, Ken, *Starseed, The Third Millennium*, Harper San Francisco, 1991, p. 145.

[7] Muktananda, *Kundalini, The Secret of Life*.

my system, times when the Divine kissed me like a warm summer breeze through visionary and mystical experiences. Some were blissful, while others were intense and frightening. The most frightening aspect was that I had no one to talk to about these occurrences. After the birth of my second son, my body began to shake uncontrollably and the nurses weren't sure what to do. It was later I would discover that Kundalini is often activated by the birthing process. When I look back at the incredible journey I have embarked upon, the openings to new awareness, the psychological healing, and the maturity both emotionally and spiritually that has evolved, I'm amazed. And it all occurred in spite of myself.

I didn't consciously set out to explore the experiences of Kundalini. Until I became aware of the spiritual process that was to reshape my reality, my life would have been considered "normal" by our Western standards—middle-class American through and through. Though my childhood was uneventful there was always a sense of *the Divine* afoot. I learned early in life, however, that to speak of psychic phenomenon was unacceptable; it was called "crazy," or I was accused of "exaggerating." Life was not to be experienced as a mystery, but rather as a cognitive approach toward desired goals. The questions produced by a child's mind were quieted unless socially acceptable. Anything outside that paradigm proved embarrassing. It was punished accordingly.

It was, however, that impeccable need to question that initiated my quest. It first took me into eduacation as a teacher. But my questioning of our educational system during the time of integration in the South only fueled my frustration with a system that appeared to have lost its soul. The system at large seemed to have become an entity that was reactive in nature and political in scope. The goal of learning through individual motivation got lost in our response to live out of our fears, and systems were born that elicited control—objectiving the personal. The original goal of the movement to bring fair and equal care to all our children got lost. The children were caught in the middle and in actuality paid the price for our unconsciousness. The results are blatant in our society today as observed in the high numbers of teenage pregnancy, drug abuse and violent gangs. During my first year as a teacher I was put on notice many times that I would be transfered to another school as part of the city wide plan. I was working in an elementary school helping to develop one of the first kindergartens in public school. The children in my class were having their first experience outside the home and were trying to deal with their own adjustment problems such moments in life provoke. In a normal and healthy environment such transitions are difficult, but add the constant threat of teacher change and political unrest, and a normal developmental time becomes traumatic. The system's response to their emotional needs was not included in the plan. They just became numbers on charts—objects shuffled to meet required ratio. My search for a system which was motivated to evolve out of a conscious response to the *individual* within that system led me into the field of psychology. In fact, my post graduate studies were aimed at exploring different models that emphasized just that. We couldn't continue to explore just the container of such programs. We had to get to know those contained within the system. In the field of psychology, I began working professionally with abused and neglected children. I would soon come to realize that these students of life were my most valued teachers, for they taught me how to identify and heal my abused child within. Even though their stories spoke of inhumane treatment beyond comprehension, there was a spirit deep within each child that wanted to survive— and did. It was through their experiences and instruction I began to explore the dark side of human nature, collectively and personally.

The American Indians say there are three kinds of warriors: those who break the ice, those who carry the dream, and those who fight the demons. The paradox may be that the clue to understanding ourselves as a people lies within the locked wards and jails of our culture. For within those walls lay our "sensitive ones," the warriors whose lot it is to fight our collective "demons."

Through such an understanding I began to struggle with my own dark side; not an easy task, but a necessary one. Did I set out to do just that? No, but my work began to make me question. It was in that questioning that this story began to unfold. I was sent into a "riotous" situation as the acting superintendent of an institution for "dependent and neglected children." Institutions such as this had served as orphanages in the past. However, due to birth control, foster care, and legalized abortions, these facilities had become a "dumping ground" for the courts and legal system. Plea bargaining resulted in a mixture of abandoned, runaway, or psychotic children, aging from six to eighteen years old. These children had broken the law. Their offenses ranged from runaway to felony. All of them had been neglected or abused in some way. Their case histories revealed inhumane treatments of sexual and physical abuse to such degrees that one wondered how they had survived. Placing children with such wide ranges of disturbance resulted in total chaos; with children arming themselves and often "raiding the village," so to speak.

After two years of very intense work and restructuring, the facility had acquired a new face, and geared towards treatment, *based on loving* instead of locking them up. Just as the students were beginning to feel good about their program, and about themselves, the state decided to sell the institution to the mental health system. This proved devastating. I stood at my office window one night near dusk asking, "What is this all for anyway?"

An inner voice said, "You are throwing your stone into the wrong pond. You must now climb the ladder within your own labyrinth to reach the ocean of the collective. Then when you throw your stone it has the possibility of bringing change. For if enough individuals do likewise, a wave will splash out of this pool, spilling over your existing reality, and a new way of being will unfold."

I had learned previously to listen to and trust that "inner voice." I contemplated the meaning of "climb the ladder within your own labyrinth" and realized that as long as I took my energy to shape things outside myself without first looking within, the outcome would not be sustaining. The collective could not undergo transformation until enough of us individually had made the journey.

Little did I know when all this began that what I was truly in search for was reconnecting with my own deep femininity. My culture held in high esteem all the traits needed to survive in a masculine oriented society—analytical skills, focus, achievement. In other words, the *doing* side of our nature was over stressed and the *being* side of ourselves was ridiculed and misunderstood. In his book *Transformation* Robert Johnson describes three levels of consciousness: simple, complex and enlightened. Simple consciousness was more the standard for mankind's awareness in primitive times and is related to the Garden of Eden. This was a time of acting instinctually and living a two dimensional awareness. Complex consciousness is the usual state of educated Western man and is characterized by a time of worrying and states of anxiety. He relates this stage to Hamlet.

> To understand Hamlet is to gain invaluable insight into the emptiness and loneliness of modern existential life. Hamlet is three-dimensional man: he has no roots in the instinctive world and his head is not yet in the heavens, where he can gain the nourishment of enlightenment. He is the forerunner of a new man whose characteristics will be the healing of the paradox of masculine and feminine, doing and being. Lao-tse, the Chinese sage, commented on this: "He who understands the masculine and keeps to the feminine shall become the whole world's channel. Eternal virtue shall not depart from him and he shall return to the state of an infant."[8]

Johnson goes on to say:

> It is characteristic of complex man, caught between functioning by instinct and acting by enlightenment, that he often destroys everything feminine within his grasp.[9]

---

[8] Johnson, Robert A., *Transformation: Understanding the Three Levels of Masculine Consciousness*, Harper San Francisco, 1991, p. 42.
[9] Johnson, Robert, ibid, p. 43.

If we take a moment to look at what's happening on our planet today, we can easily see what Johnson has suggested. I had to be willing to go into the chaos while being nurtured by the heavens, or the enlightened realms. The doing and the being had to become one action. Our task then is to return to the Garden and know we are there. It is Psyche (the feminine) that will guide us there. If I have no relationship to her then I am lost. When we look back at history, or even biologically, we see that it is woman that births our people and therefore our evolution. It is with this in mind that we must each approach and enter into our new consciousness through the doorway of the feminine. We must realize we have been in a deep denial that is poisoning our air and waters, killing endangered species at an alarming rate and threatening nuclear destruction of our Mother Earth. When we no longer need to rape our earth, we will no longer need to rape our women and children who inhabit her.

I had been married to a man for eight years and bore two children by him. After four years of a rather happy relationship, he decided he would get a vasectomy. The man I loved and knew did not return. It would be many years later that a family member would share with me the family secret of physical and emotional abuse that had been inflicted upon my husband during his childhood years. The surgery had served as the vehicle that reopened pandora's box. He had a second personality which we called Ralph. When Ralph was "out" I was in trouble! At first, it was mostly emotionally abusive, but with time it deterioated until he became a physical threat as well. My self esteem was so low I didn't know where to turn. My shame overshadowed everything, making it hard to ask for help. There were times when he would become violent and my friends would lock the door, afraid to get involved, afraid they might get hurt. If you called the law, there was little they would do in a family dispute. He refused to get counseling on an ongoing basis. He did agree to visit a psychiatrist once. We went several times, after which the doctor suggested I seek divorce. This was in the seventy's and in the south where there were no laws or social support for women in these situations. I'm not sure we've come much further today. I was watching a show on abuse last year, 1990, and at the end of the telecast they reported that six times the number of people who died from AIDS in this country last year were women beaten to death. Beaten to death! What does that say about our culture, about our very values?

I as a woman caught in that web stood frightened and alone one spring shaking with fear and torn inside about what to do. I only knew one thing. I didn't want my two boys to grow up in this kind of environment. Something inside screamed, "No more!" He had told me that if I tried to leave he would blow my head off. I knew that day that I was already dead living like this, so there was nothing for me to loose except my soul and the souls of my children. That decision changed my life. It wasn't easy, for there weren't many people who would talk with me. The denial was so thick that even my family said things like, "If you didn't work and would stay home, your marriage would work out." When I talked with my husband's family and shared my real concern for his mental health, his mother said to me that such things happen and if I would give it more time it would pass. Everyone and everything around me seemed to support the craziness of abuse rather than the healthiness of "right caring." I wonder what would happen on this planet if enough of us said, "No more!" In stepping away from abuse as a collective, would we step toward our healing, toward our power rather than our abuse of power? The answer is obvious, so what keeps us from it?

My father's death, which I describe in detail in Chapter One, had somehow opened something in me which sought health and well being. At some level, I had claimed my right to be, and in so doing, the forces that shape us began to work in my life. At first, I was unconscious about such things, and merely called it following my intuition. My life changed dramatically—divorce, career changes, single parent, graduate school. No sooner had my basic life style been altered than the inner workings of the mystical realms began to appear. Still it would be many years before the Kundalini would manifest in more obvious ways. Shakti would heal me of false images of myself and help me integrate the broken off pieces of my personality. The work is difficult at times, but always moves you into more empowering and life enhancing spaces. I've come a long way, and it took the Divine Mother to show me the direction. I wasn't sure where I was going, I just knew I wanted to be whole—to stand in my power from that place of wholeness. What did that mean? I wasn't sure. I just know that when times got hard and felt unbearable, I would meditate on an image of my self standing in wholeness. When times got difficult and I wanted to quit, I would remind myself that I wanted my boys to inherit my healing, not my wound.

Kundalini is a process in which Spirit fuses with matter. A process in which the individual is taken on a journey into the Divine through the body. After the fire within (Kundalini) purges and purifies the vessel (the body and mind), the divine elixir (samadhi states) will then cool the form before Divine Being incarnates within it. This process, defined in detail in the following chapters, is what this book is about. I am not writing this account to label or to be labeled. I am not here to declare myself anything other than what I am—an ordinary woman who is striving to integrate both heaven and earth, both father and mother God, into her waking reality. It was through the acceptance of both realms that my healing occurred. When these two realms meet, anything is possible. One such incident was reported by Peggy Tabor Millin. She wrote in *Mary's Way* about the apparitions of the Virgin Mary that appeared to six young people in Medjugorje, Yugoslavia, beginning in 1981 and which is continuing to this day:

> In early Judaeo-Christian history, miracles of this sort abounded. Many Biblical stories are about people who have had visitations from angels, dreamed transformative dreams, heard God's voice, or experienced foreknowledge of events. Even people who are very literal in their belief of Biblical stories, however, have difficulty accepting that angels, visions, and other miracles can

happen today to ordinary people. We have no difficulty accepting electricity in our homes, although few of us can explain or even conceive of how it works. Radio waves filled the air before radios were present to receive them. At any point in history, most of us believe that our present science is infallible and that we actually can explain the workings of the universe; at the same time we laugh at the misconceptions of the science of the past. The true scientist, however, is engaged in journeying into the mystery of the unknown rather than in proving that which is believed to be true, *is* true... We, however, remain attached to our philosophy of what is "real."[10] [*That very point of attachment is usually where our work begins.*]

And so my journey continued to unfold. I discovered that Shakti's path is not just one of vertical ascension, but rather forms a spiral. In my experience Shakti found her way up my spinal column, opening each chakra, purging issues accumulated at each center, and then went over the top of my head, falling down into the third eye, the throat and filling the "golden hara," located in the belly region. (In Chapter Eight I will detail more the occurrences in the golden hara [or the manifestation of what some have called my "Buddha belly"].) In my visions I have seen that it will culminate when this new body that has been gestating is ejected out of the heart region to encase my physical form.

Russell Park explains Kundalini in relationship to the chakra system:

> Kundalini is seen as the personal manifestation of the active energy of Shakti which is called *prana*—the universal life force in the yogic traditions. [*Prana, as described by Gopi Krishna, is the* intelligent *force behind all chemical actions and reactions of a bio-logical organism.*][11] "Kundalini is the static support of the entire body and all of its pranic or energy forces" (Rama, 1979, p. 29).
>
> Prana is the subtle electric energy which comes from the breath and travels through subtle nerves known as *nadis*. Nadis connect

---

10  Millin, Peggy Tabor, *Mary's Way*, Celestial Arts, Berkeley, Ca., 1991, p. 33.
11  Krishna, Gopi, *The Awakening of Kundalini*, E. P. Dutton, New York, 1975.

the body and mind through the *meridians*, common to the Chinese and Japanese medical system of acupuncture, and are organized around common centers known as *chakras*, meaning "wheels." Traditionally, there are six or seven chakras, depending upon which Indian system you consult.  Chakras are located along the spinal column from the base of the spine to six inches over the crown of the head.  Chakras are not physical centers, but rather vortexes or psychospiritual energy circles [*centers*], that maintain, organize, and are responsible for the quality of consciousness.

In some forms of the Indian spiritual practices of yoga there is an intent to awaken the latent potential of Kundalini.  Upon awakening, the unleashed energy of Kundalini begins an ascent up the subtle energy channels toward the chakras removing blockages and impurities while impacting, or raising, the consciousness of the organism...[12]

Bonnie Greenwell reviews the broad symptomatology that accompanies this process.

The manifestations of the movement of consciousness is primarily perceived as a phenomena of energy.  The classic symptom of Kundalini awakening is a energetic vibration or pressure up the spinal column associated with flashes of light, visions, spasms, or shaking.  There maybe extreme variations in the felt-sense of body temperature, eating habits, sexual desires, and emotional stability.  There may be involuntary sounds, movements, postures (asanas) or hand positions (mudras).  Physical pain may be experienced in various parts of the body, usually without an organic basis, with irregularity in location, frequency, duration and severity.  There is often an associated emotional component including waves of depression or ecstasy, orgasmic rapture, anxiety, or overwhelming feelings of pending death or insanity.[13]

I don't think I had ever pondered the question whether consciousness forms the body or whether the body takes form

---

[12]  Park, Dissertation, p. 55, 1991.
[13]  Greenwell, Bonnie, *Energies of Transformation*, Shakti River Press, Cupertino, Ca., 1990.

around consciousness. As I've watched my body change shapes during these past years, I have come to understand that the later is what prevails. An example can be easily observed in reviewing man's development physically during the caveman era. At one point man was bent over and could not think cognitively. Amongst him a new species began to appear: he stood straight and could count. The tribe was frightened. Little did they know that they were standing side by side with their evolved "self." So it is today. A new species of human is standing amongst us. Will we again meet this new "self" with fear?

## THE STORY STIRS

I have learned a new meaning of the word surrender and the depths of letting go that must accompany deep transformative states. In addition, a great trust in the Divine Intelligence behind these processes has developed, in ways I will go into later, leaving in me an unshakable core of faith and love in the Mystery. One realizes after a while that you have entered the Divine Play and are consciously participating in its unfoldment. Though the path has been difficult at times, the healing has been so profound that gratitude wells up in me when I speak of it.

This story is about reclaiming a relationship with myself; of learning to trust an inner knowing and to follow it into new dimensions. This experience is not limited to a psychological change, but a physical one as well. Let me use the metaphor of a train going down the track, stopping at each station. With each stop there is an emptying and a refilling, but the momentum is geared toward its final destination. Each chapter highlights the stations Kundalini took me to during my journey; each serving as a mile marker. I have written in narrative form so as to share the unfoldment of this experience, describing my reactions with the deductions and conclusions they evoked. It is my hope that such an open review will help you recognize similar occurrences that may become active in your process. Just knowing what is happening can give you the courage to let go and surrender into it.

I have often wished to read material about Kundalini as written, perceived and experienced by a woman. Unfortunately, there is very little available. It is for this reason many have asked me to share my story. Kundalini is a very individualized inner process of healing, therefore, my experience is only one possible course of many.

It is time for the storytellers to speak. Through such sharing, we can begin to glimpse the new reality birthing itself into today's times. In olden days, storytellers roamed the countryside sharing parables that served to arouse the imagination of others, speaking of happenings collectively experienced. It is my belief each of us has a story living within—waiting for its time to awaken.

When the story stirs, it demands to speak; asking only to be heard. If one hears the call and answers, a Mystery begins to reveal itself. You follow the clues, discovering as you go. You must embark empty handed, expecting no outcome. Following such a path will test your faith and reform your perception. The story is never-ending, with new chapters each step of the way.

This is a story that narrates a process of healing. One that is not told to enliven the superhuman in us, but rather one told as a reminder of the need to return to our true nature, to give reverence to the divine birthright inherent in each of us. Alan Richardson in the *Priestess* describes this journey:

> In effect she had had none of the classic journeys through madness, going through the three stages identified by Joseph Campbell as, first, *Separation*, whereby the whole personality falls apart. In many Eastern systems of occult training the guru deliberately humiliates his disciple, constantly and in public, with the intention of smashing the hapless wretch's ego in order to begin again anew. In the West, however, life itself is the guru. Then there is *Initiation*, whereby a piece of personal courage or achievement enables the individual to reconstruct his personality along better and more flexible lines. And finally comes the stage

of *Return*, when this newly made heroine goes back to the very Source itself.

More significantly Richardson goes on to say:

> The stages of development into the new identity may not be as clearly marked out as I have indicated, but they usually follow this pattern: crisis, interlude of apathy and dejection, followed by visions and dreams of death, possibly by drowning, the hearing of a command to take up a new identity, and finally a "call" to reveal this new identity and the mission that accompanies it to the whole world.[14]

From 1987 to 1990, I served as the coordinator of the Spiritual Emergence Network (SEN), an international organization that helps individuals undergoing transformative spiritual experiences, sometimes in the form of a crisis. Often these people fear for their sanity and are confused, isolated, and misunderstood by their families. Unfortunately, the traditional mental health system often labels these people with "pathological" deficiencies, medicates them, or worse, locks them up in mental health wards.

At SEN, we connect our callers with holistic or transpersonally oriented therapists in their area so that they can get support for such a process and begin to integrate their experiences, resuming normal, often more healthy lives. One fourth of our callers are experiencing some type of transformative process through the body. I wonder if the time of Krishna's "collective Kundalini awakening" is now upon us. I wonder if enough of us individually have "climbed the ladder within" to bring about this collective awakening that will reshape and ultimately transform this dream we call reality.

Kundalini would appear to be the key to the transformation of the human species to its highest level of consciousness. As Gopi Krishna summarizes:

---

[14] Richardson, Alan, *Priestess, The Life and Magic of Dion Fortune*, The Aquarian Press, 1987, pp. 50−51.

The existence of a consciousness of the transcendental type at the end of a certain period, the inevitable result of the awakening of Kundalini in all successful cases, provides incontrovertible evidence for the fact that the regenerative force at work in the body is at the very beginning aware of the ultimate pattern to which it has to conform by means of the remodeling biological processes set afoot.

The existence of an empirically demonstrable power in the system not only fully aware of all the perplexing psycho-physical intricacies of the organism, but also capable of reshaping it to a far higher pitch of organic and functional activity so as to bring it in harmony with the demands of a higher state of consciousness can have only one meaning: that the evolutionary force in man is carrying him towards an already known, and predetermined, state of sublimity of which humanity has no inkling save that provided by the religious concepts of prophets and visionaries.

The inquiry is not to be approached in a spirit of conquest or arrogance with the intent to achieve victory over a force of nature, which has characterized man's approach to the problems of the material world, but rather with humility, in a spirit of utter surrender to Divine Will and absolute dependence on Divine Mercy, in the same frame of mind one would approach the flaming sun.[15]

---

[15] Krishna, Gopi, *Kundalini, The Evolutionary Energy in Man.* Shambhala Publications, Inc., Boulder, Colorado, 1971, p. 249

# CHAPTER ONE

# Death As Awakening

M Y FATHER IS DYING AFTER a sixteen month battle with cancer. For the last three days, he has been saying "uh-uh!," as if, "No, I'm not ready."

Several months before, my mom was bringing my father home from the hospital. As they entered the car, he said, "Do you see anyone in the back seat?"

"No, why?"

"There is someone there," he answered. "I can't tell if it's a man or a woman, but there is someone there."

Mom called later and told me about the incident. I had a friend who was a nurse on a terminal ward and she had shared with me that many of her patients had reported such a "visitor" when no one had been seen. This seemed a natural part of the dying process.

As time went on, this stranger became an important figure to my father, particularly in his last days. When he would awake, he would seem frightened until he could locate the stranger, and then much calm would fall across his face. He asked me once if I could see him. "No," I replied, "he's someone special just for you."

Once he awoke and asked Mom if she had seen heaven.

"No, but tell me about it."

He told her he had been to heaven, and there were many houses there, all with a crucifix on the front. He had been taken to his house. It had a living room and a bedroom. He said there wasn't any kitchen or bathroom, and then laughed and said, "But I guess you don't need to eat or shit in heaven."

I had been at the hospital three days. Each day the doctors said would be his last, but still he hung on. They also said he would lose consciousness, but he never did. He just changed consciousness. His brother had come the day before, and when he walked in, Dad, though weak, raised up in bed as if shocked. I had the distinct feeling that he was viewing a scene that marked his final hours, and he knew that they had begun. He just kept telling me he wanted to go home.

Mother, attended by her sisters, was in the hallway outside his hospital room. My uncle and brother were in his room with me. Our nurse stood in the far right corner. I had known somehow that I would be with him during the "change," and had asked her to give me a sign when he was going, so I could prepare myself emotionally. I had never been with anyone as he died. I was scared and apprehensive.

The situation unfolded in a naturally accepting and caring way. I had fallen asleep on the couch next to his bed, but around 9:00 on the morning of November 10, 1974, something woke me. As I woke, I was summoned by my father to his bed, but he used no words. All that transpired between us for the next few moments was exchanged telepathically. I felt as if we were surrounded by a cocoon of energy within which everything moved naturally. All that was happening seemed calming in some deep place within myself.

His eyes met mine. I had never experienced such concentration. His gaze seemed to create a lifeline from his eyes to mine. He used this lifeline to hold on until he had completed his final act. The intensity of his eyes was so great that for days after his death, I could not escape his gaze. It was at that moment that I knew we were not just father and daughter, but two souls exchanging and sharing something more.

He told me nonverbally that he was afraid. I responded, "I know, Dad. I'm afraid too. But let's be honest. The old body isn't what it used to be, and to continue hanging on would only cause you and the family more pain."

He conveyed reassuringly, "I know you are right, but I will need to use some of your courage."

My courage! What could he mean? This man had always seemed to display courage in all that he did. How could I add to that? Besides, I was the girl child. He had always turned to my brother in the past. I mean in the South that's just the way it's done. Girls listen, boys do. I had always bucked that system-questioning, wanting to know why. Though my struggle brought many nights restricted to my room to "think over my behavior," no real answer had ever been offered. Now, here I stood, communicating with my father telepathically with him asking me for courage! Everything seemed upside down, yet in its right order.

I responded, "Sure, I'll help, but I don't know what to do. I've never done this before, so you will have to tell me what you need."

He then sent me to get mother, but indicated that I should hurry back for he needed my eye contact to finish what he had to do. I told Mom that Dad needed her and took her to the left side of his bed. He raised up, and with his last verbal words, said, "I love you, Vada, and I always will." He kissed her on the cheek and signaled me to take her back into the hall quickly. Several of her sisters gathered around her, comforting her. He knew the depth of her sadness and took the precautions that would provide support and care for her, something he had done for twenty-six years.

When I returned, his gaze became even more intense, and for a moment, it was as if time stopped. I sensed a feeling of empathy and understanding that I had never known before. We were one in thought; it was a feeling of complete harmony.

Dad said to me that it was time to borrow some of my courage. He told me to hug him around his middle, but I knew that if I did this, he would die. My body went stiff. My heart seemed to stop. Could I do this? Did I have enough courage? Many questions seemed to spin through my mind, yet his eyes were relentless in their appeal. For a few more minutes, I just loved him, appreciated him. Then I took a deep breath, leaned down and hugged him around the middle. As I did, I glanced up at the nurse. She nodded to me. It had begun.

He suddenly jerked his head, stared up at the ceiling, and withdrew into a fetal position. My first thoughts were, "Oh, my God, what have I done? Where have you gone?" His face looked as if he had seen something horrifying. The next moment, it was as if someone called his name—he again looked up. At that moment, I suddenly felt myself both sitting on his bed and hovering above this scene, standing with my father gazing at a most magnificent Light. He said, "Aaah!" I looked down at him in the bed as if I were watching a movie. Yet, at the same time I had the great privilege of watching my father walk into this Light. When he disappeared into the Light, I returned to one consciousness as an aura of great peace seemed to prevail. Suddenly, Dad's body sat up in bed, his jaws clenched as his eyes looked directly into mine, and then he went limp against the pillow. Somehow, I knew that I had just witnessed the reaction of his body to his "death"—the point at which his soul withdrew and went into that beautiful Light.

The next days were full of preparing for the funeral. His preacher had been out of town and knew nothing of these events leading up to his death. I entered the funeral home numb, feeling somehow in a state of suspension. The preacher told the story of a young boy who was going to visit his grandmother for the first time. She had sent a black man in a carriage to escort him safely. At first, he had been afraid of the stranger, but later realized that this stranger was a guide to ensure his safe passage.

Dad's "stranger" popped into my mind. How could this man who wasn't even with Dad during his final hours have known what he had seen and experienced? Why was he picking *these* metaphors? Was it just a coincidence? The surrealistic nature of these happenings seemed to spin me around. Though one part of me seemed to know and understand such phenomena as natural, the rest of me was in a state of pure conflict and confusion. I wanted desperately to share what was happening, but had no way to articulate. (Carl Jung described genuine synchronistic phenomenon in connection with archetypal processes in the unconscious. "It is a term coined by Jung to designate the meaningful coincidence or equivalence of a psychic and a physical state or event which have no causal relationship to one another or of similar or identical thoughts, dreams, etc. occurring at the same time in different places.")[16] The air seemed to be impregnated with such happenings. Each example the preacher used seemed directly related to Dad's death experience. Just about the time I was able to rationalize some of it away, another incident would happen; pulling the rug out from under me. I could only sit frozen, as if caught up in something much more than what appeared to be. Yet, beyond all the questions and confusion, I knew that Dad was safely home.

The preacher then went on to quote a passage from the Bible, John 14: 1−3:

"Let not your heart be troubled: ye believe in God, believe also in me. In my Father's house are many mansions: if it were not so, I would have told you. I go to prepare a place for you, I will come again, and receive you unto myself; that where I am, there ye may be also."[17]

Dad's view of heaven spoken through this preacher's mouth! I knew somehow it was Dad letting us know he had made the voyage safely. Not only was he safe, but he had given me a gift. I would never again view death as a finality.

That night I could not sleep. I felt that my father would appear, materialize somehow. I just couldn't absorb any more. I moved from the bedroom into the den to lie down on the couch. About an hour later, my three-year-old son came into the room and said he

---

[16] Jung, C. G., *Memories, Dreams, Reflections*, Vintage Books, New York, 1965. p. 400.

[17] *The Holy Bible*, King James Version, Collins World, Great Britain.

wanted to sleep with me. When I asked him what was wrong, he said, "I can't sleep. Pop's [his name for my father] keeps moving his shoes, and it keeps me awake." Kirk went on to describe how he saw Dad in his closet, sorting through his shoes. Something in me knew that Dad had come to say goodbye and remind me that he was always close. His appearance also underscored an awareness of the continuation that our souls experience.

I share these situations to amplify the synchronicity of events that followed his death—a death that shook the foundations of my world as I had known it, impregnating a new reality into the depths of my consciousness. If death was not as I had been told, what other generally accepted beliefs would prove to be untrue?

These events took many years to process and integrate. The experience had shown me our physical life is continuously revolving, while something else within us goes on, always moving toward something. I didn't know what the something was or where *it* was taking me. These thoughts would later evoke questions that would stir my soul and open me to a compulsion—a yearning to be with God and know who I am in such union.

I could not talk to anyone about them for fear of being misunderstood. As a child, I had glimpsed the "other world," but whenever I tried to relate such experiences I was told not to lie or exaggerate. Therefore, my identity—who I am—stood in question in my mind at an early age. What do you do when how you experience the world is said to be a lie? Once again I was struggling with the same issue, yet ironically, this time I had been led by a father who had told me not to speak of such things. My father's death became my awakening. It was the beginning of my life's transformation. The years that followed brought me countless confrontations with myself, and through their resolutions a redefining of who I am. At that time, however, I turned inward, as did the child. It would be eight years before I shared this death episode with anyone.

The following excerpt describes how the Koreans would explain the passage just related to you.

The Koreans talk about a "bridge of people" (*indari*) that comes into being when a member of the family is chosen to be a shaman and another member has to die as a result of this. They refer to this process as "spanning a bridge over a human being" (*indari nonnunda*). A God has "entered into" the shaman and, in return, demands another human life. However, if the clan is willing to submit the member destined to become a shaman to the requisite ceremony of initiation as soon as the first symptoms of obsession or sickness manifest themselves, indari is not inevitable. But most families are unwilling to have a shaman in their circle, so the indari phenomenon occurs quite frequently. According to the investigations made by Cho Hung-Youn, indari occurs on average seven or eight times in every twenty cases of shamanic vocation.[18]

---

[18] Kalweit, Holger, "When Insanity is a Blessing: The Message of Shamanism," in Grof, Stanislav and Christina, *Spiritual Emergency*, Jeremy P. Tarcher, Inc., Los Angeles, p. 96.

# CHAPTER TWO

# The Seduction

DURING THE NEXT EIGHT YEARS my life went through radical changes. A marriage that had become very destructive to me ended. I would come to know the hardships inherent in being a working single mother to two wonderful children under the age of four. I returned to school to complete my master's and took advantage of career opportunities that seemed magically to appear. I remember saying to a friend once, "I don't know where I'm going, but something is pulling me. I've decided not to fight it, and just let go and see where it takes me."

And take me, it did! I became one of the first women to administer residential programs for delinquent youth in the state of Texas. The entire juvenile justice system was going through enormous upheaval. In 1974, a class-action suit had been filed demanding that correctional facilities become more humane. Children had been whipped; hunted down with dogs and horses. There had not been enough state-appropriated funds to provide adequate care to children in state custody. The result was that many new and courageous people responded to a call. Though the times were life-threatening due to children rioting and the total chaos that such a reformation brings, many new and innovative programs were initiated to promote care rather than abuse. There were many nights I prayed and felt lost in the pain that such responsibility demands; times when I wasn't sure if I would be able to meet my bills; times when I felt as if no support could be found anywhere. A woman, a mother, an administrator, a student. "Too much," I would scream. I wanted to quit. I wanted to die. My body responded to the stress with illness and bouts of depression, yet something in me went on. It was like swimming upstream against the current. In those days there were no laws in place that acknowledged a woman's plight in the marketplace. In fact, there was a great deal of anger because we were there. What I discovered was that, in the long run, it made me stronger. It developed the masculine side of my nature and helped me discover the strength of my "warrior" personality. The irony of it all is that I had embarked upon my "quest" and didn't even know it. These tests were initiations that raised my awareness and pushed me still further up the path, deeper into the labyrinth within.

Finally, I reached a plateau. I married again and secured a job that allowed me to actively lobby in the state legislature, bringing into law many of the ideas for which we had fought; laws to protect our children rather than abuse and devour them in our state systems. It was during this period of completion that new beginnings evolved. "New beginnings" is putting it mildly. How about "end of old life—new one coming!"

In May, 1982, I was in California attending two seminars back to back. I was standing on my balcony looking out over the ocean. Though the sun was warm, the sea breeze invigorating, I became aware of this empty space within me. This place that seemed to house an ache that just wouldn't go away. I reflected on my life. It seemed full. I was in love with a man who cared for me and my children. My children were happy and healthy. I was financially secure—the swimming pool, fancy car, nice house: the American dream through and through, but this emptiness wouldn't allow me to rest. The material things weren't enough. What else was there? It was like an illusive whisper that I couldn't quite hear, yet it demanded that I listen.

I said, "O.K. God! I think I've figured this step out. What's next?" Once you truly understand that the physical world doesn't provide satisfaction to your spiritual self, you begin to examine what will.

Well, you'd better be careful what you ask for because God will always give it to you.    It just may be in a different form than you expect.    Hyemeyohsts Storm, in his book *Song of Heyoehkah*, writes about a young woman, Estchimah, who is taken to a medicine woman in preparation for her Vision Quest announcing her development into womanhood.    The old woman describes to Estchimah the box of mirrors. Mirrors serve symbolically to represent soul.    As J. C. Cooper writes in *An Illustrated Encyclopaedia of Traditional Symbols*, "The universe is the mirror of God... man is the mirror of the universe." He goes on to say, "Mirror is the reflection of the supernatural and divine intelligence [*the Great Mirrors*]; the reflection in the mirror is the manifest and temporal world, also man's knowledge of himself [*the little mirrors*]."[19] The old woman explains this concept quite eloquently, and in so doing gives us a map to the journey ahead.

> "The Vision Quest is a marriage with ourselves," the old woman said gently.    "And it is a marriage with the Earth.    Let me tell you of the four walls."
>
> "The four walls?" Estchimah frowned.    "I feel trapped just hearing the words."
>
> "It is common for all People to build the four walls," the old woman smiled.    "The Buffalo Teachers call it the Place Where All the Mirrors are Hidden."
>
> "How is it possible to hide the Great Mirrors?" Estchimah asked.
>
> "Not the Great Mirrors," the old woman laughed good-humoredly, "but the little ones.    To the South, in the place of trust and innocence, is the wall of childhood.    The powers that make up that wall are all the children you grew up with.    The wall grew as you grew, a living wall of beginning years.    You, my daughter, are afraid to walk through that wall.
>
> "To the North is another wall.    That wall is made up of every teacher you ever had.    There is every kind of teacher there, living

---

[19] Cooper, J. C., *An Illustrated Encyclopaedia of Traditional Symbols*, Thames and Hudson, London, 1978, p. 106.

and dead. Everything that ever taught you is there within that wall. You, my daughter, are also frightened to walk through that wall.

"To the East is another wall. That wall is made up of everything dead. All religions are there. You, my daughter, are frightened to walk through that wall.

"To the West is the fourth wall. That wall is the wall of dreams. A portion of that wall is reflected into the wall of the East, just as the North and South walls are reflected into one another. Those things of the dead that are mirrored into the West wall are the many dreams that you have let die. You, my daughter, are afraid to walk through that wall."

"Is there no way out?" Estchimah asked emotionally.

"There is," the old woman smiled. "But first we will speak of the many tiny mirrors from which the floor of that place is built. Many of those tiny mirrors are from the world into which you were born. Some of them are from the world of your Mother," the old woman explained. "There are old images in that world, the world of remembrance. Each one of these tiny old mirrors blinds you to the path that can free you from that world."

"What is the path?" Estchimah asked with fear.

"If you truly begin to question each of the mirrors you have placed in that world," the old woman answered, "or question who it was that placed those mirrors into your world, then you will see the path through the West wall."

"But you said that I was frightened to walk through that wall," Estchimah said with emotion.

"You will walk through that wall on your Vision Quest," the old woman smiled. "There have been many who have walked through the West wall. They have walked through that wall in as many ways as there are People. The West wall is the wall of dreams. Many fear that there is nothing beyond the wall and they will be alone," she chuckled, "but these, of course, have never questioned and have never walked through the wall. Beyond the wall is reality. Within the enclosure of the walls is unreality. Beyond the wall is the great world of your own mind. It is a world as beautiful and varied as this one we call earth."[20]

---

[20] Storm, Hyemeyohsts, *Song of Heyoehkah*, Ballantine, New York, 1981, pp. 255–57.

I was beginning to understand that my reality as I had known it was the shadow of what was real. If I wanted to reach my Truth, I would need to walk through the wall of dreams. Would I have enough courage to face my false self? How does one begin such a quest? I seemed to have lots of questions, but how could I discover their answers?

## UNCORKING THE "GENIE" IN THE BOTTLE

The *Psychology of the Tao* says that when the pupil is ready, the teacher will appear. Two days after asking my "What's next?" question, Larry appeared, a wise and kind gentleman who became my guide through the West wall, the wall of dreams. I was seated at the conference. When I looked up I noticed that on his name tag was written the Texas Youth Council, the organization whose transformation I described earlier. It was unusual for them to send representatives out of state. I approached him and introduced myself. We immediately connected and began to share.

He asked me, "Do you remember your dreams?"

"No! I dream sometimes, but remember them? No."

"Do you meditate?"

"No. I pray, but I've never meditated."

To my surprise Larry lived two hours from me in Texas. He introduced me to a man by the name of Carl Jung; an introduction that affected my life beyond description. June Singer in her book *Boundaries of the Soul* describes Jung's work in the following way.

> Close to the beginning of *Memories, Dreams, Reflections* there is a short passage which establishes for the reader the basic attitude with which Jung approached his life, and with which Jung approached the phenomenon of Life, and it is this which has seized so many readers and refused to let them go until they had lived with Jung for a long enough time to make him the friend of their soul. The passage follows:
>
> Life has always seemed to me like a plant that lives on its rhizome. The part that appears above the ground lasts only a single

summer. Then it withers away—an ephemeral apparition. When we think of the unending growth and decay of life and civilizations, we cannot escape the impression of absolute nullity. Yet I have never lost a sense of something that lives and endures underneath the eternal flux. What we see is the blossom, which passes. The rhizome remains.[21]

Jung developed a psychology that through the use of dreams accessed the collective unconscious or universal consciousness. He presented an approach that included the spiritual dimension as well as the psychological one. Jung identified inner psychological figures such as anima, a man's inner feminine, animus, a woman's inner masculine, and shadow, the unknown or unacceptable parts of our personality. Larry, a trained psychologist who had studied Jung's works for eight years, was bringing a tool that would help me through the "box of mirrors."

Larry began to work with my dreams and a river began to flow. He would listen to the dreams and then ask me how they made me feel. We would explore the symbols presented; first by association (memories stimulated from my past) and then by research (meanings described in various cultures and mythologies). The exploration expanded my awareness on every level—intellectually, emotionally, and psychically. Each dream, once explored, stirred the psyche, drawing me deeper into the labyrinth.

He kept asking if I wanted to meditate, but I was frightened. Looking back now I realize some part of me knew that meditation would be like uncorking the genie in the bottle. I finally told Larry of my fears and asked him if he would meditate with me at a prescribed time. I trusted him and somehow felt protected in this way. And so it began. A whole world opened before me. Since I did not know any particular method of meditation, I listened and was given instruction internally. I would lie down on the bed and clear my mind by envisioning a blank screen. A feeling of stillness would descend covering my body. As I relaxed deeper into this

---

[21] Singer, June, *Boundaries of the Soul*, Anchor Books, New York, 1972, p. xiv.

feeling, another part of me separate from this scene would emerge looking back on me with a sense of clarity and objective viewing. It was an interesting feeling to see myself looking back on myself. This part I call the Witness. When the Witness was evoked, I could hear instruction auditorally. Where was this voice coming from? It was always helpful and gave me a sense of comfort and well being. I have since come to understand that I am clairvoyant, clairaudient and psychically feel through the body. The instruction comes from my inner teacher and/or guides depending on the given situation. The discrimination as to who is helping comes with time and familiarity, much like knowing a good friend's voice on the phone.

I had no prior knowledge of the chakra system, out of body experiences, or spiritual happenings. I was being taught from the inside out. In fact that is the way this process has continued to unfold. Each step introduced new terrain, new concepts and new phenomena. After each new experience, usually a book and/or a person would appear in my life to give validation and assist with the integration such happenings require. Let me go on.

While lying on my bed meditating, I was led to image the Lord's prayer interfacing with my body from foot to head in the following manner:

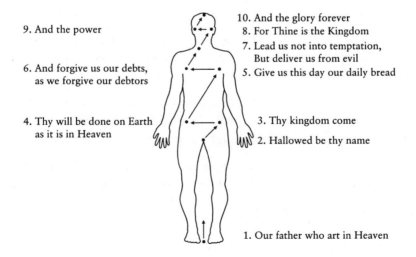

9. And the power

10. And the glory forever
8. For Thine is the Kingdom
7. Lead us not into temptation,
   But deliver us from evil

6. And forgive us our debts,
   as we forgive our debtors

5. Give us this day our daily bread

4. Thy will be done on Earth
   as it is in Heaven

3. Thy kingdom come
2. Hallowed be thy name

1. Our father who art in Heaven

Spirit told that me that this practice would serve as a blueprint in mapping my development. I was told that if I transfered this pattern onto the Tree of Life presented in the Kabala, it might give some insight into the paths "being taken." Then suddenly I heard a song, "When the Saints Go Marching In."

I studied the the Kabala and added that to what Kundalini was teaching me, it proved quite helpful. I refer you to Halevi's book *The Work of the Kabbalist*. I will refer you to the diagrams in this book which when laid over the diagram that came in meditation proves enlightening for they describe the stages of development that have to be passed and the tests initiated. Halevi states,

> To know one's projections upon oneself, others and situations is to recognize the ego's power to transmit or block what is coming from deep within the psyche. To observe and have command over the processes of action, thinking and feeling that fluctuate within the ego is to be able to use it rather than be used by it. This requires the capacity to rise above the opposing tendencies of willfullness coming from the right side of the Tree and will-lessness from the left. To be able to lift consciousness, at will, out of the purely yesodic personal into the triad of awakening is to achieve mastery over the four lower halls of the psyche, and come under the will of either the self or *Tiferet*...[22]

He further states,

> ...the process of evolution or return to the Light, as against that of creation or descent into matter, follows the path of the Lightning Flash, but in reverse.[23]

The lightning path that had been given to me in meditation was clearly a map of events to come. To give further validation to this process and how it unfolded, let me quote Halevi once more.

> To draw the Tree and the sefirot is a contemplative act. It connects one with the geometry of its structure, so that one begins

---

[22] Halevi, Z'ev ben Shimon, *The Work of the Kabbalist*, Samuel Weiser, Inc., York Beach, Me., 1986, p. 31.

[23] Ibid, p. 11.

to perceive during its construction the form and dynamic that compose it. To use another person's Tree or study it from a book is not enough. One has personally to enter into contact with the Tree and participate in its extraordinary beautiful symmetry... In some kabbalistic groups to draw one's own Tree and then one's own Jacob's Ladder of the four worlds, is considered an initiation in itself because it is done as a formal ritual to indicate a commitment to the Work.[24]

I don't want to go into much more interpretation with these examples, but rather just present them and allow their lessons to unfold with the story. In fact, I have found that has been one of the main teachings throughout this adventure. Rather than allowing the mind to analyze everything and categorize it too quickly, it proves beneficial to hold the experience and see where it will lead you-what it will magnetize to enhance the depth of learning.

Psychic phenomena became a daily happening. Somehow I had wandered into the place where two worlds kiss. For the next year, I would run home every night with the excitement of a young girl and lie down on my bed to meditate. For as many hours as I wanted, a parade of images would be shown to me. It was just like being at the movies. Scenes of Egypt and other exotic places would appear as well as images of birds with eyes all over them and other such intriguing symbols. Larry kept loaning me books and sure enough there would be the image I had seen and some information about its meaning and historical origin. I kept seeing a hole that was shaped like an eye; the "God's eye" is how it was identified. Behind the hole an illuminated world with bright colors seemed to exist from which an old man with white hair peered through at me smiling. It felt as if I was under a microscope and he was examining me. The experience was more lifelike than anything I had previously known.

*Once during meditation a beautiful being with a golden light emanating all around him appeared. His eyes were highlighted*

---

[24] Ibid, p. 61.

*and seemed to reach into the depths of my soul. A quick flow of energy created an orgasmic feeling that spread throughout my body. The Light was everywhere. It appeared like a moon or a ball of light that moved in and out of my field of vision. An energy of love surrounded me and as this "Christ-like" image merged with mine an ecstatic orgasm rolled through my body like nothing I had ever experienced.* (Nine months later I saw a picture of him and discovered he was named Gopal Das.)

On another occasion, a vision appeared.

*I seemed to be in my car on a black tubal-looking track that curved like a snake. I could see that the end of the curve went around a bend. My attention turned to a crackling noise. It seemed to be coming from my head. Accompanying this sound was the sensation of a line being drawn from the top of my head down my spine. It actually seemed to be creating a crack in my torso. A pressure or force pushed down the crack, extending it to just below my solar plexus. I flashed again on the car, which was now nearing the curve just around the bend. The pressure intensified, pushing my body up and cracking it open—just like one would crack an egg. As the crack widened, I had the sensation of being both above this image as an observer and within the image participating. I could see myself in a cocoon, much like a larva. From inside the cocoon, I could see out through the cracked body shell. I wanted to push out, but couldn't. The elastic film or sealer substance prevented me from breaking through. I seemed to understand that I was constructing my new vessel.*

I had never had an out-of-body experience and this one was mixed with visual images as well. Realizing that consciousness can be in more than one place at a time is quite an eye opener. Viewing it in this way also gives new meaning to its relationship with the body. The vision had given me a feeling of watching a butterfly releasing itself from its cocoon. Was that my soul? What would this new vessel be about?

The outer physical world and the inner world of spirit were commingling in a dancelike manner, one blending into the other, each enlivened by the play. In the meantime, I went on leading my life as usual, tending to the children, working as a professional, cleaning and cooking.

## THE HOODED ONES

My dream world was becoming just as animated as my meditations. I was given deep instruction in a very lucid manner. In fact, lucid dreaming became a regular occurrence. In lucid dreams, the dreamer is conscious of the fact that he or she is dreaming, therefore, interaction with the dream "reality" is active rather than passive. I have found that such states of awareness present a far more intensified sensory experience. Smells, tactile sensations, visual imagery and auditory experiences are more alive. So much so that that reality makes this one take on a flat and shadowy appearance. Dreams have multiple levels of meaning to me. Not only do they help us heal on the personality level, but they provide access to archetypal realms and open the door so we can meet our soul. (The Carlos Castaneda series does an excellent job of exploring the dream state and how one can access deeper layers of the unconscious.)

I was introduced through the dream state to the "Hooded Ones." They were beings that wore white monklike robes. They always appeared in a group of about twelve or so. Their heads were hooded, covering their faces so that no particular identity was visible. Their energy was so full of love and compassion that the atmosphere itself was filled. They never spoke to me, but communicated telepathically. Each time they appeared, dramatic changes in my life followed.

Our first meeting was on January 24, 1983, in a lucid dream.

*I was in a large house, as if preparing for a ceremony. One of the Hooded Ones stood in a white boat. Water was filling the house, running through a long hall that lead down into the basement. I stood behind the boat with another Hooded One assisting me. The water had the appearance of a river with a waterfall rushing down to the underground. I was given a rope that was connected to the boat and asked to place its noose around my neck. I was to*

*submerge myself under the water and allow the boat to drag me.*
*I was sure I would drown. I was then handed a fishing net and told*
*that they would wait until I was ready to begin. Although I was*
*afraid, their patience and strength gave me courage. I visualized*
*the task, then started down the descending hallway. Suddenly,*
*the water became shallow, and I was able to descend the stairway*
*barefooted. (I realized that the difficulty is in the initiation of*
*a task, for by making a decision and taking action, the "doing"*
*becomes easier; I would be given assistance.) The area I found*
*myself in was dark and lit by candles. There was a ceremony*
*about to be performed and I was the guest of honor. I was led to*
*the center of a circle. At that point my consciousness was held at*
*two levels of awareness: one part of me was participating in the*
*ceremony while the other part observed the happenings. They cut*
*off my head and, to my amazement, replaced it with Gandhi's. It*
*was a very humbling act, and the awesome responsibility of such*
*action filled my being. Afterwards dancing and gaieties followed.*

Little did I know how prophetic this dream would become.

This dream speaks to the descent each of us (male and female)
must embark upon to retrieve our femininity. Sylvia Brinton Perera
does a wonderful job of describing this passage in the *Descent to*
*the Goddess*. She states, in summary:

> The implication for modern women is that only after the full,
> even demonic, range of effects and objectivity of the dark feminine
> is felt and claimed can a true, soul-mate, passionate and individual
> comradeship be possible between woman and man as equals.
> Inanna is joined to and separated from her dark ancestress-sister,
> the repressed feminine. And that, with Ninshubur's (Inanna's
> faithful servant) and Enki's (god of Wisdom, god of water) and
> Dumuzi's (Inanna's mate) help, brings forth Geshtinanna—a model
> of one who can take her stand, hold her own value, and be lovingly
> related to the masculine as well as directly to her own depths;
> a model of one who is willing to suffer humanly, personally, the
> full spectrum that is the goddess.[25]

Little did I know how prophetic this dream would become.

---

[25]  Perera, Sylvia Brinton, *Descent to the Goddess*, Inner City Books, Canada,
1981, p. 94.

## THE INITIATION

Shortly after this dream experience, during meditation I was instructed to buy a copy of Carl Jung's autobiography, *Memories, Dreams, Reflections*. I was to write the following on the front cover:

> It's not what you do in life,
> It's why you do it,
> That is the eye in the needle.
> It's not that your work is your life,
> Rather, it's your *life* is your work.
> That is the path out of the trap!
> Think about it!!!

More dreams and meditations followed insisting that I attend the Jung Institute in Zurich, Switzerland. Now how was I going to do this. Where to even start was in question. I went to Richard, my husband, and said, "I keep getting these dreams and visions about our going to Switzerland. Is that crazy or what?" "No," he said, "I've always had a dream about going there. Why don't you check it out?"

Boy, what a surprise. Sometimes when there is no resistance there is immediate fear. Nothing is in your way but yourself. Remembering the dream with the Hooded Ones gave me courage and some direction. I began to explore who in the area was Jungian-trained and, more specifically, who had trained in Europe. To make a long story short, I found such a man living about two hours from me in Austin, Texas. He began to see me and instructed me on how to apply to the Institute. Within four weeks of preparing and mailing my application, I received a letter inviting me to attend the Jung Institute as a "matriculated auditor." Everything else went just as quickly. Realtors said we wouldn't be able to sell our house since the market was moving very slowly, but within one week from listing, it was sold! Richard, a dental hygienist, contacted a lady who was responsible for placing dental hygienists in Switzerland; it was one of the few jobs still requiring importation of personnel. The problem was that they had never hired a man in this position before and we were met with their bias and misconceptions about Richard, especially focusing on his sexual preference. To them a man doing a hygienist's work must be gay. The paradox thrown at him was interesting to watch. It was certainly fascinating to watch the discrimination work in reverse. This became our hurdle. Time grew near. The boys were finishing school and we were to leave in June. Should we make such a large jump with no secure platform under us?

Everyone told us we were crazy. Some said that they weren't letting families into Switzerland due to overpopulation problems. I said, "But, I had a dream." They said that Richard would never find employment. I said, "But, I had a dream." They said that housing was hard to come by and we could never find a place for just a few years—the Swiss don't move like we do, they rent a place usually for ten to twenty years. I said, "But, I had a dream."

Richard and I talked it over and we both felt strongly about going. So with a bit of fear in our hearts and lots of head shaking, we set about preparing for the journey. Now, Larry had become quite a support mechanism for me during this amazing process that certainly had a life of its own. I felt like a small child. How would I manage without him? Would I find someone who could honor this process for the good inherent within it without calling me crazy? My fear was that if I couldn't find someone to help me withstand the dynamics of this birthing, the intensity would drive me mad.

Before leaving for Switzerland, an incident occurred which paved the way for our new beginnings, but in what ways and to what extent, we would not fully discover until we were in Europe.

*On the evening of April 30, 1983, I was taking a shower when a loud buzzing noise began. It became so loud I felt sure that everyone else could hear it. I poked my head out of the shower door and asked Richard why the shower was making such a strange noise. He replied that he could not hear anything. Strange, I thought!*

*This must be just for me. So many things were happening out of the ordinary these days, one more didn't surprise me. The loud buzzing seemed to reach a peak at which point a bright Light appeared above me. A beam shot down from it and poured into the top of my head, traveling throughout my entire body. My body seemed to be drawn forward. I felt totally nurtured and the process went on for quite some time. I fell deeper and deeper into an altered state of consciousness. After a while, I returned to a more functional state, but I still felt altered in some way. Richard and I decided to meditate together. This was the one and only time we would do so; such experiences were intense and made him too uncomfortable. We sat down on the bed, sitting upright with straight postures. The energy was extremely strong, and again the loud buzzing returned. The Light returned, hovering over my head. As it descended, a sense of calmness and beauty seemed to fill the room in an all-encompassing, ever-present glow. I felt great empathy with it. Four figures in white hooded robes appeared, one on each side and two at the end of the bed. Their form was wavy like heat coming off a road, but their appearance was distinct. They stood quietly and serenely, as if in ceremony.*

*At this point, Richard and I layed down on the bed, extending our bodies in a comfortable and flat position. Although Richard could not see what I saw, he certainly had the distinct feeling of the profundity of the experience we were immersed in. Again the energy returned. I visualized it as a white light that drew a circle around us encompassing our bodies. The energy seemed to flow across both of us. I found myself in a white swirling tunnel that had a bright red sphere at the other end. Its light radiated out and filled the tunnel with a red glow. People were standing in the tunnel. They disappeared leaving only one man, who began to walk toward me and then motioned with his arm to come. Suddenly, I saw the familiar circular hole with the old man looking through at me—the God's eye. It was directly above me and closer than it had ever been before. He looked at me for a moment, then moved away from his "window." The "window" then moved to eye level. The scene changed, and I was looking into the corner of a living room with a couch, a chair, and a lamp. The scene changed again, and I saw a city street scene. It appeared to be European with trees lining the area between the street and sidewalk. It was a busy street with cars rushing to and fro. Each scene seemed so distinctly different that no connection could be made. Again the scene changed, displaying a beautiful, sunny landscape. The sun began to shine more brightly and filled the scene with such a brightness and intensity that only the silhouette of a tree in the center remained.*

*Following this scene, I found myself flying over a terrain of rolling hills. I enjoyed the sensation so much that I began to indulge in it, flying closer to the ground—up and down and over the hills. Suddenly, something pulled me up. I realized that I was in outer space looking down upon what appeared to be the planet earth. How in the world did I get out here? Outer space wasn't dark, but rather produced a sense of clarity. The earth was breathtaking in her hues of blue and green. Ahead of me was another planet or moon that was barren and rocky. As I landed, I began to feel my vision narrowing. I had the distinct feeling that I would soon realize my true origin. At that moment, I sensed my concentration being broken.*

I got up and went over to the plate-glass doors and sat in the light of the full moon. A Voice spoke saying, "Once your hands are on the plow, you can never look back." Somehow, I knew I had made a commitment that must not be broken. The realization of the impact it would have on my life was felt throughout my body. My head was confused and my heart full. I sobbed for hours not knowing why.

Upon returning to ordinary reality, I was filled with completeness, fullness and total commitment. Although Richard was not able to visually experience what I had seen, he had felt the impact of the strong energy. We sat and held each other for hours afterwards. I am not sure I will ever be able to verbalize the intense meaning this evening held for me. It had begun at 10:30 p.m. and the initiation was completed around 4:00 a.m. the following morning. I can only say that Spirit shook my world once again and impregnated me with an overwhelming essence of love and wholeness. The next day we discovered that the bricks on the exterior wall of our garage had completely buckled out from the wall, confirming the reality of our experience. It appeared that a strong force had forced the metal belts that hold the bricks on the connecting garage wall to bow out. The repairman could not give us an explanation. Was the manifestation of the energy we experienced the night before the reason for the damage or was it all just a coincidence?

Shakti had once again made herself known. The second station for the train would signify a psychic opening, removing the veils that keep us from "seeing." Our perception changes, our world view expands and our transformation begins. My sense of self had been radically altered. Not only was my definition of who I was shifting daily, but my outer reality was about to change in ways I could not imagine. I mean here I was—a woman from Texas about to become a graduate student in Europe. That alone was mind altering!

# CHAPTER THREE

# Jumping Into the Void

IT WAS JUNE WHEN OUR PLANE arrived in Zurich. I don't think we had any idea of what we had actually done until that moment. I mean when you can't figure out how to use the phone or flush the toilet, you know you are in for a major change! None of us knew how to speak German, so our first challenge was how to communicate and navigate in this new land—a bit symbolic to say the least. As Joseph Campbell writes in *The Hero with a Thousand Faces*:

> The call to adventure signifies that destiny has summoned the hero and transferred his spiritual center of gravity from within the pale of his society to a zone unknown. This fateful region of both treasure and danger may be variously represented; as a distant land, a forest, a kingdom underground, beneath the waves or above the sky, a secret island, a lofty mountaintop, or a profound dream state; but it is always a place of strangely fluid and polymorphous beings, unimaginable torments, superhuman deeds, and impossible delights.[26]

Shakti would begin to teach me about faith at this station on our journey. As is stated in a marvelous book, *Talking With Angels*, "Faith is only a word unless it has action, and action is only misdirected unless it has faith."[27] The air around us seemed to be

---

[26] Cousineau, Phil, ed., *The Hero's Journey: The World of Joseph Campbell*, Harper & Row Publishers, San Francisco, 1990, p. 1.

[27] Mallasz, Gitta, *Talking With Angels*, Watkins Publishing, London & Dulverton, 1979.

electrified with synchronicities abounding. Within two weeks of arriving Richard secured a job and had to return to the United States until his work permit was processed. We were selected as a family to rent an apartment that was a ten minute walk from the Jung Institute. The lovely couple that had it would be traveling to Saudi Arabia on a visiting professorship. Ironically, they would end up being gone the exact time needed for our stay in Europe—three years. They would not be leaving, however, until September and this was late June. We found another furnished apartment to lease for the summer. All the obstacles others had said would block our way had been met and magically resolved.

Richard's absence brought a deep loneliness. Here we were, two young boys and myself, living in a one-room efficiency apartment. We knew no one except the family who had befriended us and assisted in placing Richard in his new job. Though this was a trying time, magic was in the air! The country was beautiful. Flowers were everywhere. The forest was as magical in its appearance as the Alps were majestic in theirs. I felt strangely at home here, as if I had rediscovered a lost land—one I had visited before. Once the physical necessities were attended to additional pieces of the puzzle began to reveal themselves.

## NEW TEACHER, NEW NAMES

I contacted a group of people connected with Eckankar, an organization whose purpose is to assist taking soul by Its own path back to Its divine source. It was founded by a man named Paul Twitchell under the direction of the ECK Masters in the Himalayan Mountains. Their teachings contained "the wisdom and ecstatic knowledge of those planes of the spiritual worlds, beyond the regions of time and space."[28] I had joined just before leaving Texas. I called to see if anyone knew of an analyst who was

---

[28] Twitchell, Paul, *The Shariyat-Ki-Sugmad*, Book Two, intro., IWP Publishing, Menlo Park, Ca., 1971.

Jungian-trained. I hoped that I could find someone to continue the work I had begun with Larry. They gave me the name of a woman, Cornelia Brunner. What a treasure I was about to discover.

When the higher Self is activated and you walk in the realm where two worlds kiss, you have a sense of crossing a psychic threshold. It's as if you enter an altered state and the world around you feels different, more animated. Such a time was activated the day I met Cornelia. Fate kissed me and the world stood still. Cornelia was 84 years old, was writing her third book, had a full practice, and could beat me to the top of the mountain and back. She had transcribed much of Paul Twitchell's work from English into German and had studied with Carl Jung for over thirty years. What a combination! Upon leaving her home, I was walking to catch the tram when suddenly, like a bolt of lightning, I was struck by the obvious. There I stood looking down the street suddenly transported in my mind back to the night in Texas when the Hooded Ones had appeared. The visions I had seen, the ones that seemed to make no sense loomed alive and in front of me. The foreign street and the living room scene belonged to Cornelia! Could this be? Could I have seen something across the ocean, across time that was now present in this reality? It was the first time I had experienced the fulfilment of a precognitive dream and I understood. I had definitely found my analyst. Cornelia had given me the name of another woman who was connected to the Institute and could guide that part of my process. Later they both would laugh and say that Cornelia would pull my head into the clouds while Liz would put my feet on the ground. In this way, they would stretch me a bit—and stretch they did!

As you might perceive, my new container was slowly and magically coming together. Of course, when you have a pot more stew gets cooked. So, Psyche brought me new material. One night in a dream the Hooded Ones once again appeared.

*Their small group was escorting me up the side of a mountain. I, too, had on a white robe, but my hood was pulled back off my head. I was riding a donkey. My sons, Kirk and Scott, were walking behind us along with several others. Again, I had the distinct feeling that we were in a ceremonial procession. We proceeded past the tree line until we came upon a round hole in the ground. I got off the donkey and upon exploring the hole discovered a white spiral staircase that descended into the ground. I became a bit nervous, but was told that I could take as long as I needed— they would wait for me. Such patience only encouraged me to go on. I began the descent. The others followed. About half way down, the Light appeared in all its splendor—golden white light. It shined so brightly that I couldn't see the others behind me any longer. The Voice said, "Only Princess Gopal can go to these depths." I had never been given a new name before. What did this mean? I continued down the staircase and at the bottom discovered a hollowed out white cave. Sitting in the center near the cave wall was a huge oyster shell, silver in color. It lay open, and lying in it were numerous round, white stones. Each shone in its own lustrous, white magnificence. The Voice spoke, "You are responsible for these!"*

*Next, a vision appeared on the wall of the cave. A silver cross appeared. It was ornate in appearance. The Voice said, "When you awake in the morning, drive your car with what you call your »head open«." (I used to refer to intuiting things in this way; you know, driving and just letting your intuition choose the way.) The Voice went on, "When you feel it is time to stop the car, do so. After parking, you will discover a store with a large picture window. In the window will be this cross. Go in and talk to the clerk. You will know you have the correct cross when she tells you that it is very, very old and hand carved by Indians."*

I awoke! What a dream. Could this really be true? Faith and action were being called upon again.

When the boys woke up, I told them of the dream and we decided it sounded like an adventure. Once in the car, I "opened up my head" and proceeded to drive instinctively. We ended up in the old section of Zurich. Remember, we were brand newcomers— we still did not know our way around, but something was directing our steps. Suddenly, I had a strong impulse to stop the car. We parked and walked just up the street when there, in the showcase, was the cross. It sat in the center of a large collection of old jewelry and artifacts. I shook all over. I went inside and asked the clerk to tell me a bit about the cross. She said, "Oh, this is an interesting piece. It is from South America. There is so much civil strife and unrest that many families are selling their very old artifacts to fund moving their families out of the country. This is such a piece. It is very, very old and hand craved by the Indians of South America." I, of course, bought it but not without arguing some with my resistance. I had been given a totem by Spirit. I wore it constantly and felt protected.

As I witness the story as it occurred, I will attempt to interpret what I have learned and come to understand, in hopes that within your own knowing such telling will stir a personal meaning in you. Kundalini is a very individualized path. While its goal, Self--Realization, is the same for each of us, the paths vary according to the evolutinary needs of the individual. Therefore, look at your experiences and interpret them according to your framework. As one friend once said, "When Kundalini awakens, she opens your blossom on the Tree of Life. Your blossom is distinct, unlike any other."

Each new experience stirred more in me, revealed new depths of my being that I had been unconscious of. Sometimes that learning was exciting, mysterious or just plain frightening. Yet, still within me a yearning grew, a passion to know my truth. The dichotomy lay in my fear that I might find out.

This was the first of three spiritual names I would be given. The other two came from people in this waking reality rather than in a dream. Their significance would mark other plateaus my personality would be required to attain—plateaus that would alter my outer reality still more. Halevi speaks to this occurrence in *The Work of the Kabbalist* in the following way:

> When the Kabbalist touches and is touched by the Divine, then it is said that he is known by name. The meaning of this is profound when you consider that a name is the acknowledgement of a particular being by themselves or others. To possess a name is to become individual, to be quite separate from others who might be quite similar to oneself. And yet this is another mystery: in this

very uniqueness is an intimate solitude that can only be known by that self. This self is a spark of Divine consciousness. It is in this state of isolation because it was divided out from Adam Kadmon so that it might experience separation from the Divine and so be able to look back at its own reflection. Thus each self is a photon of Divine Light removed from its normal habitat in the World of Emanation and embodied in the lower Worlds of Creation, Formation and Action. When an individual comes to know and be known by the Holy One, then something Divine begins to manifest and this dissolves the sense of isolation that many people feel, but know not why. To be known by name is the prelude to acquaintanceship, then love, and eventually union.[29]

Secondly, the cross in the Mayan culture as defined by Cooper in *An Illustrated Encyclopaedia of Traditional Symbols* represents the "Tree of Life and the Tree of Nourishment." In the Mexican culture, he goes on to say, "God is sometimes represented on the cross and his sacred victims as crucified."[30] The personality undergoes a deep crucifixion in order to individuate. Again the vision in Texas sang out. The silhouette of the tree in my series of visions within the vision seemed to be mapping this passage. The unconscious had provided me with a map of sorts—a map which in the vision promised to return me to my true origin. Many questions leaped out at me. Where was all this taking me? What was real and what wasn't? What I had been taught as "real" seemed only to be a surface view. I couldn't argue with the "realness" of the dream and the cross I held in my hand. I was beginning to learn a new way of living. I very slowly was awakening in this dream we call reality.

As I pondered all of this, I received in meditation an objective view of a systematic process that would continue to carry me further on my path. I must understand it as a process and avoid over identifying with the stages of the process itself. I was shown that as I move from one level of awareness to the next, I would

---

[29]  Halevi, Z'ev ben Shimon, *The Work of the Kabbalist*, Samuel Weiser, Inc., York Beach, Me., 1986, p. 187.

[30]  Cooper, J. C., *An Illustrated Encyclopaedia of Traditional Symbols*, Thames and Hudson Ltd., London, 1978.

follow a five-step process. In this way, I could better maintain my center by focusing my attention on each step as it progressed, thereby not being lost in the material needing integration. Let me take a moment to describe that process.

In the first step, I have a feeling of birth, as I imagine a new-born baby must feel. As my integration occurs and I move another notch, my perception changes, and I look at this world in another way. The perception changes as I do. I take time to be a quiet observer, adjusting to the new awareness. I notice that these changes in perception affect *all* the senses in varying degrees.

The imprint stage follows, in which I acquire some insight into an image. We are all like one large jigsaw puzzle, scattered about the table, or as Don Juan pointed out, the "tonal" reality. As a new piece of that puzzle comes into focus, additional knowledge is "remembered." A new piece is added to the conscious image one has constructed, thus moving one closer to the core of your true identity.

The following phase brings about integration. During this phase, I experience volumes of energy, and my thinking becomes clear and quick. My whole being seems to be tuned to a high level, and my sensitivity to all forms of communication is increased.

Each time one experiences a high, one must prepare for the equal and opposite reaction in the descent. For in order to maintain balance, one must know and experience the opposites of each new thing. If the opposite is avoided, one then only acquires partial knowledge. I am confronted with this reality of experiencing the opposites.

As my experience nears completeness, I must prepare to give it away. In the fourth stage I experience the death of the image of my "now" self in order to allow a new piece to be added. In so doing, I bring about again the first stage, the birth of the "new" self. This phase usually has resistance and sadness. I experience a loss; although paradoxically, the give-away becomes the gain. The learning then begins to flow naturally, as my ship is carried always towards its destination. Since space and time are an illusion of the "tonal" world, I begin to grasp the fact that my destination is in the total "Beingness," remembered here where I stand.

The final stage brings me to a confrontation of the opposites. I am both giving birth to the next step of awareness and being born at the same time. Each time I stand upon this fine point, I become aware of the tension such confrontation evokes, and the release of new energies such friction generates. This cycle then repeats itself, constantly spiraling through the density of my unknowing.

The following excerpt from the *Song of Heyoehkah* written by Hyemyohsts Storm further exemplifies what I have just described. He begins by explaining what the "dance" is about.

> It is this time that is called The Time of Dreaming the World Awake! The symbol of learning is the Maze. You wander as a guest of your world within the wonderful Maze. It is like a great magical garden where you are the principal person. You are protected there. You are the shadow of light, of the flowering tree. You were dreaming the world awake! You dreamed what the world was to be like. You were remembering the future with the power of the past, a past that reached back into ten millions of suns.[31]

It will behoove you to take some time to reflect on your own process. Start by looking deeply at what is going on for you right now. Explore it in its entirety. What is present in the emotional field? What are the characteristics of your energy? Are you confused, tired, sad, clear minded? What are the physical manifestations? What clue from the unconscious is up for investigation? How did it present itself? How is it altering your current perception? Become conscious of how your process presents itself. Become the watcher as well as the doer. In this way, you become the participant in a divine play, not the victim in a drama. Our process is like a river constantly flowing. If I learn to let go, my resistance is lessened and the journey less tumultuous. So, watch the flow of your process. Don't try to

---

[31] Storm, Hyemeyohsts, *Song of Heyoehkah*, Harper and Row, San Francisco, 1981, pp. 52−53.

figure out the beginning or the end of the cycle. Just watch! It will shift bringing you into the next phase. Continue to watch, observing particular characteristics of this stage. At some point you will realize you have returned to the point you started. You will have, however, moved up on the spiral and a new piece of the puzzle will have presented itself. Both Stanislav Grof's book, *The Adventure of Self Discovery*, and Ralph Metzner's, *Opening to Inner Light*, provided maps to the unconscious that helped me to understand better how deep personal change transpires. In addition, *Spiritual Emergency*, edited by Stanislav and Christina Grof provides insightful commentary on the possible phenomena spiritual awakenings can exhibit.

Now as you can see in what I have just described, my new container had been formed and a map provided with lovely and wise guides to support the process. As the dreams and visions continued, their guidance led me to the discovery of the Black Madonna in a small Swiss village called Einsiedeln. I would come to discover that the Divine Mother walked more closely to me than I had ever realized. In fact, looking back, I can see that she anointed me and changed my vision each step of the way. The site of the Black Madonna in Einsiedeln started as a hermitage in the late 900's. It has since become known as a pilgrimage, a place of healing. Upon the walls of the cathedral are many pictures illustrating the miracles that have occurred through the Grace of the Divine Mother. I spent many hours in prayer and meditation there. Though I had little understanding of the "call" that brought me there, a feeling that is hard to describe absorbed me and strengthened me. It served always as a reminder of the wholeness I sought. As Christin Lore Weber writes in *WomanChrist*:

> There is a mystery that women must enter into if we are ever to become wholly ourselves and know God. We need to find that secret, rooted place. We need to enter the mystery of descent.
> We must descend individually and collectively—and we must eventually bring our brothers and fathers and spouses along. It is the descent of each woman to join womanbody with womansoul.

> It is the descent of humankind to the place where the essential
> feminine waits in darkness. It is the descent of the Christ to
> become earthed, fleshed.[32]

The American Indians say you must travel around the hoop and
learn from each of the four directions before you can enter the
center of the mandala and claim your power. As I look back at
my path as it unfolded, it weaves the way of my Cherokee walk
with my Christian upbringing; always fired by Shakti. I still did
not know about the concept of Kundalini, though my body had
begun to demonstrate some of the physical manifestations. I would
awaken at night with mild body tremors and heat rushes running
through me. They were not noticeably painful, but psychologically
scary. The most noticeable happenings were parapsychological in
nature. I guess I had always believed in such things as "ghosts,"
but I hadn't directly encountered any, particularly in my adult
years. Suddenly, the apartment seemed full of unseen spirits.
The phone would ring at odd hours and no one would be there.
The same thing was going on with the doorbell. Doors were
opening and shutting with no apparent reason. Many others on the
path of awakening have reported a time when parapsychological
phenomena become activated initiating the neophyte into the
"other" worlds. I have two such incidents that I would like
to share. Each happened spontaneously. Each shook old realities
leaving many questions and new perceptions of what could be.

In the spring of 1984, Richard and I decided to go to Rome.
We were both excited. What a special place. You have a sense of
standing in a place where two cultures, two times meet. Amongst
the ruins of Rome, the busy traffic scurries in the haste of our
everyday world. One minute we were standing in front of
a Michelangelo statue caught in total humility by the presence
of something so divinely beautiful. The next we were meditating
in the catacombs feeling the devotion of the Christians who were

---

[32] Weber, Christin Lore, *WomanChrist*, Harper & Row Publishers, San Francisco, 1987, pp. 23–24.

buried there. It was like being caught in dream time. My romantic self loved it. The Italian people create an ambience that's hard to describe. Feeling and emotion are in the air with red poppies accentuating the color of the mood. We were only planning to be there a few days, so each day was filled with more to see. It was the second day of our trip, early morning. We were just about to go out for breakfast. I picked up a pair of earrings on the table and started across the room to the mirror to put them on. Suddenly, a loud sound shrieked through the air. The next thing I knew I was in a dark passage and a man was speaking to me in a language not from this planet. I seemed to know and understand him quite well. I spoke to him in an authoritative manner demanding that he leave—get out of me. My vision returned at that moment and I realized I was standing at the mirror leaning on the sink, speaking to myself in this unusual language. Then in a loud voice, I said, "Get out! Get out now!" Just at that moment, the entity left taking me along with it. I found myself above my body, watching it begin to fall. I realized in that split second that if I didn't want to return, I didn't have to. Death was just that simple. With that realization, I popped back in, catching myself with my hands on the sink. My psychologist self came out running around doing a mental check list to see if my thinking was in tack. What had happened? Nothing like this had ever happened before and it was scary. I looked at Richard, who sat on the end of the bed with his mouth open. I went over and sat down by him and asked him to share what he had seen. It matched. Neither one of us could talk about it until much later in the afternoon. It felt as if I had been given an opportunity to be a medium for this entity, but some part of me had very emphatically declined. I was clear that if I was going to be asked to do such work, I wanted to be conscious simultaneously. What did that mean? I didn't know. The rest of the trip was relatively uneventful. There was a silence between us that seemed to say it all.

Upon my return I hurried over to see Cornelia. She had a friend who had worked with these states of consciousness. She set up an appointment for me to go see him. When I walked up to his front door I recognized the entry way as one I had seen in a dream a few nights before. This meeting would prove to be one of those arranged by fate. He shared stories of work he had done with souls he described as "caught in the astral plane." He gave me some guidance and told me to trust my inner guidance. I would be protected. This was just the beginning of several "cases" that came to me introducing me to another level of work. Strangely enough, one part seemed frightened and child-like, while another part seemed to remember and know. Was this my split I was healing? The astral world is described as the emotional body of the earth. Mary Summer Rain in *Phantoms Afoot* says,

> The existence of finer dimensions of reality is not a matter of debate for the learned men of physical science. The related issue that is frequently considered is the possibility of what exactly these delineating dimensions consist of, and what precise manner of altered forms constitute the vast realms of differing vibrational rates... The existence of spirits cannot be stupidly ignored or eradicated by skepticism or atheism, for spirits are not affected by either, but continue to exist in spite of them both.[33]

She goes on to say, "Spirits are a fact of life. Spirits who are unfortunately caught between dimensions cannot be logically disputed. And the most beautiful and emotionally-moving experience one could have is being actively instrumental in freeing a confused and lost soul."

The next case exemplifies just that! A lady I had known at school started coming around more frequently. She asked a great deal of metaphysical questions, seemingly out of curiosity. She had sent her husband back to the States that year, but didn't share much about why. She seemed introverted and shy. One evening, I went to have coffee with her and another friend. We were talking and enjoying a night out with the girls. Suddenly, my body moved, as if to plant itself. By now, I knew that meant

---

[33] Rain, Mary Summer, *Phantoms Afoot*, Whitford Press, Pennsylvania, 1989, p. 1.

something was about to come in psychically. Again, the loud sound announced the happening. All of a sudden the image of a small man jumped out of my friend and on to the table. He was about three feet tall, bald headed and white in complexion. He rolled back and forth in front of me cussing up a storm. He went on and on in a nonsensical manner, and then rolled back into her shutting a door. The atmosphere returned to normal. No one at the table seemed to notice anything. "O.K.!" I said to myself. "You've finally lost your cookies." I had been working with Spirits caught in between dimensions for several months, but now one accompanied my friend. I mean what do you do? How do you tell someone you think they're possessed? I took my friends home shortly after, choosing not to say anything for the moment.

I paced the floor most of the night, praying and asking for help. I began to get inner auditory instruction. I was told that this was a case involving a family karmic pattern that had gone on for many generations. The karma was now completed and could be cleared. I was to assist. Needless to say, I prayed and paced some more. Finally, morning came and with it a telephone call to Cornelia. She supported the process, asking me to trust myself. I asked if I could bring Ellen over to share what I had seen. My friend had been seeing Cornelia in therapy. I felt this might give her support, since what I had to share might be upsetting. I called Ellen explaining I had something I needed to talk to her about, but I would prefer to do this with Cornelia. She agreed, surprisingly, with no questions. When I arrived at her apartment, she invited me in and proceeded to show me a family album. She spontaneously showed me the pictures of her family disclosing that there had always been one "crazy" aunt each generation. Was this the family karma I had been told about? I listened, but didn't respond. We drove over to Cornelia's.

This was one of those moments I will always remember. I was nervous; sweaty palms, dry mouth, and all. My responsibility was to share what I had seen. That was all. She then would have to decide how she wanted to proceed. My teachers have always taught me that a good healer goes into any given situation with no expectation for outcome. In so doing, one becomes an instrument for Spirit. I took a breath and jumped in with both feet explaining what I had seen the night before. Her reaction was what surprised me. She leaned back in her chair and began to cry quietly. She said, "I am so relieved. Let me tell you of a dream I had about a year ago. In the dream, I walked out on a balcony. At each of the four corners stood a statue of a little man, approximately three feet tall and bald headed. One of them became animated and started to laugh saying, »At least now you know who I am!«" Since that time bizarre things had begun to happen. Many of them had sexual overtones. She would catch herself urinating on her sacred objects and the like. Several incidents occured where knives were involved. She wouldn't go into the details. She had become frightened and sent her husband away for fear she might hurt him. She had been frightened to tell anyone, because she knew they would only call her crazy.

I think there were times when I was just as frightened as her, but something in me carried a memory of how to work with such phenomena. I would go into an altered state and our sessions would unfold spontaneously. Although I was present and quite aware of the goings on, my body was used as a vehicle in the healing. I was a witness to these proceedings as much as anyone else. In the beginning, Little Man Darling (that was my name for him), would sit in my lap and talk to Ellen through me. As time progressed and a relationship evolved between them, Ellen, who was quite psychic herself, began to communicate with him. We came to discover that many years ago he had committed a crime against another on his planet. His home was not in this galaxy and such crimes were taboo. He had been sent to Earth, a more primitive culture, to learn about such things. Since a similar crime had taken place in this family, their karma was linked. Little Man Darling had become enamored with Ellen. He was jealous and angry and had become caught in the unconsciousness of this plane. To make a long story short, it took three weeks of continuous work. The emotional clearing for Ellen was an important part of the work. Someone can be psychically attacked when they are ill or emotionally defenseless. Her mother had died two years prior and at that time our friend had entered. Much of the therapy at this point dealt with the grief process around her Mother's death and the wounding their relationship had possessed. Part of Ellen's work was to own responsibility for her own psychic gifts and begin to use them in a more integrated manner.

As was happening in those days, I would work with the case, taking it right up to its stage of completion. Then, someone with years of expertise in the field would appear to assist in its closing. And so it was in this case. Three women from London came to town. Cornelia called to let me know and to suggest that Ellen go to see them. I informed Ellen and she set up an appointment. The next morning around 6:30 a.m. a vision awoke me.

> *There in a golden round bubble was Little Man Darling working in the fields. It was so bright that I could only see his silhouette. He looked up at me and said, "Thank you! I'm finally home."*

The vision burst. Little Man Darling was gone. Ellen called about two hours later. She reported that the ladies from London had confirmed all that we had discovered and had completed the healing.

And so this station as visited by Shakti had pierced yet another veil! As Holger Kalweit writes in his article, "When Insanity is a Blessing: The Message of Shamanism,"

> Resistance to psychophysical change and a disintegration of the normal structure of existence has always been part and parcel of the aspect of every rite of transformation. Rejection of the new and unknown is a standard human response. True, existence itself is change, but the leap from three-dimensional to multidimensional perception and experience is the most fundamental change.[34]

---

[34] Kalweit, Holger," When Insanity is a Blessing: The Message of Shamanism," in *Spiritual Emergency*, edited by Stanislav and Christina Grof, Jeremy P. Tarcher, Inc., Los Angeles, 1989, p. 93.

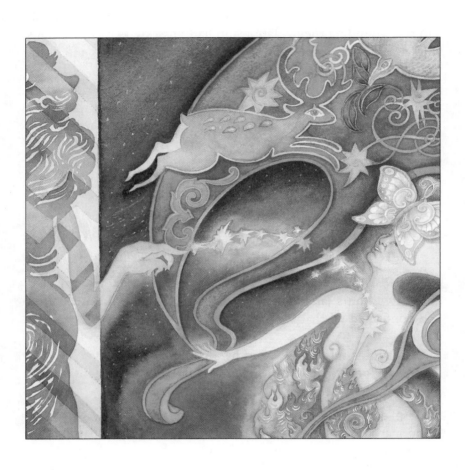

# CHAPTER FOUR

# The Induction

## SHAMANISM AND KUNDALINI

W HAT IS SHAMANISM? How does it relate to the reality shifting that was at play in my life? Jean Houston describes it in a book entitled *Shamanism* by Shirley Nicholson:

> Why is there so great a renewal of interest in one of the oldest forms of the religious life—the practice of shamanism? I believe that a good part of its fascination lies in the fact that it is prepolitical, for all religions begin as spiritual experiences which then become politicized and bureaucratized. Each level and dimension of reality is available to the one who will make the effort to learn and practice the ways and means of the spiritual journey. Thus, in shamanic practice one can have one's spiritual experience and revelation direct and unmediated by structures ordained by church or doctrine. This appeals immensely to those who seek autonomy in the spiritual journey.
>
> The shaman's ability for self-orchestration on the continuum of states of consciousness enables him or her to serve as a bridge between ordinary reality and transpersonal realms... The way of the shaman calls for initial steps of radical disintegration and dissociation, as well as procedures for consciously entering into chaos. Living at his edges, standing outside and beyond himself, the shaman experiences ecstasy as a condition of his mastery, although the ordeals and voyages into shadow worlds bring with it a harrowing of the soul that few but the shaman could endure.[35]

---

[35] Houston, Jean, "The Mind and Soul of the Shaman," in Nicholson, Shirley, ed., *Shamanism*, Quest, Wheaton, Ill., 1987, p. vii.

Ralph Metzner describes shamanism in its relationship to other traditional systems of consciousness transformation.

> I suggest that there are three traditional systems of consciousness transformation, of belief and practice, in which the exploration of these non-ordinary realms is pursued with discipline and intention: shamanism, alchemy, and yoga... Alchemy, which developed independently in Europe, the Near East, India, and China, shares with shamanism the goal of consciousness transformation, the quest for healing, knowledge, and power, and profound respect for nature.
>
> Yoga, like shamanism and alchemy, comprises a certain kind of world view and a systematic technology of changing consciousness. There is less emphasis on nature, animals, plants, minerals, the environment, and more focus on interior higher states of consciousness.   In some of the Indian yoga teachings there is a kind of detachment from and transcendence of the realms of nature, matter, the earth, the physical body. Important exceptions to this general tendency are tantra yoga ... which emphasize the transmutation of the physical body and practices of regeneration and longevity, along with the seeking of higher, transcendental states of consciousness.[36]

The ultimate goal of all paths is union with the Higher Self—the return to the source.  The soul (the divine feminine) merges with spirit (the divine masculine) bringing about the wholeness both seek.  Each individual journey is unique within itself.  Although Kundalini is described more completely in the Hindu texts, I would only come to know of that later.  For the moment my process began at my roots, my American Indian heritage.  Shakti was engaged in the weaving of my healing garment which would result in a universal pattern.  I was once told by an American Indian that we must travel around the hoop learning from each of the teachers of each of the four directions.  Then and only then would you

---

[36] Metzner, Ralph, "Transformation Processes in Shamanism, Alchemy, and Yoga," in Nicholson, Shirley, ed., *Shamanism*, Quest, Wheaton, Ill., 1987, pp. 233–234.

be ready to step into its center to claim your power. And so the journey had begun. Holger Kalweit describes how the induction into such states begins:

> For traditional cultures sickness, suffering, and death are manifestations of the body's inherent wisdom, to which we only have to surrender to reach areas of perception capable of revealing the true basis of our earthly existence.
>
> They also see sickness as a process that cleanses us of the bad habits we have accumulated by our false attitude to life. To die and to suffer a severe sickness are part of the basic experience of the shaman's path... We must learn to look death in the face and come to understand sickness as something resulting from an inner imbalance... Sickness is a call for self-realization, self-development, and in extreme cases—as the following narrative shows—a variety of shamanic initiation.
>
> On his travels through Siberia, the Hungarian explorer Vilmos Dioszegi collected many reports about shamanic vocations experienced as a result of sickness. Once he asked Kyzlasov, a former shaman of the Sagay tribe from Kyzlan on the river Yes, how he had acquired his powers. Kyzlasov reacted with a stony silence. But then his wife began to tell her husband's story:
>
> How did he become a shaman? Sickness seized him when he was twenty-three years old and he became a shaman at the age of thirty. That was how he became a shaman, after the sickness, after the torture. He had been ill for seven years. While he was ailing, he had dreams: He was beaten up several times, sometimes he was taken to strange places. He had been around quite a lot in his dreams and he had seen many things... He who is seized by the shaman sickness and does not begin to exercise shamanism, must suffer badly. He might lose his mind, he may even have to give up his life. Therefore he is advised, "You must take up shamanism so as not to suffer!" Some even say, "I became a shaman only to escape illness."[37]

---

[37] Kalweit, Holger, "When Insanity is a Blessing: The Message of Shamanism," in Grof, Stanislav and Christina, eds., *Spiritual Emergency*, Tarcher, Los Angeles, 1989, pp. 80–81.

## THE RESTRUCTURING PROCESS BEGINS

I marvel as I look back and realize the wonderful teachers who have appeared in my life to assist me in this awakening. Their teachings have varied in culture and ideology, stirring in me understandings of universal origin and scope. Many have told me that bodily changes occur as Kundalini rises through the different chakras culminating finally in a union. The American Indian shamans describe it as dismemberment and rebirth. The body is often seen as being torn apart in some way and magically restructured in preparation for a destined task. This process expresses itself either in the imaginal realm, the physical realm or seeks manifestation through a combination of both.

The next phase of my journey would initiate a period of body restructuring and illness that lasted over eight years. My experience of such physiological changes began our first Christmas in Switzerland, December, 1983. Some friends of ours had invited us on a ski trip. After arriving and settling into our rooms, excitement rose as each guest anticipated the afternoon's adventure in the sparkling snow covered mountains. The house was full of busy sounds as everyone gathered their equipment and packed lunches for the trip. My right arm began to ache. My throat became sore and my body felt feverish. I took my temperature, but all seemed normal. As time went by, my condition worsened. It became quite evident that I must remain behind. Hopefully, it would pass. About mid-afternoon, I went to lie down. Silence filled the house as everyone drove away. My arm began to hurt so badly that I placed a pillow under it for support. It felt as if a great pressure was pulling it out of my body. The pain mounted in intensity until I could barely stand it. My arm felt somehow separate from the rest of me. I felt myself drift into an altered state.

A great Light, golden and oval in shape, appeared. Although it looked like a flying saucer, it was only about a foot long. It hovered above my head and began to shoot a laser of golden light into the top of my head, creating an immense heat that radiated throughout my body. The Light seemed to run into my head, down into the heart region, out through my arm, and completing its circle back at the saucer of Light. Following the same path it recycled continuously for several hours. The pain increased at such a high pitch until finally I lost consciousness. Upon awakening, to my surprise, I realized the sun had gone down. Somehow I had lost track of time. The achy feeling in the body was gone. My sore throat was cured, and all pain had disappeared. My arm seemed renewed and stronger. In fact, I had the strange sensation that it was somehow different from the rest of my body. In actuality, it was considerably stronger. I could lift heavy objects with it that I had not been able to left before. How could this be? What in the world was happening to me? Was there no one who could help me understand such bizarre happenings? Little did I know that this was only the beginning of many such occurrences.

The left arm went through transformation in a less severe but equally effective manner. I had a dream in which a huge prehistoric butterfly appeared overhead. As I pointed to it with my left hand, it came to me. It wrapped itself around my whole hand, stinging me. When I awoke, a burning sensation ran from my little finger down my arm to the elbow. Although the results were more subtle in nature, I seemed to experience a sense of balance between the two sides of my upper body. I did not have any knowledge of Kundalini at the time, and so when the visionary experiences began to have physiological manifestations, I became frightened. Gopi Krishna speaks to such visionary awakenings in the following way:

> The whole organism now begins to function in a most amazing manner which cannot but strike terror into the stoutest heart. Tossed between the old and yet incompletely built new conscious centre, the subject, unprepared for such a startling development, sees himself losing control of his thoughts and actions. He finds himself confronted by a rebellious mind and unruly senses and

organs working in an inexplicable way, entirely foreign to him, as if the world, suddenly turned upside down, had dragged him to a topsy-turvey existence as weird and bizarre as the most fantastic dream. It is for this reason that the ancient teachers of Kundalini Yoga, taught by an experience extending for thousands of years, insisted on a exceptionally robust and hardy constitution, mastery over appetites and desires, voluntarily acquired control over vital functions and organs, and, above all, the possession of an inflexible will as the essentially needed qualifications in those offering themselves for the supreme undertaking of rousing the Shakti.   An excellent condition of both body and mind, difficult to achieve in the unfavorable environment of modern civilization, is absolutely necessary in an enterprise of this nature to prevent the brain from giving way completely under the unbearable strain.[38]

## ALTERED STATES OF CONSCIOUSNESS

The archetypal energy was electrifying my field, creating synchronicities that seemed to merge the inner and outer realities. It was like walking around in a dream or waking up in this one we call life.  I couldn't tell which!  The following events only further animated that feeling. In February of 1984, I accepted an invitation to the south of Switzerland. Just before going, I had a lucid dream.

*I was in the house of an old man, who had been instrumental in teaching me many things. He had the appearance of Father time— wrinkled, with white thinning hair that always seemed astray. He was stern yet patient with me.  He possessed great wisdom and a physical strength that was incongruent with his physical appearance. His house was wonderfully earthy, with a hearth and all natural surroundings. Ivy curled its way around the exposed beams in the roof, and slid down the packed earth that were the*

---

[38] Krishna, Gopi, *Kundalini, The Evolutionary Energy in Man*, Shambhala, Boulder & London, 1971, p. 164.

*interior walls of the cavelike room. A fire was burning in the hearth, creating a flickering light that danced around the room spreading a feeling of warmth in all directions. We sat talking as the night stirred outside. Just then the door blew open and in stepped an old woman. Although she seemed old in appearance, I sensed her strength and realized her power. She came and sat across from me and said, "Now tell me of the experiences that have brought you here."*

*As I began to talk, she got up, walked around to my left side, and began to whisper in my right ear. "I don't believe you," she said. "I can't see anything yet." As she said this, my consciousness shifted into an altered state. I was aware of what they were doing, but was rendered helpless to interact in any way. They laid me on the ground and began to "work" on me. The old woman knelt beside me and began to blow into my belly button. As she did, a spiral of energy began to turn within my belly and grow larger until it completely engulfed me.*

*The next thing I remembered was awakening by the fire. I felt like a new calf after birthing. I shook myself, trying to regain my orientation. I then walked over to the old woman and sat on the floor at her feet and looked up into her face and asked, "What was that?!" Just as I spoke, I realized that a luminous light flowed from each of her eyes. I again shifted into an altered state. I said, "Please help me!"*

*They stood me up. The old man took my right arm and the old woman took my left arm. They began to pull until I could feel a tension growing between my breasts. The spiral of energy began to turn again, this time originating from my heart. It grew until it engulfed me. I was in a place of darkness. I could not see, but could only hear our voices. I said, "I'm not ready!"*

*"Yes, you are!" they said.*

*I repeated, "NO! I'm not ready!"*

*"Yes, you are!"*

*They pushed me into a place I cannot describe with words. I became one with that dimension. I felt as if I had no boundaries. I was everywhere, yet nowhere at all.*

*I said, "Jesus be with me," and awoke.*

I revealed this dream because it played a major part in the events that followed. I had been invited to Locarno in the south of Switzerland by Frederick LeBoyer to view his film "The Art of Breathing." Frederick is a physician from France who has literally revolutionized birthing by reminding us of its nature and developing techniques that enhance the process— water births, soft lighting, etc. His film was to be viewed in a school auditorium in Locarno. I went with a friend. When we arrived, we discovered Frederick had reserved us seats down front. He came over and greeted us. He was obviously excited about the event and told me to pay close attention. The film began. There were no words, just beautiful images symbolizing the journey of birth. An East Indian chant echoed throughout the movie as we watched a mother prepare herself for the birthing of her infant. Frederick had developed a series of chants to train expectant mothers in the art of meditation. Through this form of meditation, the mothers were able to participate in delivery with no pain. As the film reached the climax of birth a large ocean wave representing delivery seemed to spill out of the screen and onto me. It felt as though it washed through me, leaving me in a trancelike state. The film ended. The lights came on in the auditorium, but no one moved. All of us seemed to have entered an altered state. Frederick went on stage and asked if there were any questions. No one moved. He made several jokes, but still no one moved. He thanked all for coming and left the stage. A small group of people formed a circle around him. As I looked around the auditorium, I noticed no one was leaving. Small circles were forming around the room, as if the audience was unconsciously replicating the small group that had formed around Frederick. How strange! I mean, there were around 1000 people in this auditorium and no one was leaving. Finally, Frederick motioned that it was time to leave. We were invited to eat with a group of his friends at a local pizzeria. As he left with our small group out of the back doors, the spell was broken. People began to speak more loudly and wander out of the auditorium. I have never before or since experienced such a group dynamic. We as a group had obviously been inducted by the sound and imagery of the film. In the film we had been left with the image of a new born wide eyed child. In some way a similar dynamic had been tapped in our psyche's leaving us in a preverbal state.

In the car riding over to the restaurant, Frederick asked enthusiastically how we liked the film. I shared that it had put me in an altered state and I needed a little time. I rode the rest of the way speechless, trying to stay centered, with an inner "knowing" instructing every step of the way. Shortly after we had ordered, my inner guidance said to share the dream of the old man with Frederick, so I did. He pushed his dishes back and moved closer to me, facing me. As I told the dream, the trancelike feeling intensified—something began to take over. I told him that I was experiencing a feeling of no boundaries, a feeling that I was everywhere, but nowhere at all. As I said this, a small tear ran down my face.

He said, "Don't hold back—let it come."

A gush of energy rolled up from below, bringing with it waves of emotion. A ball of light appeared overhead and emitted a light beam that entered the top of my head, and then surrounded me completely. The heat was incredible. I felt I was on fire. I could hear it making an electrical whirring sound as it burned, similar to neon lights or those electrical gadgets that kill flies. I began to sweat profusely. A rumbling sound ascended from the earth up my torso as the light cascaded from above. They met at my heart region sending convulsive movements throughout my body. My breathing became labored.

Frederick told me that it was important to say what I saw and felt at that moment. I felt as if I were a ball of light whose essence poured through the pores of my body radiating outward. As a wave of emotion rose through me, my body experienced involuntary convulsions—epileptic in appearance. Mucus and sweat poured. My clothes were wringing wet. Although Frederick could not visually see what I was seeing, he had some sense of its magnitude. Frederick asked if I was going to be all right.

Something quietly spoke to him from inside, "Don't worry. When she gave birth to her second son, the body reacted in the same manner. She birthed too quickly. The body must adjust." It was true, for after the birth of my second son my body had gone into involuntary convulsions and body tremors that lasted for several hours. The medical crew hadn't been able to explain what had happened. I know now that many women experience Kundalini phenomena during childbirth, but our culture has not yet come to understand it. After a few more minutes, he had me raise my arms and breathe slowly in and out. All seemed to pass.

I knew somehow that we were in "protected" space. One part of my consciousness seemed to do a physical check of the surroundings. It was as if the world had stopped. Our group seemed to be in a different space than the others. Here we were in a pizza parlor, and no one seemed to mind the commotion or even notice that it was happening. How could that be? I sat in my wet clothing wondering what had just happened. I had a sense that I had crossed over a threshold of some sort, but to what avail I had no clue.

Frederick invited me to stay over an extra day. We talked almost non-stop the next day, reviewing what had happened, trying to make sense of it all. A voice kept whispering in my head, "What is birthing but breathing in. What is dying but breathing out. Isn't it time we put the two together?"

The experience had left me changed. My view of the world around me had changed. Everything seemed a part of me, or I a part of it. I seemed to know things before I actually saw them or was told about them. Frederick suggested I visit his guru, U. G., in Gastad on my way home. He gave me directions to a chalet called Little Sunbeam located on the outskirts of the village. Though I was still a bit disoriented, I managed to find my way. U. G. was very gracious and listened to my story as I rambled on and on. Finally, he leaned forward and said, "You are a pioneer on the new frontier. Go home and wash dishes!" As

I prepared to leave, he gave me a book entitled *The Mystique of Enlightenment — The Unrational Ideas of a Man Called U. G.* that told of his awakening process. He suggested I read it. It would help me understand.

There was so much to ponder on the way home. I felt like Dorothy in *The Wizard of Oz*. A huge tornado had just picked me up and left me in a new world. I was disoriented. I had difficulty remembering, and cognitive practices of any kind, no matter how simple, were monumental. Still, I went home and washed dishes, continued to go to school and managed my daily affairs as best I could. For the next two weeks I was out of my body, floating above it with a sense of expanded awareness. My body operated on "automatic." I had to make a conscious effort to feel the soles of my feet. Only in this way could I maneuver the physical self. Trying to operate from two levels of consciousness took incredible energy. The aloneness I felt was overwhelming. Sometimes the fright would feel overpowering. Was I going to have to learn to live like this? It was too much! My senses were so expanded that it felt as if they were on overload. I could smell things cooking down the block, hear others thoughts and sense their feelings through my body as if they were my own. I was able to manage on my own for the most part. When I tried to share what was happening with my husband he became frightened and just shut down. I had a dear friend who I confided in who helped me get my grocery shopping done and other daily routines that involved a cognitive process. Remembering schedules, grocery lists and the like seemed to be the most difficult. I know now that what I was experiencing was a unitive process that many of the saints and mystics have written about. Evelyn Underhill in her book entitled *Mysticism* describes the unitive state in much more detail. Then, I just thought I was going crazy. Walking in the woods and staying close to nature was the only thing that seemed soothing.

How do such transcendental states of awareness effect us? Though my personality (egoic self) was struggling with the events, "the witness" in me was calm. Emma Bragdon in her book, *The Call of Spiritual Emergency*, explains it in this way:

> Having an experience of any of the higher realms does not necessarily mean that people will be in a crisis. However, even when they have openness, trust, and flexibility, it is still a challenge to let go of their habitual ideas of the world and enter a world of psychic phenomena, timelessness, boundlessness, limitless energy, and inspiration. Approaching these realms, even though they offer ecstasy and love, is often disorienting and can cause profound fear.[39]

James Hillman, in his commentary on Gopi Krishna's Kundalini process, states:

> The other world has become terrifyingly, experientially real; he has felt its power, not just known of it from books and teachings. He becomes the "homo religiosus" through the very fear itself, which is nothing else than awe, the primary religious emotion.
>
> Now he can say that the movement to the other world is not a one-step matter. It is not crossing a threshold from a small room to a larger just like that. This is an old debate in spiritual disciplines. Is enlightenment achieved step by step as a pilgrim climbs that mountain? Or is it achieved in a break-through flash of illumination? Gopi Krishna's observation (is) that enlightenment has a process character.

Hillman goes on in his commentary on Krishna to describe one step that he calls the *extension of consciousness*:

> Consciousness and the "I" are no longer identified. The ego "instead of a confining unit, now itself encompassed by a shining conscious globe of vast dimensions"... the formulator (the ego) cannot grasp the totality of the event. In a nutshell, "There was ego consciousness as well as a vastly extended field of awareness, existing side by side, both distinct yet one."[40]

---

[39] Bragdon, Emma. *The Call of Spiritual Emergency*, Harper & Row, San Francisco, 1990, p. 7.

[40] Krishna, Gopi, *Kundalini, The Evolutionary Energy in Man*, Shambhala, Boulder & London, 1971, pp. 154–155.

Shortly after my experience of extended fields of awareness, I began noticing a strange feeling in my right eye. It burned and felt irritated. During meditations I was told that it was being rebuilt to be used as an instrument in allowing the "energy" to flow through to others. How this could happen, I did not understand. Several days later, after my eye had returned to normal, I was at a party with several friends. Suddenly, I began to receive instruction from Spirit about one of the guests. I was told that she would be approaching me in a minute and would relay her personal distress at several things happening in her life—in particular, health problems. I was instructed to tell her to hold out her hands, palms up. I was to place mine palms down just about an inch above hers. She was to look into my right eye; in this way, a "gift" would be given. As I listened, I fought with myself. Should I risk telling her what I had been told? Would she think it crazy? Though it was validating for me at some level, it felt risky at another. "Trust the process. All will be revealed," a voice spoke softly.

No sooner had I received this instruction than the scene that had been described unfolded down to the last detail. When she had finished sharing her problems, I told her of my instructions from Spirit and asked if she was willing to experiment with me. She answered, "Sure, let's give it a try." We stood face to face in the position that had been suggested. As she looked into my right eye, a sudden flash of psychic energy, much like a laser, shot from my eye into hers. She was startled as a chill-like reaction descended through her body and out of her toes. She jumped back saying, "What was that! It went right through me to my toes." I was as amazed as she. Several days went by before I contacted her again. She had been through quite a process, experiencing extra bleeding during her menstral cycle, chills, and general bodily feelings that were flu-like in nature. It took about a week before all reactions seemed to clear. Her health improved and solutions for the other situations in her life presented themselves.

During such spiritually transformative processes, it is important to stay consciously aware of your physical and mental states. Therefore, as the energy works through the body manifesting physical symptoms, it is helpful to consult with a physician to investigate any possible diseases or ailments that could be "flushed up" during, or as a result of, the process. It is important to try to find one with a holistic perspective so that a supportive environment for your healing can develop. Remember that the "energy" is working towards your healing on all levels and will provide you with the necessary tools to facilitate that process. It is a cooperative operation. In surrendering to the process, you do not give up your responsibility in it. Quite the contrary! The healing inherent in such a process is multidimensional. As you witness, you begin to see that the dress and the dressmaker are the same. The weaving of the new garment requires that you stand back and "watch" as each different color finds its place to blend with the other colors of varying shades and thicknesses, creating a pattern distinct from all others. And so it goes as Shakti animates within your psyche the varying memories that stir the alchemy of the individuation process. In my case, the "body restructuring" served to stir past-life memories. It's my belief that such remembering serves us best if we realize that these memories surface to remind us of the strengths developed during previous incarnations and/or the unfinished work left for the soul to complete in this lifetime. This is simplifying a deep field of study, but for further information I would recommend that you complete your understanding of reincarnation by seeking texts on this subject.

Bear with me, I will continue to describe the "dismemberment" process as it presented itself before I propose any further interpretations. I next experienced another dream.

*I was in a circle surrounded by Indians. A ceremony was in progress. One of them handed me a staff made of bamboo that had a handle shaped like a snake in a circle. He handed*

*the staff to me with the handle pointing to my uterus. I began*
*to experience menstrual cramping.   When I awoke, the pain*
*continued.*

I began to bleed profusely.  In meditation I was told not to
worry, this was a purification process; all would be fine.  The
bleeding continued heavily throughout the next day.  Finally, in
late evening, I called a doctor and described my symptoms.  He
prescribed medication to shrink the uterus which was suppose to
stop the bleeding.  It had no effect.  I was becoming continually
weaker.  Around 2 a.m.  the next morning, I prayed for help.
I needed rest.  The bleeding stopped, allowing me to sleep for about
five hours.  Again, it started, continuing until early afternoon.  By
the time I reached the doctor, all symptoms had subsided.  I relayed
my story of the events.  He became concerned, fearing the worst—
cancer.  He ran many tests and did a physical exam.  I will never
forget the irony of it all when he walked into his office and said,
"What can I say, all seems fine.  Yours is just a unique experience!"
A unique experience—boy, if he only knew!

I find that one experience usually prepares us in some way for
the next.  A "purification process" would suggest a preparation for
something.  I don't really think I understood that in those days,
but I can see it now as I look back on the events as they unfolded.
About one month later, I attended a workshop on healing by
Gloria Karpinski.  At the conclusion of the day, we performed
a ritual to heal the earth.  During this rite, I felt my energy change.
I went out in the hall to be alone, thinking it would shift.  Rather
than diminishing, it intensified.  Once again I began to feel the
surge of an energy wave that came from below and moved over
me, bringing with it overwhelming emotion.  I paced the floor,
wondering what was going to happen.  Suddenly, my feet became
planted, and instead of Light surging from above, Sound came.
A loud roaring shot from above and rang through my body.  It
seemed to come out through my hands with a humming sound
much like a tuning fork evokes.  Gloria, who is knowledgeable of

such happenings, came to my aid. I felt that I was being born and giving birth both at the same time. I could actually feel the membrane above my head, and after two tries I was able to break through this unseen wall. I felt like a new born baby who had just exited the womb!

The period afterwards was experienced much as before with Frederick, only I was able to adjust to the newness more quickly. I took some time to regroup and drove Gloria and me home. This wasn't such a good idea since the brakes seemed to be affected by my energy surges; I had to have them repaired shortly afterward. Later that evening, I kept feeling a kicking sensation in my belly. Others could feel it too. We assumed it was the energy kicking, reminding me of its power. My belly became extended and remained that way for several hours. Little did I know that I was being given a preview of events to come, but that is another part of the story. I began to understand the meaning of "walking the razor's edge" and knew that I sometimes hung between life and death, sanity and insanity. As my body continued to transform, so also did my psyche.

In the months that followed, I began being awakened around one or two in the morning with my body shaking and jerking. I would later discover that this is called kriyas on the Kundalini path. It is defined as a pranic activity that displays physical symptoms such as involuntary jerks, shaking, vibrating or spasms. Bonnie Greenwell, in her book *Energies of Transformation*, further describes *kriyas* as the resulting "jerking as a major flood of energy comes up the body originating from the big toe, the foot or the base of the spine."[41] When these convulsive activities were happening, I could feel an energy running through me. My spine felt as if it was being realigned. This usually went on for an hour or so, and during each episode, I felt as if I were above my body watching the events below.

---

[41] Greenwell, Bonnie, *Energies of Transformation, A Guide to the Kundalini Process*, Shakti River Press, Cupertino, Ca., 1990, p. 31.

In addition to these nightly sessions, I experienced a severe headache from the neck up. It lasted continually for six weeks and felt as if I had one of those old iron deep-sea diving helmets over my head. My head felt weighted down. My neck was painfully stiff. It felt as if the weight of the helmet rested on my shoulders, making the smallest movement of my head constricted and painful. Finally, one evening I awoke to sense many unseen presences in the room. The room felt stuffy and very cool. My body began to run energy—activating *kriyas*. Suddenly, I began feeling a pushing and rolling motion that began in the pelvic area and continued up the body. It felt like a tube being uncoiled. Slowly the uncoiling continued up my torso. When it reached my head area, I had the distinct image of a white larva-shaped object falling out of the left side of my head onto the pillow. A quietness followed. I fell back into sleep. Upon awakening, I realized my headache was no longer present on the left side of my head. The next night exactly the same procedure took place, except this time when the uncoiling reached my head I had the image of a cobra spreading wide its hood and resting on the top of my head as its tongue licked my third eye. The image was accompanied by a loud high-pitched ringing. The next morning the headache was completely gone. I again realized a change in my senses. I could see things in their energy form. All of my senses were enhanced, more finely tuned.

Until these experiences I had no knowledge of Kundalini. This rebuilding process as I have described it took about a year and a half. Much of the experience had been frightening, but my therapists assured me that my sanity was in tact, that I must keep going. With the presentation of this last image Cornelia gave me Gopi Krishna's book, *Kundalini, The Evolutionary Energy in Man*. For the first time I began to feel ground under my feet. I still wasn't sure where all this was taking me, but I knew I had no choice but to follow or risk loosing myself all together. Later as I began to study more about Kundalini I found that the phenomena I had been experiencing followed a traditional path. As Bonnie Greenwell writes:

Generally a Kundalini experience is first identified because of the unusual physiological activity it generates. It is difficult for western medicine to grasp the connection between body symptoms and mysticism, even though a cursory glance at the writing of Christian mystics makes it clear that they commonly endured dramatic physical problems. These have been considered a consequence of a weak physical disposition by those who have no framework for understanding the relationship between energy, the body and religious experience. If we can theorize that spiritual awakening involves an intense movement of energy and a restructuring of the physical system in order to handle it, then we can begin to appreciate the impact on the body and the strain of the system trying to integrate it.[42]

Greenwell goes on to say:

Da Free John wrote that the emotional problem of self--division is the root of all suffering and delusion. People are not relaxed in the heart, and are afraid and contracted against the experience of being in contact with divine being which is manifest everywhere.[43]

She presents a statement by him:

Heartfelt release of fear is the secret of passing through the spiritual process without going mad. To the degree that you are full of fear, you limit your experience—and if experience is forced upon you, then you have no ability while fearful to view it sanely, to relax and surrender within it. You cannot surrender by relaxing and trying to feel better. You can surrender only by giving yourself up, relaxing your self-hold, surrendering your mind altogether to the Transcendental Consciousness in which it arises, and yielding your body to the All-Pervading Current of Life, of which it is but a temporary modification.[44]

---

[42] Ibid, 1990, p. 31.
[43] Ibid, p. 266.
[44] Ibid, p. 266.

It had been a difficult passage in many ways, yet I had begun to discover a depth in me I had not known existed. No sooner is the vessel emptied than the filling begins. My friends and therapists had been my mainstay during this part of the journey, but more new teachers and spirit guides were soon to appear.

CHAPTER FIVE

# *The Marriage of Self*

L OOKING BACK ON THE TIME PERIOD I am about to describe, I realize that this phase of my learning was based in ritual. As Joseph Campbell states, "A ritual is the enactment of a myth."[45] Jean Houston elaborates, "Like all real art, ritual provides organic order, a pattern of dynamic expression through which the energy of an event or series of events can flow in an evolutionary process toward larger meaning or a new stage or level of life. *It offers ways in which your transitions are illuminated.*"[46] Ritual is born out of the culture in which it resides and therefore reflects the cultures heritage. It sets a container for the divine to initiate the practitioner through a direct experience; an experience that enlivens the entire being of that individual activating new levels of consciousness and expanding one's awareness. In my case each ritual activated another part of my personal myth initiating me into new ways of "seeing." There seemed to be an alchemy afoot. One ritual stimulated my Christian mystic side, one spanned the human-spirit divide, while the other enlivened my Cherokee memory. Though their cultural differences were obvious, all were rituals performed for the Earth ignited by my deep passion for her healing. The intensity of these initiations changed my life in

---

[45] Campbell, Joseph, *The Power of Myth*, Doubleday, New York, 1988, p. 82.
[46] Houston, Jean, *The Search for The Beloved*, Jeremy P. Tarcher, Inc., Los Angeles, 1987, p. 42.

63

ways I still do not completely understand. Was this to be a year of ceremony and pilgrimage for the purpose of awakening something in me? There had been no conscious intent to seek out initiation, but I found myself deeply within it. Hearing the call, I answered.

## FIRST INITIATION: THE DIVINE MOTHER

My friend Max and his wife Theresa told me of a place in Yugoslavia where the Madonna was said to appear to six young people. They knew a woman who was arranging groups of people to visit there. She had come from the village of Medjugorje and knew the children and their families. She had been so moved by her own experiences there that she had devoted herself to helping others make the same pilgrimage. She shared with us the information as she knew it to be: on June 24, 1981, one of the small children was on the hillside above Medjugorje near a cross that looked down upon the village. The Madonna appeared to her. She wanted to share the "beautiful lady" with her friends, so she ran to get them and brought them to the cross. The Madonna appeared again and began to speak to the children. They then sought out the parish priest. As people began to hear of the apparitions, thousands began to gather. The Yugoslavian government did not like such activities and seeking to quell them, placed the priest in jail, but this only stimulated more publicity. The government, caught in their own web, told the priest that they would release him if the Madonna would agree to go into the church. The priest spoke with the children and they with Mary, and she agreed. The word spread quickly to all corners of the world, generating thousands who sought to attend High Mass daily. Ironically, some 20 years prior to Mary's appearance a large church had been constructed, as if in anticipation of its future need. When you arrive in this very small remote village and see this large church reaching up to the sky, it's size alone is astounding because it doesn't seem to fit. Yet, it stands filled each day with thousands of visitors.

The children were brought to the chapel each day around 6:00 p.m. for High Mass. They held prayer separately in a small antechamber to the left of the main alter. The priest would begin mass in order to prepare the people. About midway through mass, the children would cross before the alter and enter another room just off to the right of the alter. It was in this room that the Divine Mother would appear. In a lovely book entitled *Medjugorje, A Portfolio of Images*, her divine mission is described in this way:

> Through these youngsters, the Blessed Virgin is bringing her message of conversion and peace to the world, saying that these will be her last apparitions on earth. And she has invited all men and women of good will to fast and pray, to frequent the sacrament of the Eucharist and that of Reconciliation, for too long neglected: *"Take my message seriously, for God is not joking with mankind."* She is said to have promised that she would entrust to the six seers ten secrets and that she would leave a tangible and visible sign on the hill of the first apparitions for atheists, that they, too, might come to believe. She has likewise assured the children that humanity will be freed from the power of evil when the contents of all the secrets have been fulfilled. Then a new era of peace and a faith-filled return to God will be initiated on the earth.[47]

The author goes on to say,

> The Blessed Virgin has not come to predict catastrophes, but to teach us how to avoid them... At Lourdes, the Virgin appeared at the break of dawn; at Fatima, she appeared at noon. In Medjugorje, she appears as the sun begins to set. History's clock stresses time's inevitability. "Happy the servant whom the Master finds watching when he returns."[48]

In the summer of 1984 I decided to make the journey with Theresa and Max. When we arrived, I became the quiet observer,

---

[47] Emanuele, *Medjugorje, A Portfolio of Images*, Alba House, Staten Island, New York, 1987, p. 7.
[48] Ibid, p. 71.

watching the happenings as they evolved each day. There were people of all colors, all faiths, from all countries. Humanity itself was certainly well represented. Priests sitting in chairs outside the church heard confessions and administered to the people. Nuns in their traditional habit rallied around being available to those present. A sense of reverence was in the air.

I spent my first day in meditation in the chapel, not completely sure why I had been drawn to this remote place, but having a sense that the Divine Mother had called me. The room in which she appeared to the children could only hold around 20 people. Some were given special invitation and others merely walked up to the room as the children entered in hopes of being among those allowed in. My intuition strongly suggested that I would experience this vision along with the children. I knew that if I was supposed to be there, things would happen to arrange it. I continued to pray and meditate. A stillness was in the air that seemed to permeate one's very being.

The following day my friends and I walked the mountain path leading up to the cross where Mary had first appeared. Theresa wandered off the path and got lost in the bramble bush of the hillside. The bush was full of thorns and difficult to maneuver through, so that it took several hours before she was able to find her way out and back down the path to the church. In the meantime, Max and I had become quite worried. We looked frantically everywhere. We went to the nuns and priests and told them of our predicament. It was getting late and the sun was beginning to set. Our fear was that we would not be able to find her before dark. The land was primitive and could prove dangerous to someone not accustomed to it. 'One of the priests made an announcement to the congregation asking Theresa to come forward if she were in the audience. No one came. It was decided that if she did not return by the conclusion of High Mass, we would form a search party to walk the land. Max and I were beside ourselves. A small inner voice quietly suggested we go to mass and know that all would be all right.

Max and I entered the church and proceeded to the front where we were to sit if we wished to enter the antechamber with the children. The priest came to the center of the alter and welcomed all. The church was full to overflowing. About halfway through mass, the children entered the sanctuary from a small room just off the main alter area. They walked across the front of the church and entered a room on the opposite side. People stood and began to walk, pushing, anxious to get in. A strong feeling of trust descended on me and reminded me of the sacredness of such moments, so I walked in a state of prayer. Just as I got to the door, the priest put his arm across the door halting any further entry. I entered an altered state. The world around me took on the feeling of dreamtime. A small brown skinned girl of about 5 years turned around looking up at me. Her brown eyes were deep and warm. I felt her connect with something deep inside my soul and the next thing I knew out of my mouth came the words, "Bambino!" My arm, with a life of its own, reached out for the small girl child. She reached up and took my hand. The priest turned and looked at the child and then back at me. Much to my surprise, he lifted his arm and allowed me entry. The door to the room was then closed, allowing no one else to enter. The young girl seemed to melt into the crowd and I never saw her again. I had been taught that "a child will lead you" into heaven, and on this particular day, one had.

The room was quiet as the children stood before a statue of the Blessed Mary. We stood in close quarters, perspiring from the heat of the day. Suddenly, I sensed the room filling with an unseen presence. If you've ever been in a spirit-filled room, you will sense an energy that feels like cotton in the atmosphere. The children all simultaneously fell to their knees and looked up. I saw what appeared to be a tiny blue dot that moved closer to the children and then stopped. For a moment we were all suspended in time. Then as quickly as it had begun, it ended. The children rose to their feet, moved through the people and reentered the church sanctuary. We all followed.

I don't think I realized the impact of the environment created by Mary until I left the room. The air and climate felt very different. How to describe this with words is beyond me. My body felt weak and for a moment I thought I would pass out and go into convulsions, but something in me resisted. I was still very concerned for Theresa and placed her in my prayers. The children finished the mass by chanting. You could actually see a room full of strangers melt into one body. As the message for love was shared, strangers embraced and hearts opened. The service over, I found Max and we proceeded to the entryway. Small tremors played through my body and my head began to ache. We had met with the priests and were about to put a search party together when Theresa came walking in. She was scratched and bleeding all over from her battle with the thorny landscape, but she was all right. Each of us in our own individual way had received something.

We decided to drive to Dubrovnik, a coastal village about two hours away. About halfway there, my head began to ache so badly that I couldn't stand it any longer. I could feel the energy mounting, demanding release. I asked Max if we could stop the car for a few minutes. I needed some time alone to surrender to the process at hand. Max stayed with me. My body began to shake and perspire profusely. A loud sound moved through me ascending from my feet, up through my body and out of my head. I became very nauseated. After about 20 minutes or so, the energy quieted and we were able to continue. But later that night, as I lay in my hotel room, waves of emotion flowed through me. Again, a sense of the dreamtime altered my reality. A deep stillness descended and a giant being entered my space. He was so tall I couldn't see above his chest. His body was made of gold dust with a red background. He walked toward me and passed through me. My body began to convulse and I lost consciousness. When I awoke, it was morning. I felt different, but in what way I wasn't quite sure. I spent the day lying next to the sea, bathing in the cool clear waters and drying by the warm sun.

This would be the first of three initiations I encountered starting in the summer of 1984 and ending in the summer of 1985. I do not presume to know more than what I actually witnessed. Each time I received an inner instruction to go; each time a mystical state descended and transported me into the dreamtime; each time my system was impacted as I entered an interdimensional reality. Why or for what purpose, I did not know.

The feminine archetype of the Divine Mother had massaged my soul initiating a process of unfoldment that lay deep within my core. Jean Houston in her book *The Search for the Beloved* describes that process in the following way:

> Philosophically, in the reality structure of the feminine archetype, Great Nature is just as important within as it is without. The principle of the unus mundus, the unified reality stream, is operative here; the realm of inwardness has as much ontological status as the external world has. [*The feminine principle expresses itself as an unfolding of levels of existence, not as the conquest of facts.*][49]

She goes on to explain how the ancient Asclepian[50] is the great Western model for transformation.

> On very deep levels it asks us to remember who we are— to know again our sourcing through the sacred. It provides an opening through which the emerging myth and archetypal energies may enter into time, renewing the individual and the larger context in which we live.[51]

---

[49] Houston, Jean, *The Search for The Beloved*, Jeremy P. Tarcher, Inc, Los Angeles, 1987, p. 16.

[50] Ibid, p. 11. "In the Asclepian mode, the growth of consciousness as well as the healing of the body-mind was encouraged by a rhythm of dynamic input through theatre, philosophy, athletics, and so forth, followed by experiences. of the sacred dream [*the Madonna experience being a good example*] Such experiences created a context for the body and mind to shift into a more complex, coherent state of being. This state organically effected healing by reconstituting the reality of body and mind into a high order."

[51] Ibid, p. 12.

## SECOND INITIATION: THE VISION QUEST

When trying to incorporate spiritual realities into a consciousness programmed not to recognize or accept them, it helps to have a frame of reference with which to analyze, categorize, and process them. This frame of reference could appropriately be called "sacred psychology"—a psychology that helps bridge the two worlds that must be integrated. It helps categorize spiritual experiences by using terms and references familiar to us through traditional psychology. Jean Houston explains sacred psychology in the following way:

> In the cartography of human experience, sacred traditions have tended to map three major realms of experience. Doubtless there are many more realms, with levels upon levels inside each, but three stand out as significant: the realm of the historical and factual, the realm of the mythic and symbolic, and the realm of the unitive or source level of being. To suggest their nature, I have called them the realm of THIS IS ME, the realm of WE ARE, and the realm of I AM, respectively... The first and certainly most familiar realm, the THIS IS ME reality, refers to everyday, ordinary existence... The WE ARE realm functions as the contact point for sacred time and sacred space, the container of that which never was and is always happening... The place where the self joins its polyphrenic possibilities, including the gods and goddesses and their courts... Beyond and within the other two realms is the realm of the I AM, that is, Being itself, pure potency, a realm of love and organicity, the very stuff of reality. It is the realm many of us know as God... God as the Unity of Being.[52]

With Houston's realms in mind, let us once again enter the WE ARE realm—the realm of the mythic and symbolic experience. It was January of 1985. Snow was falling heavily; in fact, it was the heaviest snowfall in 100 years. For several months the idea of doing a vision quest kept entering my mind. (A vision quest, as described by Native Americans, is when you marry yourself to

---

[52] Ibid, pp. 23–25.

Mother Earth. It is a rite of passage which knocks at the door of Great Spirit and asks for direction in the THIS IS ME factual realm.) Like a fly this idea wouldn't go away. The final kick came when I received a letter from a shaman of the Pomo tradition—she said it was time for my vision quest. Her instructions: find a place of seclusion, begin to fast, and wait for my vision—the biggest vision I had ever experienced. Well, that made me nervous! She said to set aside 9 to 21 days. After the vision had visited, I was to spend one more night before returning home—end of instruction.

I called a friend and arranged for a cabin in the Alps. Friends helped me cart wood and coal, plus some juices. As they disappeared over the ridge, I first felt a sense of relief. It was the first time in my life I would have so much time alone. I didn't have to cook or wash or see to anyone's needs but my own. The snows were so heavy that I couldn't walk except on a rather short trail I had made getting up to the cabin. It took a full day before the cabin got warm. Everything, plumbing-wise, was frozen, so it was outside for toilet privileges. A small stream that ran close to my front porch, provided me with drinking water. The first few days were restful, changing into boring. I came to realize how much I enjoyed being with others. My mind talked incessantly about everything and nothing. It was an interesting paradox: I found me quite boring at one level, and yet something in me anxiously awaited at another. I then began to find the need for ritual to create a connection. Though my rituals were very simple— fetching water, walking meditations, tending the fire—they began to enliven my sense of connection with my body and with the earth. As my appreciation for ritual deepened, magical encounters with the animals occurred. An example of this happened one afternoon as I sat on the porch sipping my tea. A blizzard was blowing in quite hard. I couldn't see but a few feet in front of me. Suddenly, a bluebird appeared singing and flying, making the shape of figure eights in the air. He disappeared. When he returned, he brought his whole family. There in front of me were four birds flying in and out and amongst each other, playing as if it were a warm summer day. Their visit warmed my heart and melted my loneliness away. I also had a family of rats that lived under the floor. At night they would roll things. It sounded like they were bowling! The last night I was there they really raised a commotion. It was as if they knew I was leaving. When you connect in these ways with nature, your inner child becomes animated and a deep belonging emerges, a sense of unity with all of your surroundings unfolds.

During the first six days all of my dreams and visions disappeared. It was just me looking at me. When my dreams returned, they were archetypal in nature, and I sensed an energy shift. On the ninth day, a great being came for tea! An inner voice said, "It is time. Enter the cabin and wait for instructions." I was frightened and a bit resistant: "I'll just finish my tea then I'll go in," but the instruction was persistent, so I went. Once inside I laid down on my bed. My breathing seemed to take on a life of its own— breathing first rapidly, then slowly, and finally stopping for long intervals. As the process continued, a deep trance state evolved. I felt the approaching presence of the same large godlike figure that had appeared and passed through my body in Dubrovnik. The earth seemed to quake with his every step. This time he appeared in a golden body of light. The experience took on a very intimate and sexual tone. It was so personal that I prefer not to share its details. At the conclusion of the experience a loud deep voice roared, "And now you are the ravished bride!" Just as quickly as it had begun, it ended. About three hours had passed. The sun was setting, the room was still. I cried for several hours. I felt much like I did when I lost my virginity. Though something had been given, something had been lost. A profound change in my life began that day; it took years to even begin to comprehend and in fact, I am still in search of its full meaning.

This would be my last night in the cabin. I decided to take my evening walk to express my deep thanks to this special snow-covered hideaway. The night was clear with stars brightly lighting the night sky. I walked slowly, feeling a growing warmth spread through me. Then something very quizzical happened. It had never happened before. As I walked, I began to notice a soft candlelike glow on the snow. I looked around trying to discover its source. To my surprise it was coming from me. Whatever had transpired that January afternoon in the Alps had left a radiance in its path. My mind was confused, amazed, and bewildered. How could I speak of such things? Who could help me understand what had happened and why? This same figure has continued to appear in varying forms. Many years later based on my descriptions of his unique appearance and behaviors, a dear friend would tell me his name, Metatron. Until then he had no name, only "my Beloved." (Metatron, as described in a *Dictionary of Angels*, is the link between the human and the divine.)[53] I later discovered in the writings of Lynn Andrews and Mary Summer Rain that each of them, at a certain point in their training were introduced to their spirit teachers, Windhorse and Dreamwalker. Was Metatron mine? A poem by Kabir appeared in an article by Ram Dass entitled "Promises and Pitfalls of the Spiritual Path." It seems to capture the essence of this experience.

> Friend, hope for the guest while you are alive.
> Jump into experience while you are alive...
> What you call "salvation" belongs to the time before death.
> If you do not break the ropes while you are alive,
> do you think
> ghosts will do it after?
> The idea that the soul will
> join with the ecstatic
> just because the body is rotten—
> that is all fantasy.
> What is found now is found then.
> If you find nothing now,
> you will simply end up with an
> apartment in the city of death.

---

[53] Davidson, Gustav, *A Dictionary of Angels*, The Free Press, A Division of Macmillan Publishing Co., Inc., New York, 1967, p. 192.

If you make love with the Divine now, in the next life you
will have the face of satisfied desire.
So plunge into the truth, find out who the teacher is,
Believe in the great sound![54]

The months that followed were spent with my teacher and
friend, Cornelia, trying to integrate the experience and understand
what implications it had for my life. Though it stirred my psyche,
the deeper memories would not surface until 2 years later as
the dark night of my soul purged me.   Understand that the
impregnation of new consciousness is only the beginning—the
old must break away to make room for its growth. The dance in
the WE ARE realm opens the door to the I AM realm where unity
can occur. And so the Gods kept dancing!

## THIRD INITIATION: THE SUN DANCE

I met Tigre during the summer of 1984 at a five day retreat. He
was a Native American Indian who had been trained by a Lakota
Indian chief as a Sun Dancer.   His work as a medicine man
was known amongst his people.   His life had been hard, yet
his courage and compassion formed an ambience around him.
Though he was a man of few words, his actions demonstrated that
he was a teacher.   It was like meeting an old old friend; there
was something so familiar.   There are times in one's life when
such a meeting marks a predestined encounter with fate. And as
you embark upon the inner journey, you reclaim parts of your
heritage that have been lost. My meeting with Tigre was just that.
The Taoists say that when the student is ready, the teacher will
appear. And so it was with Tigre. He was only in Switzerland for
a short while, but we continued to correspond sharing dreams and

---

[54] Ram Dass, "Promises and Pitfalls of the Spiritual Path," in Grof, Stanislav and
Christina, *Spiritual Emergency*, Jeremy P. Tarcher, Inc., Los Angeles, 1989.

visions as they appeared, reminding us of other lives and work not yet completed. It was this predestined meeting that led to an invitation to attend the Sun Dance at Big Mountain located on the Hopi mesas in Arizona. The Navajo Indians would be our hosts. Richard and I had planned a trip to the United States for August of that year, 1985. We visited family and friends. Richard and the boys returned to Switzerland and I made plans to attend the Sun Dance before rejoining them. Tigre was secretive about the Sun Dance since those in attendance were by invitation only. I wasn't sure how I would get there until a few days before my departure when a friend of a friend asked to take me. I called Tigre to work out the arrangements. I was to meet him at a small diner and he would guide us from there.

I had received a psychic reading the week before and among other things had been told that the ritual I was about to attend would signify my marriage to God. My first question was, "Will I know it when it happens?" The answer, "Oh, I'd say so!" What does such a proclamation mean? How will I know it? How will it effect me? Many questions gathered in my head. Others have said that it's not the answer that is important, but rather finding the right question. In so doing, the teaching can arise. In addition, I was told that White Eagle would be there to assist me through the initiation. I knew nothing of White Eagle or what such a guide might signify. On White Eagle Grace Cooke writes,

> I believe I am right in saying that White Eagle, our well-loved messenger from the spirit life, has been coming to us now for forty years, giving us, through all the years of fire and conflict, comforting and inspiring messages, gently leading us on to a higher conception of life's purpose. He explains to us that this teaching comes from the sphere of John, who is the herald of the New Age of Aquarius, the age of world-wide brotherhood, which will bring a fresh revelation about the purpose of man's life on Earth and his soul's potentialities. A note that may be important at this time of the story states, "In the light of recent scientific discovery it needs to be pointed out that throughout his teaching White Eagle emphasizes that the »real world« is not the material one which

we inhabit, but the spiritual world, what we sometimes call the »inner world«."[55]

It seemed that I was to be guided by the most impeccable spiritual warriors.

The Sun Dance is a ritual for the Mother Earth and her people. There is much preparation in the year preceeding the ceremony. The excitement and a palpable sense of Spirit surrounds all those involved. Each dancer has received an image of how he will dance. A Sun Dancer is sponsored by a warrior that has danced before him. He works closely with a sponsor during the year before the Sun Dance to prepare. Once he pierces at a sacred site, he is expected to pierce there for the next four years. As Jamie Sams shares in her description of the Sun Dance in her *Sacred Path Cards*,

> The purpose of the Sun Dance is to allow young Warriors to share the blood of their bodies with the Earth Mother. It is understood that women do this through their Moontime, or menstrual cycle. Women give of their pain through childbirth and the men through the Sun Dance, so the people may live. Women nurture the seeds of the future generations and the men commit their lives to the protection of that future through the ceremony of Dancing the Sun... This ancient ritual is considered a strong act of love. It teaches us how to Walk in Balance and let go of the parts of ourselves that are only interested in the personal "I".[56]

With this knowledge of the Dance I left for Arizona. My friend and I traveled several days to reach a small diner in the desert. After a couple of hours, Tigre arrived and we followed him the rest of the way. We reached our destination late in the night, so I had no idea where we were until morning. The sun was hot and the air dry. The wind stirred the red soil of the mountain and

---

[55] *Wisdom from White Eagle*, The White Eagle Publishing Trust, England, 1983, pp. 7–8.
[56] Sams, Jamie, *Sacred Path Cards: The Discovery of Self Through Native Teachings*, Harper San Francisco, 1990, pp. 75–79.

then dropped to a stillness while all settled. The sacredness of Big Mountain and of the people who reside there permeated the atmosphere. The roughness of the land and the primitive living of the people reminded one of times long ago and a connection to the land that has since been lost.

There was trouble in the air. The U. S. government wanted the land for mining coal and uranium. What they did not seem to understand was the sacredness of this land and the imbalance that could occur if it was not honored. Our government has been taking the red man's land for centuries. When will such obvious disregard of personal and civil rights be stopped? When will we get in touch with our greed and open our hearts again? In my eyes, what we do to the Earth is what we do to the women on her. When we quit raping the Earth, we will quit raping our women and children. When we quit poisoning her air, we will create a more healthy atmosphere in which to live. If we don't wake up soon, we will succeed in killing ourselves. We will die in our own filth! We as a people are on the endangered species list and it is up to us—the choices we are making will determine the outcome. Mother Earth will survive! The Sun Dance was being held at Big Mountain so we could pray for healing; so we could stand together in support of the Navajo and Hopi people and their way of life.

Though most of those in attendance were the indigenous people, some were of other colors. Many whites present were there because of their deep love of the Native Americans and what they represent. All had come great distances and made great sacrifices to be there in response to a call by Mother Earth—this great being who supports us and endures our pain. The camp was being built. Outhouses were dug and temporary kitchen space constructed. This would be the first Sun Dance held on this sacred space where all the colors of the rainbow would be represented in its people— blacks, reds, whites, and yellows. When you bring that many tribes together there is some discord before resolution. So it was in the camp days before the dance. The dancers continued to prepare, praying and entering "sweats," a process of purification performed in a sweat lodge. The dance began.

I watched as the dancers entered the arena. There were about 64 dancers that year. All had sage wreaths around their heads, ankles, and wrists. They danced around the great tree which stood tall in the center with ribbons of all colors blowing in the breeze. (Ribbons had been tied on the tree representing requests for healing and prayers.) In the first round, the Sun Dance Chief, Leonard Crow Dog, sang prayers to the four directions. Each day would begin this way. Drums beat and chants echoed across the land while people of all ages gathered in the shade of the arbor—grandmothers, mothers nursing their young, children restlessly afoot, and men and boys standing in silence. As a round of prayers came to completion, the dancers would rest momentarily and then begin again, stopping at sunset each day. The length of each round was orchestrated by the Sun Dance Chief, so many rounds were performed during a day. The dancers who participated had been called by Great Spirit. Their vision usually revealed in what manner they would pierce and on which day. The Chief would then pick the time of day. Two men had visioned that they would pierce the first day and stay attached to the tree throughout the four-day ceremony, breaking on the fourth and final day. When the second round began, several men with red marks drawn on their bodies were selected to pierce. One at a time the Chief would come and select them, bringing them over to an area that was purified with cedar and sage. The dancer would lay down on the ground while his family and friends gathered around. The chief would cut or pierce the skin with a knife or the claw of an eagle. He would then slide the cherry stick under the tissue and tie it to the rope connected to the tree. The dancer would then rise and depending on his style, as revealed and dictated in his vision, break the tissue, freeing him to merge with Great Spirit. Several dancers were usually piercing in one round. Some were hoisted up in the tree suspended by their own tissue until it broke. Some pierce in the chest, others in the back. Still others tie to horses and have the horses run, thus breaking the hold. One dancer was pierced in the back and had six buffalo skulls tied to him. He pulled this weight around the circle many times before he broke.

Though these pierce-and-break scenes were hard to watch, a great compassion filled my heart for the dancers. I did not see why our Christian brothers and sisters called this "savage" when Christ walked this same path. At first it was hard to understand how anyone could subject themselves to such pain, but then my own prejudices seemed to melt and I realized that they made me look at pain with connected eyes. I had to confront the confusion that such close examination stirs. It wasn't important to judge the rightness of such acts, but to honor what they were helping us to see, and this would be a different experience for each in attendance.

The night of the second day a very tall dancer walked into our camp. He had a gentleness about him that caught my attention. My inner voice instructed me to ask him about White Eagle. When I did, he replied, "What makes you ask about the chief of the Lightning Beings?" I went on to share some of the experiences that had been happening to me. He listened and then responded, "If you are here to bring White Eagle into your heart, you must pay attention, because you will be given only one chance." He turned away and began talking to Tigre. What did he mean? How do you bring White Eagle into your heart? My confusion only mounted and my fear of failure grew in size. Only one chance?! There was just a little pressure.

The third day when I arose and started toward the ceremony, I was amazed. Everywhere I looked White Eagle symbols appeared—white eagle necklaces, white eagle earrings, white eagle insignias on the back of blue jean jackets. What was going on? And how do I pull this into my heart? I figured White Eagle was letting me know he was near and I should pay attention.

The morning of the fourth day came. I said a prayer in camp and asked for guidance and then let it go. If this was going to happen, (whatever *this* was) it was not something I could control. I must just be open and ready. Tigre was to pierce today, but neither of us knew the time. I entered the arbor and started to dance in place like I had the last four days. I had been fasting for 10 days and could feel the lightness that results. An older Indian woman accompanying a younger white woman came and stood in front of me. Suddenly my ovaries began to burn and ache. Two young women were standing beside me and they too could feel something stirring. The opening prayers came to a close and just as they did a great invisible energy hit me in the heart region of my chest with such power that I fell backwards onto the ground and landed in a sitting position. My consciousness shifted leaving me in a deep altered space. The Indian woman approached and asked how she could help. A voice speaking through me said, "You know why you have come today. You have come to assist me in my birthing." She smiled and leaned over and began to chant in my left ear, "Let go of the ego and move into the higher self. Let go of the ego and move into the higher self." As she spoke I fell deeper into a trance. My body began to rock and I began to chant, "This is for the children. This is for the children. This is for the children." As I did, the women formed a circle around me and began to chant softly with me. I could hear the old woman telling the others that it was O.K., I was just having a spiritual experience. Every time I would become concerned about what was happening, she would chant in my ear releasing my ego to the process. My body began to perspire profusely and mucus oozed everywhere. Two huge balls of energy began to form around my hands; they became the size of basketballs. The energy originating from my hands began to flow up into my arms, across my chest, and down into my belly. At the same time energy from the earth started to enter through my feet extending itself up my legs and into my belly. Although I tried I couldn't seem to get the two flows of energy to come together. That seemed to be the ultimate goal, but try as I did, I couldn't achieve it. The old woman got Crow Dog—at least that's what others told me later, I never saw anything but his feet. He asked me if I had fasted and began smudging me with sage. He then asked me to tell him what I was experiencing. I did. He then did some movement in my abdominal area and leaned me forward asking me to push like a woman in labor. Once again, I had the distinct feeling that I was being born and giving birth all at the same time. I saw a light that looked like white tail feathers. A loud sound roared through my body as I went into the light or it went into me, I couldn't tell which. I remember saying, "Oh, my God!" I then went limp and all sensation left my body. I could hear and feel things, but I could not move. Crow Dog leaned down and said, "Keep the power within you. Do not speak or open your eyes for a while. Your new name is The Star." He instructed the women to leave me there for about 10 minutes and then to turn me over and lay me spread-eagle face down facing the east door so that the healing could be shared with the rest of the circle. This they did. After turning me over, my feet and hands began to tinkle and I could move them a little. Just about that time a man whispered in my left ear, "You are my spiritual sister. Not many understand what you have done today, but I have seen and I thank you." With that he turned and left. I could barely move my head, but I managed and peeked. An Indian man with long dark hair was walking away and on his back was the emblem of White Eagle. I lay still a few minutes more while feeling returned to my body. I then stood and leaned against the pole of the arbor and danced as my friend and teacher, Tigre, was pierced.

After completing the piercing, the dancer returns to a bed of sage and the chief cuts the tissue and cleans the wound. The dancer places his flesh offering in a medicine bundle and offers it to someone for empowerment and healing. He then returns to the circle to continue the dance until the closing ceremony. Tigre sent his medicine bundle to me. I treasure it dearly! He later said that I pierced in the etheric while he pierced in the physical that day—a healing we offered to Mother Earth and her children.

I left the arbor and went back to camp. Three of the elders came later and sat with me. They never spoke, nor did they have to. I felt quite honored. A young man brought me a pin to attach to my shirt; it was of a bluebird. Again, this lovely winged creature was with me. Coincidence? I don't think so.

I tried to find the Indian woman and man who had so mysteriously appeared, but to no avail. Later when sharing my experience with other indigenous healers, they reported similar experiences when "spirit puts on skin" to assist. For many days after this experience, I could not close my eyes without reliving it as vividly as the first time. Waves of emotion brought tears. I still had no idea what had happened or what results it would bring. I just seemed to know that my life was not my own, but had been committed to a higher purpose. It would be many years before I came to understand just what that meant.

A friend and client once wrote to me these words: "The light and dark of it all lies in the shadows movement. Can we rest in its shade as we hide among its darkness? Can we befriend the enemy? Can we be filled with gratitude that in our loss is gain? Perhaps our gain was the loss itself. I've never felt so little and so much. I want to keep learning that I might teach. I want to teach that I might keep learning."

Larry had once told me that no matter how high the mystical highs would take me, I must be prepared for their equal and opposite lows. And so the purging must begin. Little did I know when I reached home and was met by my three guys screaming that they would not stop until they had all gone their own individual ways. Some part of them must have known what I did not, for it was at this time that I entered the part of the labyrinth known to the mystics as the "dark night of the soul."

I first heard it as a whisper,
someone calling me softly from a distance.
I paid no mind to it and thought it the wind,
and indeed—the wind it was.

It next came as a murmur,
a chant drifting down gently through the darkness.
I raised my head and called it the wind,
And the wind—called me.

Then came the rumble, shaking my door,
demanding I honor the power of its force.
I defied the wind, and the wind—defied me.

Now comes clearly the howling of the vortex
with the cries and the wails of those consumed before me.
My stone walls tremble,
for the wind knows no home—and honors no home.

I flee to the open spaces
but find no refuge there.
For even the stones of the earth bow in it's path,
and my pursuer—is upon me.

I turn to face my Victor,
and as my body wilts to the earth,
I yield to the wind,
and the wind—blows through me.

                              Larry Rue

CHAPTER SIX

# The Dark Night of the Soul

## INTO THE BELLY OF THE BEAST

I S INSIGHT ACHIEVED GRADUALLY or suddenly, as the Zen Buddhists claim? Here again both claims are correct, if taken together as parts of a larger and fuller view. We have to begin by cultivating intuitive feelings. These come to us infrequently at first and so the process is a gradual and long one. Eventually, we reach a point, a very advanced point, where the ego sees its own limitation, perceives its helplessness and dependence, realizes that it cannot lift itself up into the final illuminations. It should then surrender itself wholly to the Overself and cast its further development on the mercy and Grace of the power beyond it. It will then have to go through a waiting period of seeming inactivity, spiritual stagnation, and inability to feel the fervor of devotion which it formally felt. This is a kind of dark night of the soul.[57]

This quotation describes the stage of development that I was entering. For if you can imagine being struck by lightning, and the aftereffects such an incident would evoke, you can begin to sense the shake-up I was experiencing both intrapsychically and interpersonally following the Sundance. The images imprinted during the ceremony continued to replay themselves every time I closed my eyes. Some part of me knew that I had participated in a rite of passage which had created an irrevocable change.

---

[57] Brunton, Paul, *Enlightened Mind, Divine Mind*, Larson Publications, New York, 1988, p. 38.

What would be the outcome? I had no idea. I could only sense its power.

When I returned home I was literally met at the door with my husband and boys screaming at me. Their visit home had stirred a deep desire to return. In addition, looking back, I know we were also reacting to this new level of consciousness that had penetrated our lives. Little did I know that their screams would continue until they were all gone. Did they know at some deep unconscious level that our lives as we knew them then would never be the same?

No one wanted to know about what had just happened to me. The experience pushed me into a place of isolation. What is so difficult about deep transformative processes is that our culture has no place for them. Anything that has that ambience of "the unknown" connected to it is met with suspicion, exclusion, and in most cases anger at some level. Carl Jung teaches that when you step away from the collective, you must be prepared to experience their wrath, but you must keep going until you retrieve from the unconscious that which has called you in. Upon your return, the fruit of your quest becomes a gift to the collective—then and only then will their anger be appeased. I came to realize that I had dedicated myself in service to psyche. I knew to try to turn back now would prove disastrous to both myself and those I cared most about. I know it must be hard for family members to watch someone they love going through such indescribable experiences. It seems to activate the unconscious parts of the family pathology. You begin to experience your split so loudly that it tears at your very fiber. The tension of holding the opposites feels like it will break you: the inner experiences begin to constantly interplay with outer reality. The constant battering by the unconscious wears you down, and the pain seems rooted in your very soul. When you reach out to those in your most intimate circle, they retreat. When you reach out to Spirit, a stillness pervades that profoundly overwhelms you. The silence is so loud it hurts. Evelyn Underhill writes in *Mysticism*:

Psychologically, then, the "Dark Night of the Soul" is due to the double fact of the exhaustion of an old state, and the growth towards a new state of consciousness. It is a "growing pain" in the organic process of the self's attainment of the Absolute... The machinery of consciousness, overstretched, breaks up, and seems to toss the self back to an old and lower level, where it loses its apprehensions of the transcendental world; as the child, when first it is forced to stand alone, feels weaker than it did in its mother's arms.

"For first He not only withdraws all comfortable observable infusions of light and grace, but also deprives her of a power to exercise any perceptible operations of her superior spirit, and of all comfortable reflections upon His love, plunging her into the depth of her inferior powers," says Augustine Baker.[58]

The year that followed was filled with endings. My husband had met a woman during that summer and continued to correspond with her unbeknownst to me. I had many dreams that spoke to his affair, but whenever I inquired or struggled to understand what was happening to our relationship, his rage intervened. I remember one such dream.

> *I saw myself dressed in a very regal Aztec costume. I was lying in an open tomb. Although I was conscious of what was happening to me, I was unable to move my body to intervene on my behalf. A hand with long metal claws descended from above me and ripped out my heart. In horror, I watched my dripping heart beating as it was held above me. My final realization was that my executioner was Richard.*

I awoke knowing that I had viewed a past life, and that it was reoccurring, just on an emotional level. My whole body shook as I sobbed. When I shared my dream with Richard, he simply discounted it and said there was nothing wrong. My intuition plagued me, yet I continued to discount it and believe in the illusion that Richard painted. Owning my own inner authority was

---

[58] Underhill, Evelyn, *Mysticism*, E. P. Dutton, New York 1961, pp. 386–387.

foreign to me. I had always sought validation outside of myself, but now as I lay in the middle of my own life's tomb, I watched as the heart of my false self was ripped out. As the months went by, things grew worse. I could feel everything slipping away, but there was absolutely nothing I could do to change it. The dream had been more prophetic than I had realized. My analyst said that when things are happening to you that make no logical sense, you can bet that the Higher Self is stomping through your life. Surrendering is the only thing one can do beyond enduring the process.

I remember how it felt when I realized that our divorce was inevitable. My own pain was overwhelming, but when I realized what this would mean for my boys, I wept. If only I could have stopped their pain! But I also had a great trust in Spirit. I knew deep within that this too was part of our healing, but in that moment, the wound yelled out threatening to swallow me. All of my fears and self-doubts attacked as if they had been given form. In my desperation, I cried out, "What is this all about anyway?" The Voice answered, "To give love when none is given, this is the true test of love." I said, "This is not going to be easy! When will it be over?" The Voice replied, "All will be resolved on the night of the blue moon." Though this statement didn't make much sense to me at the time, it would come to mark a major part of the journey which will be explained in more detail in chapter eight.

Through all of this I continued with my analysis and my studies. I had begun preparing for the oral exams, studying up to five or six hours a day, six days a week. Because Carl Jung's individuation process was so actively invoked in my life, I studied his writings with a great desire to understand what was erupting from within. In the midst of these trials, I experienced a vision.

*In the vision, there had been a death and all were coming to visit. I went to the bathroom and looked in the mirror to discover that my face had been burned and was black. I began to peel off the blackened skin, and to my surprise the skin underneath looked like a black-and-white snakeskin. When my face had been peeled completely, I stood facing my new self and a rose appeared between my teeth.*

At that point I bolted out of the vision and tried to shake it off. I could not. A trancelike reality settled around me creating a feeling of disorientation and great sadness. Try as I might I couldn't shake it. As time passed, it seemed to intensify. I sought help from a friend. We walked and talked, but nothing helped. It felt as if another deep blow was about to strike. I was frightened, but it made no sense. The next morning I received a letter from the Jung Institute. It was written in German and said that I was not going to be allowed to take my exams until I became fluent in German. Although they encouraged me to reapply at a later date, I knew it was time to leave.

Everything I held dear was leaving. Everything! We were being asked to jump into the Void with nothing more than faith as our companion. During the period of time leading up to our departure, I had a series of dreams in which I both took my oral exams and passed them. One of those dreams presented the essence of what was to come.

*I had chosen Arnie Mindell, a psychoanalyst who works with the dream body, to be my examiner on Dreams. As the dream began I was sitting in a classroom with several other people. Arnie was lecturing. His wife (an unknown character) walked slowly over to me and sat in my lap and began to suckle my breast. As she did, a swirling sensation of energy seemed to spiral out from the point of contact encompassing me and forcing me into an altered state of consciousness. Arnie asked, "What is faith?"*

*I struggled, but had difficulty utilizing my cognitive functions while in this altered state. Finally, a realization brought clarity. I said, "I know! Faith is like a rose. When all the petals have fallen away, that is when you are left with its core. Then and only then is when faith turns into commitment."*

A friend once told me that it is during such great tests that love is forged, for once the spiritual warrior endures and survives, faith is evoked and a deep trust is formed.

I would be returning to Waco with no job and a few thousand bucks in my pocket. With two teenage boys to feed, the money wouldn't last long. Some part of me seemed to give up the fight and a numbness prevailed. A dissociated state walked me through the next month of preparing to go home. Little did I know that this had all just been preparation for the next stage that Underhill calls the "spiritual crucifixion." She writes,

> The consciousness which had, in Illumination, sunned itself in the sense of the Divine Presence, now suffers under an equally intense sense of the Divine Absence: learning to dissociate the personal satisfaction of mystical vision from the reality of mystical life. As in Purgation the senses were cleansed and humbled, and the energies and interests of the Self were concentrated upon transcendental things: so now the purifying process is extended to the very centre of I-hood, the will. The human instinct for personal happiness must be killed. This is the "spiritual crucifixion" so often described by the mystics: the great desolation in which the soul seems abandoned by the Divine. The self now surrenders itself, its individuality, and its will, completely.[59]

## THE SPIRITUAL CRUCIFIXION

We all prepared for our return. I was offered two promising positions in other states, but Spirit was relentless. I had to return to confront the old self. My boys wanted to return to Waco, to friends and a familiar place. Richard was going to live there as well. We were still playing at the possibilities of a reconciliation. My dreams and meditations kept saying I must return there to meet my power. I had experienced Waco as an ultraconservative place which would have little understanding of either this process working through my body or of Jungian approaches to healing. But argue and kick as I might, my urge to follow Spirit is too strong to ignore for long.

---

[59] Underhill, Evelyn, *Mysticism*, E. P. Dutton, New York, 1961, p. 170.

Since we had vacated our apartment, we were staying with a friend the last two nights before our departure. Richard and I had decided to separate upon our return, so he was staying in the extra room and I was sharing a room with my girlfriend, Bonnie. It was during this time that the Hooded Ones came through in a lucid dream state, one in which I became awake in the dream consciously aware of my interaction with the dream figures.

> *On the first night, I watched as the dream unfolded aware that my consciousness was both in the experience while observing it as well. The Hooded Ones were gathered on the side of a mountain. They were scattered at different places surrounding a wooden cross that was standing starkly against the sky extending itself from the side of the mountain. The left arm of the cross was missing. I was hanging from the cross. My feet had been nailed to it. I was told that my left arm would not need to be pierced, but when I was ready my right hand would be pierced in the area between my thumb and forefinger. I was warned that the process was a very painful one, and therefore, I must take my time until I was sure I was ready. As usual, their extreme empathy and patience with me gave me strength, and I acknowledged I was ready. At that very moment, a great wave of pain which is beyond words rolled throughout my being and I heard my scream pierce the air. The Voice spoke saying, "On the other side of pain and suffering is compassion and understanding. Day One!"*
>
> *The dreamscape changed and I suddenly found myself inside of a large house. One of the Hooded Ones was walking silently behind me just to the right of my shoulder. The hall we walked down was dimly lit, creating a feeling of apprehension. A horribly pungent odor of vomit permeated the air. People passed us covered with vomit. Others would sit up emerging out of piles of old rags, throwing up. The Voice spoke again saying, "This is the day of the purging. Day Two!"*

I awoke with the dream still actively being experienced by my body. The Hooded Ones had only appeared to me when it was time for another initiation, which in the past, always activated the next part of my journey. I had learned that such times animated both the inner and outer reality emphasizing the material that wanted to be brought into consciousness. I must pay attention!

> *About two o'clock in the morning of the following night, I realized that I was hovering above the bed looking down on Bonnie and myself sleeping. I was aware throughout the experience of holding three levels of consciousness; one above, which had no form, but was keenly aware of all happenings; my astral body; and my physical body. It's hard to describe, but my awareness seemed to be impacted by the experiential happenings taking place below my witness consciousness. My astral body sat up out of my physical form. I began to hear demonic growling sounds coming from Bonnie's side of the room. I couldn't see anything, but I was frightened. My astral body reached over and shook Bonnie trying to get her attention, but to no avail. My fear increased. The sounds now took on shape, they became a cloudlike form. The growling sounds became louder as they grew closer. I felt alone and confused and frightened. The cloud entered my belly, and as it did, my consciousness sank into my physical form. Darkness enveloped me as the screams of the demons which had formed the cloud swirled around me. I said, "O.K., you know what to do. Stay calm and pray. I love Jesus! I love Jesus! I love Jesus!" The energy dissipated, returning all to normal. A stillness remained. The Voice said, "Transmutation! Transmutation! Transmutation! Day Three."*

As I look back now at the events which presented themselves, these two dreams become prophetic. They foretold and gave me guidance to the next part of the quest, for they outlined the stages my process would reveal as it invoked the "dark night of my soul." Emma Bragdon speaks to this stage in her book *The Call of Spiritual Emergency* as she quotes Saint John:

> This night... causes two kinds of darkness or purgation in the spiritual person according to the two parts of the soul, the sensory and the spiritual. Hence the one night of purgation will be sensory, by which the senses are purged and accommodated to the spirit; and the other night or purgation will be spiritual, by

which the spirit is purged and denuded as well as accommodated and prepared for union with God through love.

The soul, because of its impurity, suffers immensely at the time this divine light truly assails it. When this pure light strikes in order to expel all impurity, persons feel so unclean and wretched that it seems God is against them and they are against God. Because it seems that God has rejected them, these souls suffer... pain and grief.

This, precisely, then is what the divine ray of contemplation does. In striking the soul with its divine light, it surpasses the natural light and thereby darkens and deprives individuals of all the natural affections and apprehensions they perceive by means of their natural light. It leaves their spiritual and natural faculties not only in darkness but in emptiness too. Leaving the soul thus empty and dark, the ray purges and illumines it with divine spiritual light, while the soul thinks it has no light and that it is in darkness.[60]

Emma goes on to say:

The sensory and spiritual purgings Saint John speaks of are the physical and psychological purification related to samskaras.[61] The purgation is a time of darkness, of turmoil, where perspective is lost. The commitment to become one with God's love has been made and the personality has been initially infused with Divine Light. Still, there is this painful time, truly a crisis in spiritual awakening, when we focus on elements of our personality that are not yet in the light and feel a "divine homesickness" for the transpersonal states we have experienced.[62]

With the passage of time, the pain and suffering of Day One (on the cross) was like a tidal wave—inescapable and overwhelming. My heart was breaking and its pain reached into the very bowels of my soul. A primal scream continuously emoted from deep

---

[60] Bragdon, Emma, *The Call of Spiritual Emergency*, Harper & Row Publishers, San Francisco, 1990, p. 89.

[61] Samskara as defined in *The Call of Spiritual Emergency* (p. 222) is a Sanskrit word meaning "a behavioral tendency or condition brought into this life from a previous life, or acquired during present life conditioning."

[62] Ibid, p. 89.

within.   No matter what I did I could not get it to cease. Day Two (the purge) would be revealed in the development of Avalon, a residential program for young abused women. I would be forced to examine the deep seated behaviors that created abusive relationships in my life.   All levels of the psyche had to be examined—the physical, the emotional and the spiritual. And finally, Day Three (transmutation) would unfold through an experience of fusing with light as described in chapter eight. Any time we step closer to the Light we are again asked to face not only our personal demons, but our collective demons as well. Such confrontation with the shadow reveals a false self and tears away the illusions that seperate us from our own divinity. A period of continual transcendant episodes restructured my life and brought me to a period of regeneration.

We landed in Dallas, Texas and stayed with a friend for the night. The next day I put the boys on a bus to visit my mother, allowing me some time to orient myself to this new situation, find an apartment, and secure work. Richard and I drove back to Waco together. That two hour car drive was devastating. I could feel my boys' confusion and pain. I knew our relationship was over, but some part of me refused to see its truth. I was returning to a place that had a hard history in my life. Why? What would this prove? I had Richard stop the car several times. Although it was raining, I stood unprotected with my fists clenched and screamed at God. My fear of abandonment was certainly one of those demons from my dream, and now here I was being devoured by it, or so it felt.   During the next year I began to understand that stage of development in Jesus' story when he cried for his Father to take the cup from his lips and later asked why he had been forsaken.

I had a friend who kindly offered lodging in her house. When I arrived, I could not speak.   Not only was my world as I knew it blowing up in front of me with no conceivable way to stop it, but culture shock upped the ante. The paradox of cultures was obvious. I had been living in Europe doing postgraduate study, stimulated by new and innovative thinking. The environment was aesthetic with the different languages expressive of the ambience and the mood of the people. The energy in Texas was more primitive and rugged. I don't think you can compare these places, nor should you try. Each has a distinct personality and offers something unique in its own way. It's just that the contrast of old Europe and primal Texas added to the rawness of my situation.

Try as I might, I couldn't find my center. The psychic pain that I experienced felt like I was being deboweled and gutted through all my astral and subtle bodies. I found myself rolling into fetal positions a lot trying to contain it. It felt very tumultuous, very strong, very deep, and very devastating. I could feel the pain of the collective. It was almost unbearable. The scream from my soul could not be quieted; it screamed continuously for three months. All my dreams and visions left. I could feel God breathe, but I could not see his face. I felt so oversensitive to my environment that I could not leave the house. Everything felt like too much. I called a friend in Switzerland and told her I wasn't sure I could make it, that I had over estimated this phase of the process. She just kept reminding me to breathe into it, to flow with the process instead of against it. Though my friends were wonderfully supportive, they couldn't grasp the severity of it. For a few weeks, I sat rocking and trying to surrender. Though my mind wanted to surrender, something else fought to survive. I met the enemy—and the enemy was me.

Each time I have jumped into the abyss a dichotomy has presented itself; the dismemberment of the old and support for the new. The trick is to prevent yourself from falling back into old patterns, and to see them for what they are. *That's the secret!* The moment I am able to recognize the pattern, my chances of transcending it greatly increase. Next, I must maintain integrity with myself if I want to progress further. The closer I get to a core issue that helped shape my personality, the more vulnerable I feel, and the more shame I experience. I must not identify with the chaos of what was, but with the indestructable core of my being. That's certainly easier said than done, but in this case, if I refused to leave my victim stance with myself and with God, I would not survive. That was clear.


## THE DAWNING: AVALON

Following an intuition I contacted an old friend, Bill. We had worked together before. He had stood in at my wedding and given me away to Richard. He had just opened a residential treatment program for young boys and adolescents. In that process he had met a gentleman, Pat, who was interested in opening a girls' program. He owned an old building in Marlin, Texas, a small town some 30 miles outside of Waco. We met and decided to form a partnership. Bill would run the boys' program and Pat would provide the building in Marlin, cover costs for its renovation and supply monies for startup. I would develop a program for young abused women from ages 16 to 18. Securing licensing and negotiating contracts for placement would be my initial responsibility. Later I would serve as its director. Suddenly, I knew one of the reasons for my return. We would develop a holistic program providing a safe space for young women to heal and become empowered. In order to do this, I would have to integrate what I had learned in Switzerland, both from my studies and through my own inner confrontation with the shadow. I also would have to face the image of who I was in the mind of old friends and colleagues. Could I stand in my truth without compromising myself? Could I present these ideas in a way that would elicit support rather than ignite controversy? I was clear that I did not wish to polarize the issue, but rather create a space that allowed for alternative approaches in healing to be considered. Since I was able to work on my own schedule, I was able to maintain the integrity of the work dictated by my inner process. The challenge was in keeping the balance between the material and spiritual worlds as this deep disintegration took place. The stretch is a big one. We in the West are being asked to continue with our affairs: raising children, jobs, paying bills, etc. In other cultures when deep transformative processes descend upon an individual, it is seen as "the Call." There is a place in the culture which supports such happenings and a knowledge that in so doing everyone benefits. In our culture, our spiritual warriors are having to again create that space. I truly believe that when that task is accomplished, we will have a better chance of returning to balance. In the East, for example, saints, sages, and spiritual teachers are very much a part of the whole. In their culture, their paths represent an attainment of wholeness; a recovery of one's true nature. God is within, not outside of us. If we can close that gap between our spiritual selves and our material selves, a great healing will occur in this country. When our saints and sages again become a living part of our culture, we will transcend our limitations and reach new vistas only dreamed of before.

I struggled to create a safe and balanced atmosphere for my boys, while daily being bombarded by the unconscious. After nearly three months of bearing the soul-level scream, I prayed for relief, but to no avail. Finally, one day in meditation I was reminded of the tow tides that run the Texas coastline. If you are caught by one and panic, you will be pulled under and drown. If, however, you relax and surrender, rolling up into a ball, allowing it to carry you further down the shoreline, it will eventually "spit you out" and you will be fine. I was instructed to handle the waves of pain in the same way, and relief would follow. I had nothing to lose, so I began to image rolling up in a psychic ball and rolling into the pain, embracing it rather than resisting it. After a short while, I experienced a few hours without the internal scream and chaotic turmoil. What a relief! I continued to use the exercise. The periods of calming began to lengthen until finally they subsided all together. A numbness was left in its wake.

My dreams and visions still did not return, but each morning during meditation I was given instructions as to what to do that day in developing the program for Avalon. I was amazed how quickly everything came together. Within six months we had totally renovated and restored the building we would use, hired and trained staff, secured a contract with the state for placement of young women, and opened as a residential home. As with most community programs of this nature, a lot of work must go into educating the public, encouraging an atmosphere of understanding and partnership. Many of the young women coming to Avalon had been in trouble with the law. Most of them had done so in response to the inhumane treatment of, first, family members or significant persons involved in their lives, and then later, by the social systems that handled them. Unfortunately, community people fear their reactions rather than understand their outrage at vile acts such as sexual molestation, physical abuse, or neglect. As long as we continue to assign blame and judgment, we perpetuate our co-dependency and negate our possibilities for healing. We remain in denial and diminish and destroy our most precious natural resources, our children. What I found interesting was that when the initial controversy hit, it wasn't focused on some of the alternative methods we were using (i.e., dream work, herbal medicines, drumming, visualization), but rather on my need to advocate loving our children rather than locking them up. Our girls represented the different levels of our racial and economic structure. At one point, messages were sent to me (unofficially, of course) that if I didn't cooperate and consider moving the program out of town, more severe problems would be coming my way. (A woman who had fought for the rights of children in this same town a few years before my arrival had been found shot and stuffed in the trunk of her car.) People were serious. In the midst of all this, a friend of mine called who had been an actress for many years. She had an intuition to call, and wanted to know what was going on. When I explained, she said she would call back in a few days. When she called back she had lined up seven soap opera stars from the East and West coasts to host an open house formally announcing Avalon's mission. Within a few weeks the publicity for this event was making the news and local talk shows. Several hundred showed up for the open house and we publicly honored the young women of Avalon and the struggles they had endured. It was a night that touched my heart. The publicity persuaded the public officials and disgruntled citizens of Marlin to "chill out" for a while.

As with most new programs, we had our growing pains, but all in all we continued to stabilize. I was struggling with our contract with the state, trying to get a few more girls into the program so that we could stabilize financially. In programs for girls that have been on the streets a long time, a common problem is that residents run away. Ironically, although we had our runaways, they began to call and wanted to come back. The girls were claiming their space and beginning to own their own authority in their healing process.

Through this looking glass we would come to examine not only the personal abuse these young women had endured, but the collective abuse unconsciously supported by our childcare systems. Their stories spoke of horror and torture instigated by family or friends of family. Several had witnessed ritual abuse and for a while seemed caught in the spell of its black magic. Many of the children in the streets prove to be the mystics of this country; they have had to develop their intuitive skills well in order to survive. Unfortunately, some have acquired manipulative teachers who don't have their well being in mind. One example of this happened with three of the girls from Avalon. I began receiving information that black magic was being practiced in the house established at Marlin. I kept getting the image of a box hidden upstairs and the faces of three of our residents. I called a meeting and confronted the girls. At first they denied it, but as the conversation evolved they could see my information was accurate. They demanded to know how I knew these things. A discussion followed where we talked about the illusion of power that black magic paints and the seductive nature it uses to possess someone. I shared some of my experiences with the power of love. We then explored the outcome of both practices. I told them they would have to choose, but that if they chose the dark side, they could not remain with us. I was not willing to support practices that could hurt them or others. For a moment, a stillness reigned. Then one of the girls left and when she returned, she brought with her all the articles they had been using. We built a fire in the backyard and burned the articles while we said prayers and chanted God's name. I planned a field trip for the girls and in their absence did a ceremony to clear the energy of the house and create a protective envelope. When the girls returned I presented them with small crosses to be worn as necklaces. All this was done quietly so as not to alarm anyone. For the next few days, ghosts were seen wandering upstairs at night by staff and several of the residents. Many of the girls were frightened. The energy in the house seemed unsettled. Finally, it all came to a head. Several of the girls got in a fight causing a reaction throughout the house like a rage being discharged. My staff and I stayed with the process until it completed itself—some of the girls needed one to one counseling, some needed holding until they could regain their control and not hurt themselves or others, and still others just needed to be reassurred all would be alright. By late evening the energy settled down and all returned to normal. The incident proved to be a healing for the house in many ways. A feeling of family seemed to have been born out of the chaos. Girls began to work more seriously in their dream groups. Though some ran away, many returned voluntarily (a phenomena unheard of in such programs). As the three girls had faced and burned their instruments of black magic, they would now need to face and transform those memories that possessed them and robbed them of their power.

Our group sessions were a place in which the girls could talk freely about their lives and the experiences they had had to endure both within their families and while on the streets. Though such memories were difficult, the dream process we engaged brought healing. In one of the group sessions we did an exercise in guided imagery. I had them lie flat on the floor and relax. Once in a relaxed state, we imaged a river flowing. They floated with the river as it curved into a forest. As we floated into an area lined with tall trees, I asked them to look around for their special spot. Upon locating it, their sacred animal, a magical being, would come to them. They were to listen and see what it had come to share. I would like to share two of the young women's experiences, which exemplify the rest.

First, a 16-year-old black woman, who had suffered much physical and emotional abuse in her younger years said: "My animal was a deer. He looked at me and said, »We love you.« He then turned and asked me to follow. He took me to the end of the world and showed me a great abyss. As we stood there, he said, »You mustn't be afraid, for we will never let you fall in.«" A couple of days later we did a similar exercise. The deer again appeared and took her to the deep abyss. He said, "Take one small step out into it and trust us, for we will not let you fall." She did and found the ground had moved and she stood safely. She then turned to me and said, "I know now, if I take one step at a time and trust, it will be O.K."

The second, a 17-year-old white woman, said her animal was a horse. She went on to say, "The world was in complete darkness. My horse took me above the darkness to a ring of rainbow colors which seem to encircle the earth. As I stood on this ring, I experienced peace and harmony."

I am always profoundly amazed at how significantly our personal lives connect with the collective consciousness of our planet. In each of the examples I have just illustrated that connectiveness was animated; first, in the confrontation with the dark side of the three girls and how it later affected the rest of the population in the house, and later in the images expressed by the young women during dream group. We must therefore have compassion for each other as we go about the business of reclaiming our "Selves."

I was later presented a picture album depicting the stages of development of Avalon by the staff. On its first page a description of the program captured my heartfelt dream and spoke to the work that was exemplary that year both by the girls, myself and staff as we struggled to embrace our wound and transcend the times in which abuse of the feminine was bringing a death to our culture and raping our souls.

AVALON—A mystical island where women could receive psychic healing. A myth or a reality? What is it that constitutes reality? How do we define it?

Perhaps, reality is nothing more than an idea which takes shape—can be touched and experienced—something abstract converted to that which is observable. For Jeneane Prevatt (Jyoti), Avalon began as an abstract; an idea, a hope for the future. For seventeen years she watched young people searching for themselves in a world of confusion and despair. Sometimes they succeeded—sometimes they failed. But always they were present, reaching out, asking for help.

We exist in an ever-changing environment. What was true yesterday is no longer so today. Comfortable traditions have disappeared only to be replaced by new traditions. It is a difficult and yet exciting time—especially for our children. If we somehow can weather the transition and meet ourselves openly, it will truly be a brave new world. If we fail to come to grips with ourselves, our future may be bleak.

Young women (as well as young men) are faced with a society of new roles. Men no longer serve as the center of the nuclear family, nor do they fulfill totally the role of provider. Women have stepped into the world of economics. It matters not whether those first few steps were taken boldly or unsteadily with conscious effort. They have been taken! Into this new world must come a new breed. Our young women face trying times. In order to survive and become functional they must face themselves—and to do so is not an easy task.

Avalon, the center, is an idea that gained substance. From the energy of electro-chemical processes held only in the mind, it became a reality. Slowly, it took form. First, as a blueprint, then as a broken down old hospital, and finally, as a place where young women 16 to 18 years of age can come to be healed. It is a source of energy. It is a dream become real.

From the vast stretches of Texas to the snow-capped mountains of Switzerland, and back to Texas again, Avalon grew. To give a date of birth is impossible. On October 15th, 1986, the first young woman entered through Avalon's door in Marlin, Texas. Avalon is real.

## PURGING TO RECLAIM THE FEMININE

Abuse has so many faces, much like Medusa. It is said that to look into Medusa's face directly will bring death. In some myths it is Medusa who protects the golden fleece. Athena represents the female warrior. The Greeks claimed Athena was born from Zeus's head, after he swallowed her mother Metis (i.e., Medusa), "Female Wisdom."[63] Athena was said to have worn a breast plate with the Medusa on it for protection. Egyptians sometimes called Isis Athena, which meant "I have come from myself."[64] So within this archetype, we have the destroying aspects of femininity in union with wisdom and power. If we in this culture hope to confront and heal the deep seated issues that are surfacing described as physical and sexual abuse of our children, we must first embrace the Medusa within. As we dive deep into the psyche to retrieve our lost femininity, we will meet different aspects of her. We must destroy that which binds us and embrace the wisdom and power available through such work.

Day Two of my dream in Zurich (the purging) would require the tenacity of Athena to meet the challenge of reclaiming my feminine power. Avalon marked the battle ground, but the actual battle was an internal one. As Robert Johnson wrote in *Femininity Lost and Regained,*

> The Swiss psychologist C. G. Jung observed that the unconscious dimension of our psyche will show to us the same face that we first show to it. If we have been hostile to it, it will be hostile to us. So much of our psychological life is a dialogue between our conscious world—all the things we know about ourselves—and

---

[63] Walker, Barbara G., *The Woman Encyclopedia of Myths and Secrets,* Harper & Row Publishers, San Francisco, 1983, p. 74.

[64] Ibid, p. 74.

the unconscious—the murky world of our interior life, which is such a mystery to us.[65]

In an article published in *Vogue* in November, 1986, Marie--Louise von Franz said that Jung told her and a group of students who'd come to see him about a female patient who had had a vision of being on the moon. "I had been brought up to be rational, so I said, »But she wasn't on the moon.« He looked at me in the eye and said, »Yes, she was.« I got argumentative: »You don't mean that dead satellite rotating around the earth—nobody's been up there yet.« Then it dawned on me that what he meant was that what happened psychically is real, and what happens outwardly is only secondary." The reality of those words rang loudly, for my own inner psychic experiences seemed to be molding the story unfolding in my outer world. Through the constant confrontations both internally and externally, my ego grew tired. I awoke many mornings wishing I hadn't. I later found a wonderful book by Gary Zukav entitled *The Seat of the Soul* that helped me understand some of the dynamics involved. Mr. Zukav writes:

> The splintered personality is not content. The contentment that it feels in one moment is replaced by anger or fear or envy in the next moment as conflicting aspects of itself struggle with each other... If your struggle with the conflicting parts of yourself is conscious, you are able to choose consciously the response that will create the karma that you desire. You will be able to bring to bear upon your decision an awareness of what lies behind each choice, and the consequences of each choice, and choose accordingly. When you enter into your decision-making dynamic consciously, you insert your will consciously into the creative cycle through which your soul evolves, and you enter consciously into your own evolution.[66]

Roberto Assagioli expands this further when he talks about the disidentification process necessary to evolve. He writes:

---

[65] Johnson, Robert A., *Femininity Lost and Regained,* Harper & Row Publishers, New York, 1990, pp. 16–17.

[66] Zukav, Gary, *The Seat of the Soul*, Simon & Schuster Inc., New York, 1990, p. 141.

We are dominated by everything with which our self becomes identified. We can dominate, direct, and utilize everything from which we disidentify ourselves...[67] This identification with a part of ourselves is usually related to the predominant function or focus of our awareness, to the predominant role we play in life... This identification with only a part of our personality may be temporarily satisfactory, but it has serious drawbacks. It prevents us from realizing the experience of the "I", the deep sense of self-identification, of knowing who we are. It excludes, or greatly decreases, the ability to identify with all the other parts of our personality, to enjoy them and utilize them to their full extent... we gain the freedom and the power of choice to be identified with, or disidentified from, any aspect of our personality, according to what seems to us most appropriate in each situation. Thus we can learn to master, direct, and utilize all the elements and aspects of our personality, in an inclusive and harmonious synthesis.[68]

And so, looking back, that first year in Waco was a time of meeting my demons. It was a time I met my self-doubts and stared directly into a part of myself that had dominated my life— my wounded woman—she had been gutted and purged. The Shakti had opened and cleared the third chakra—my power center. Looking so closely in the mirror had brought an awareness of not only a deep commitment to my healing, but of a faith in something inside which yearned to be whole. When patterns break, the ego experiences a death, and sometimes screams from its terror. Learning how to die had taught me how to live. Moving out of my victim stance in life had brought new clarity. The new information that began to surface about my psychology helped me to discover still new parts of myself that had been buried. One such memory had to do with my childhood, focusing around age eight. I had almost no memory of that time. I could remember the kitchen of our house and my dog, but that was all. Try as I could, nothing would surface. I could remember the years before

---

[67] Assagioli, Roberto, M. D., *The Act of Will*, Penguin Books, New York, 1976, p. 211.
[68] Ibid, pp. 212–213.

and the years after, but not that year. Since both my primary relationships, my marriages, had lasted eight years, I knew this clue was important. It would be several years later after realizing this insight that a partial memory would surface revealing a deep mystical encounter with God; a time when God left an intimate impression on a small girl child. Even then experiences of "bridal mysticism" were descending upon the eight year old. To that child the experience seemed overwhelming and she had no one to talk to about it. Her feelings of abandonment loomed darkly, both then and later in her more intimate relationships as an adult. The wound she carried was a collective one as well. For we have split off our spiritual sides of ourselves and abandoned our true natures. We are told that experience of God is crazy and irrational. Gloria Steinem in her most recent work entitled *Revolution From Within* sites the Gnostic Gospels, *"If you bring forth what is within you, what you bring forth will save you. If you do not bring forth what is within you, what you do not bring forth will destroy you."*[69] It is like God winks at you at times, encouraging you to go forward to discover still more; for no sooner is something completed, than the new presents itself. In my case, it would literally be the death of my world as I knew it, and the birth of a new one.

---

[69] Steinem, Gloria, *Revolution From Within*, Little, Brown and Company, Boston, Mass. 1992, p. 153.

# CHAPTER SEVEN

# Entering the Heart

## AND THE MASTER WILL SAY, "GIVE ME YOUR CHILDREN"

THE DAY ONE AND DAY TWO EPISODES from my dreams in Zurich had certainly foretold of a process that continued to unfold. Much to my surprise over the last few years I had been able to manage the stretch demanded by my inner and outer roles, but it had taken its toll. I lay exhausted and felt something give up inside me. Some part of me quit fighting. I just kept praying for direction—and it finally came.

In 1987, a few weeks before my thirty-ninth birthday an event happened that would prove to be the catalyst to a complete life change: from Texas to California, from motherhood to single person, from traditional employment to employment grounded in spiritual synthesis and from a wounded expression of myself to a creative one. Because a young woman living at Avalon needed some medical attention, I took her to her family's home for a family conference and to secure the proper identification papers for her medical care. After concluding the conference we all went together to initiate the proper paperwork. On the way to the office I began to have a pinching pain in the right side of my neck and shoulder region. As we walked up to the building, a severe pain that felt like a sledgehammer hit me between the shoulder blades. I excused myself and went to the bathroom hoping that it would pass. The pain increased, extending down my right arm. I felt like someone had wrapped a wire around my chest and was twisting it. I could hardly breathe. I had never been so quickly overcome by something so out of my control. A woman discovered me lying on a couch that was in the bathroom lounge and called the paramedics who, suspecting a heart attack, immediately rushed me to the hospital. There I was hooked up to all kinds of gadgets, including oxygen to assist my breathing. It took all of my concentration to visualize my lungs moving in and out. Yet, I felt calm. I felt as if time were standing still and I was outside "my movie," watching.

After I had been monitored, treated, and stabilized, I called a dear friend who is a paramedic and managed an ambulance company. I knew she would be honest with me about what was going on and should something happen, she would inform my boys in a compassionate way. When Quita entered the room, I could tell from her expression that my evaluation of the situation had not been exaggerated. The doctor finally came in and said that she thought it was not a heart attack, but pneumonia and a tumor on my lungs. She felt that I should remain in the hospital for further testing and treatment. (My father had died of lung cancer and my only thought was that I might be following in his steps.) Since I was about 45 minutes away from home, I asked if I could be moved to a hospital nearer to my family. The doctor agreed and Quita contacted her ambulance service.

Realize that when you enter the territory where two worlds kiss a magical ambience envelopes the space and you stand as a witness while the inner and outer worlds interact so profoundly with one another that it seems as if you are in a dream. Such was the circumstance this March day in Texas. The ambulance driver walked up to my stretcher, put out his hand and said, "Hi! My name's Charlie. I work for God and I'm taking you to Waco." In between my gasps for air, I said, "O.K." He put me in the ambulance and for the next few minutes he spoke to me as if he were channeling: "You are being prepared for a great task. You have given and given, but it is now time to learn the next lesson—to receive. For if you do not get this part of the training, your preparation will be incomplete. In the next week women will come to assist you. Let them." He went on for awhile insisting that I listen closely to what was being shared. Needless to say, I was amazed. All I could do was take it in; I didn't know what to think.

I was to be admitted into the hospital via the emergency room. When I arrived, however, the doctor disagreed with the initial diagnosis, so he and several other physicians conferred on it. He thought I had a blood clot on my lungs instead of a tumor. As technicians prepared me for more tests, a nurse arrived to draw blood. Just at that moment, a gentle energy entered my feet and extended up my body. It seemed to electrify the air around me. The nurse complained of being warm and had to leave. The Voice began to speak from within, repeating the same phrase over and over, as if in a chant, "And now you dance the second part of your dream awake!" I had no idea what this meant.

Several hours later when all the tests were completed, the doctors told me they were puzzled. They said I did have a mild case of pneumonia, but that would not explain my severe chest pains or breathing difficulties. They gave me antibiotics and sent me home to bed for the next week. Just as the ambulance driver had said, my women friends rallied. They took care of me and my sons while I recuperated.

I've since discovered that when Kundalini enters the heart, it is often misdiagnosed as a heart attack due to their similar symptoms. Bonnie Greenwell writes in her book entitled *Energies of Transformation*:

> Latent illness erupts, or pseudo-illness sometimes arises during the Kundalini process that cannot be adequately diagnosed by medical doctors. People complain of headaches and bands of energy tightening around the skull or burning the top of the head. A few men and women have what appears to be a false pregnancy, with the belly swollen (called "Buddha belly") periodically for a number of months. Some people have chest pains and numbness, symptoms very similar to those of a heart attack. This is likely

due to the Kundalini energy moving through the anahata, or heart chakra. It may be that the nervous system, the digestive tract or the hormonal system is seriously disrupted.[70]

Stan and Christina Grof speak about these physical anomalies connected with Kundalini in the following way:

> Although the suffering that occurs during a mystical encounter may feel destructive and violent at first, with time people often recognize it as the pain of spiritual opening and growth. They may even come to welcome it as a sign of their connection with the Divine, as described by Saint Teresa of Avila:
> The pain was so sharp that I moaned but the delight of this tremendous pain is so overwhelming that one cannot wish it to leave one, nor is the soul any longer satisfied with anything less than God. It is a spiritual, not bodily pain, although the body has some part, even a considerable part, in it. It is an exchange of courtesies between the soul and God.[71]

As I lay in bed the next week, I played the experience over and over in my head. I could understand the implications of the Kundalini energy entering my heart chakra, but I was unclear as to how to integrate it into my life. Little did I know the experience had just begun, for within the next month the world as I knew it would shift. During this time I had a dream. I had cried myself to sleep asking Jesus to help me understand.

> *In the dream I flew into a small Grecian-looking village. I wandered up to a building that was two stories tall. You had to climb the stairs from the outside to enter. Once inside I found myself on a balcony looking down into a wooden paneled room which had nothing in it except two large wooden hot tubs. Jesus was naked and bathing in one tub, while his female double bathed in the other. Though I was embarrassed and self-conscious, He smiled with complete acceptance and compassion.*

---

[70] Greenwell, Bonnie, *Energies of Transformation, A Guide to the Kundalini Process*, Shakti River Press, Cupertino, Ca., 1990, p. 236.

[71] Grof, Christina and Grof, Stanislav, *The Stormy Search for the Self*, Jeremy P. Tarcher, Inc., Los Angeles, 1990, p. 69.

The dream went on to animate how my ego felt about its impurity. The paradox between His ability to accept me and my own lack of acceptance of self was obvious.

Jesus had only appeared in my dreams two other times before this. Each time had marked a major transition. And so it would this time as well. When I returned to work I called a meeting with the staff and girls of Avalon. I told them of my situation, saying, "What I came here to do was to help you create a space in which you could feel safe enough to heal; a space in which you could reclaim your own inner authority and speak out about who you truly are. I feel we have done that. I am emotionally and physically tired and must go to rest. The ball is in your court. It is up to you now." These words would prove to be prophetic. I am always amazed at the profundity with which our souls speak, if we would only listen.

I had agreed to meet several other people in Switzerland to prepare a demonstration video for a film project about children's dreams. Though only a week had passed since my hospital visit, I asked the doctor if I could go. He was amazed that my checkup worked out so clearly and he agreed to the visit, if I promised to go slowly. After completing my commitments on the film project, I felt completely depleted. That night I had a dream. The dream was lucid in nature.

> *I saw myself with my partner Bill standing outside of Avalon. He said it sure would be nice if a little earthquake happened this weekend because no one was home and the insurance would take care of everything, then we wouldn't have to go into debt. He left. About that time the earth began to shake with a deep rumbling sound. It shook for a moment and then stopped. I thought that must have been the earthquake he wanted. Just then, the earth began to shake violently until it cracked. I saw a chain-link fence and ran to grab hold of it. I grabbed it just as everything in my dream picture completely exploded and fell apart. I was left hanging in a blue abyss. Ironically, I was excited because I realized that I was in a dream and though I was hanging in an abyss, it was blue. The black was gone. Suddenly, I realized my predicament.*

*How was I going to get out of this mess? I looked up and saw a man operating a big black crane; it was holding my chain-link fence. He slowly moved me over to one small piece of ground left from the old dream image. Once I was safely grounded, I awoke.*

The dream had set an earthquake off inside of me. I knew I was being asked to jump into the abyss again, and although the dream was reassuring about the process and its outcome, my personality was scared. For several days I paced, cried, and prayed. Although I kick and scream a lot when told what's next, because I am a good disciple, I go when called. I can't not go. My yearning to be with God is louder and deeper than anything else. God had set me up, but with such compassion. Cornelia (my analyst) and her husband, Doc, as well as Max and Theresa (my friends who had taken me to Yugoslavia), were there with me in their home in Switzerland and gave me a lot of support. I told them about the dream and said I knew my part in Avalon was finished. I went on to say, "I am being asked to jump into the Void once again. I am so tired. I worry so about my boys and how this will affect them. I know this is for all our good, but in the moment it's hard to see."

Within a day, the phone rang. It was Bill calling from Texas. The state department was threatening to shut the program down. They had fired my nutritionist and were charging unsanitary practices because we had been giving the girls whole milk from a local dairy. Bill wanted me to return immediately. I reminded him that I had just been released from the hospital less than a week before, and I was not sure if my health would hold up. I told him I would call the state officials in Austin, check with a doctor and call him back the following day with my decision. When I got off the phone, I was shaking. The process had begun!

Upon calling the officials in Austin, I discovered that the claims as Bill had described them were being investigated. I explained that I was in Europe recovering from illness. They assured me that it would be fine to stay another week or so before returning. They would not take any further action until I could return. Upon hanging up, I discussed the situation with Doc and Cornelia. They felt strongly that if I did not tend to my health, I would end up back in the hospital. I called Bill back and for the first time in my life proclaimed my need to heal first. In the past I had been so rooted in co-dependent behavior that I had worked while ill rather than honoring my body. I shared with him the feedback I had received from Austin and told him I would cut my trip short a week, but I must tend to my physical needs and rest longer. As he hung up, he said, "Well, you must do what you must do, and so must I." I hung up knowing that I had made my choice.

Cornelia was lovely. She held me and just kept reminding me to trust the process. She said, "Remember that you are only stepping out of an old coat and into a new one. Though the new one may feel uncomfortable and overwhelming in the beginning, you will grow to it. As we grow, we move into more expansive states of consciousness. Trust it!" The emotions of the moment washed over me like a wave. A multitude of levels spilled through me; sadness, anger, numbness, laughter, fear. All I could do was surrender to the process and trust it. I prayed that the executioner's blade would be sharp, allowing the process to be quick and clean. And so it was.

Upon my return to the States, I discovered that my "partners" had moved all of my money from my bank account, placing it into another bank which I could not access. They called a meeting and voted me out of the partnership and gave me severance pay. Bill, with a tear in his eye said, "I had no choice. You abandoned me." Suddenly, it was as if I awoke in this dream we call reality. I could very clearly see the issue of abandonment I had been working so hard on in my own healing process. Though I could understand his feelings, I knew they were not true for me. It was as if for a moment I could see the play of life frozen in a still frame. I was somehow outside my drama looking in at myself. I seemed to be freeing myself from an old archetypal pattern and Bill was the instrument in that action. The dream from Switzerland actively played through my head, reminding me of the support from Spirit. This was the first time that such a deep feeling of nonattachment had been evoked in my life. The image was one of a wounded woman who had been gutted and rebuilt. It was now time to let her go and claim the new image that was wanting to present itself. What that would be I did not know. I don't know how to describe the feeling of completeness that I felt that day nor the irony of those words spoken by Bill in that paradoxical moment. I would later come to find out that my assistant had been reporting "Avalon's unusual practices" to Bill and the state officials. He had been taking out of context many of the incidents at Avalon I have shared and using them toward his own ends. He wanted the directorship of the program and he had gotten it. The profundity of the words I had spoken to the girls before leaving for Switzerland rang in my ears. Destiny was at play in my life. As it cut the cord to my old self, I wondered where it would take me.

The next morning while in the shower I was instructed to get out and call a friend I had met in Zurich. She lived in California but had attended a seminar at the Jung Institute one summer. During her stay we met and had lunch, but other than an occasional postcard, I had not heard from her since. I was instructed to call and explain my situation, arranging for a four-day stay in her area. I was to hold the trip as a vision quest during which the next piece of the puzzle would be revealed. I called. She gave me the names of two women and suggested I come and crash on her couch during my stay. I made plans immediately. The trip was magical. One of the women knew of a part-time position available at the Institute of Transpersonal Psychology. It was to serve as the co-coordinator of the Spiritual Emergence Network. I called and secured an interview and was offered a job. I knew nothing of the work the network did, but I would come to discover the appropriateness of my placement. Though the pay would barely pay half the rent on an apartment, I knew I must go.

I returned home and shared with my boys what had happened. They were a bit disgruntled. Neither of them particularly wanted to leave Texas. They began to share ideas of what it might be like to live with their father in Houston. Though some part of me knew that getting to know their father at this stage of their lives would be important (ages 14 and 16), another part was frightened for their well-being. Would he be abusive to them as he had been to me? If I did not honor their request, would I be enabling (i.e., handicapping) them rather than empowering them? The decision was to be the most difficult of my life. In the long run my faith in them and their power within ruled out. They agreed to come to California and stay for a month, exploring the lay of the land, so to speak, before making a final decision.

We packed a large moving van and prepared to leave. My divorce became final and the papers were signed. We started out across the country towards new beginnings. I was shaking in my boots. Though we went through the steps of our plan, something in me knew that they would be returning. I cried and prayed for guidance. On the third day of our travels, I was meditating when I again felt a wave of mourning come over me. I wanted so to make the right decision, but what that was seemed muddled and hidden. I had met Irena Tweedie, a Sufi master, who had given me her book, *Daughter of Fire*, saying that if I ever needed an answer to a question, I could pose the question and then flip randomly through the book and an answer would appear. I tried it, and to my surprise when I opened the book, in dark bold letters it said, *"And the Master will say, »Give me your children.« Some will have the courage to do so, and some will not."*[72] Needless to say, I cried myself to sleep.

After we settled into our new home in California, a vision visited.

> *A group of Indians were gathered in a circle for a ceremony. I sat in the circle with Scott in my lap. Kirk, the oldest, entered the circle dressed in ceremonial clothing. He had a short warrior's dress that was white and hung to the middle of his thighs. He wore a headdress with white feathers circling around his crown, meeting in the center of the back of his head forming a tail that*

---

[72] Tweedie, Irina, *Daughter of Fire*, Blue Dolphin Publishing, Nevada City, Ca., 1986.

*extended itself down his back to the ground. He looked powerful and magnificent. His father entered the circle next. He also was adorned in ceremonial dress, but did not have a headdress. They began to face each other posturing themselves defensively. As they did, they moved clockwise in the center of the circle, glaring at each other with their eyes. (I knew then that whatever it was the boys needed to do with their father, it was soul business. I was not to interfere, but to support each in their own way.) The contest went on until their father began to shrink smaller and smaller. Finally, he left the circle, and Kirk raised his clenched fist to the heavens and gave a warrior's cry that shook me. He had won his power; his quest had begun.*

This is one of the hardest parts of motherhood, allowing your child to differentiate and empowering them to be who they are. Shakti was encouraging us all to grow! As Joseph Campbell states:

> The call to adventure signifies that destiny has summoned the hero and transferred his spiritual center of gravity from within the pale of his society to a zone unknown. This fateful region of both treasure and danger may be variously represented: as a distant land, a forest, a kingdom underground, beneath the waves or above the sky, a secret island, lofty mountaintop, or profound dream state; but it is always a place of strangely fluid and polymorphous beings, unimaginable torments, superhuman deeds, and impossible delights.[73]

He goes on to say,

> They thought that it would be a disgrace to go forth as a group. Each entered the forest at a point that he himself had chosen, where it was darkest and there was no path. If there is a path it is someone else's path and you are not on the adventure.[74]

And so it seemed that each of us now would quest for our individual truths. Years later when the Return or the Rebirth

---

[73] Cousineau, Phil (editor), *The Hero's Journey, Joseph Campbell on His Life and Work*, Harper & Row, Publishers, San Francisco, 1990, p. 1.
[74] Ibid, p. vi.

processes would begin to occur, we would each see the inherent healing value these steps invoked in our lives. At the time, however, we just felt the pain. Within two months of the hospital incident, I stood in my new apartment on San Antonio Street in Menlo Park, California, watching my boys drive away with their father.

## THE ROLE OF SEN IN PSYCHOSPIRITUAL CRISES

I checked in at my new office, the Spiritual Emergence Network. God certainly works in mysterious ways. The Hindus teach that the first three (lower) chakras are the "hell zones" and work with your instinctual nature. The upper chakras begin with your heart and represent "the heavens." Moving from your third chakra, the power center located in the solar plexus, to the fourth chakra, the heart center, the place of truth, is an enormous leap in consciousness. My world certainly seemed to reflect that shift. I had passed a threshold. I seemed to be entering a space with more support and less struggle; less suffering and more integration; less disintegration and more synthesis. My professional world would now serve in healing the split I had always experienced between who I was in the outside world and who I was in the inside world. I experienced an enormous amount of joy. The support offered to me from those around me was consistent and unbroken. I had never before experienced this kind of total gestalt shift. Since an early age I had been taught that altered states of consciousness were crazy or weird. Now suddenly I was co-coordinating an international organization that was formed to connect holistic practitioners and helpers with people who had undergone a spiritual emergency. Let me take a moment to explain this work, for I found it to be most instrumental in my own healing process as well as others.

The Spiritual Emergence Network (SEN) is a non-profit inter-national organization which seeks to support people undergoing certain types of psychospiritual crises. In 1980, in response to an increasing recognition of and need for further information and support for those undergoing psychospiritual crises, SEN was formed by Christina Grof at the Esalen Institute, Big Sur, California. SEN operates a free information and referral service and works to inform the lay and professional community about the nature, incidence and treatment of transpersonal crises. SEN is the only international organization to serve people undergoing a phenomena not yet recognized by the standard psychiatric and psychological establishment. Should you need to contact them yourself their address is:

> Spiritual Emergence Network
> 930 Mission Street
> Suite 7
> Soquel, California 95060−3653
> (408) 426−0902

This phenomena is called "psychospiritual crisis" or more commonly "spiritual emergence or emergency." People undergoing these crises are usually undergoing altered states of consciousness, disorientation, strange bodily sensations, and other symptoms commonly associated with mental disorders. These people are often confused, isolated, frightened, and afraid of being crazy. SEN, along with many leaders in the transpersonal movement, proposes that many such experiences are natural, painful stages of development which have been clearly documented within the world's great spiritual traditions. With the proper contextual information and support, these individuals can begin integrating their experiences and resume normal, often more healthy lives. SEN is in a unique position to observe various forms and manifestations of spiritual and psychological phenomena occurring around the world. Being the sole network concerned with these issues, SEN serves as a "window" to such paranormal and pychospiritual crises as they arise. It is an organization that sits on the leading edge of our quest for wisdom and knowledge—in this case an inner, psychological and spiritual quest. As such, SEN's work is not recognized or supported by the general populace or even the mainstream psychological community. Yet, clearly SEN is responding to an increasing need for alternative mental health support. It is SEN's contention that being drugged, labeled, and treated from a psychopathological perspective may not be the most beneficial (or economically viable) means of approaching individuals undergoing these psychospiritual crises. The individual and social implications are just beginning to be defined and the pragmatic exploration and research of psychospiritual experiences just beginning. In fact, in 1994, such experiences were defined in the DSM IV (a diagnostic manual for health care professionals) as "religious and spiritual problems." It was classified in the V codes which are areas of our mental health needing support and attention, but not considered pathological.

In the field of transpersonal psychology, spiritual values, concepts, and experiences are incorporated into the predominate paradigm and theories of psychological functioning and developmental processes. Indeed, this spiritual aspect is one of the characteristics that differentiates transpersonal psychology from other schools of psychology.

One of the contributions that transpersonal psychology has made to the understanding of human development is the recognition that during the course of normal human development, psychological crises of a spiritual nature may arise. *Spiritual*, in this sense, refers to experiences that seem of a higher order—those beyond the personal/personality level of experience.

> Spiritual refers not only to experiences traditionally considered religious but to all the states of awareness, all the human functions and activities which have as their common denominator the possession of values higher than average—values such as the ethical, the aesthetic, the heroic, the humanitarian and the altruistic.[75]

So, in this context, people experience crises which seem to arise from an expanded realm of human experience—experiences

---

[75] Assagioli, R., "Self-Realization and Psychological Disturbances," in *Revision, The Journal of Consciousness and Change*, Volume 8, Number 2, 1986, p. 21.

which reflect the spiritual nature of the phenomena.   One of the contributions made to the understanding of such states has been the categorization of these phenomena into various types of experiences.  Some of these various types have been recognized and accounted for in traditional religious and spiritual literature.  This has served as a great source of information and validity in regard to such experiences, psychological states, and phenomena, helping many people understand their experience and thus removing much of the associated fear.  Stanislav and Christina Grof's book, *Spiritual Emergency, When Personal Transformation Becomes a Crisis*, describes these phenomena and their individual manifestations, Kundalini being one such expression.[76]

While these categories of experiences are distinct in nature, they do tend to create a generalized response.  People experiencing psychospiritual crisis are usually undergoing disorienting phenomena such as a feeling that another reality "bleeps" in during the waking state, a burning sensation on the hands or feet, electrical sensations in various parts of the body, hearing inner voices or having knowledge of events before they happen.  Some of these symptoms are commonly associated with mental disorders, causing people to fear for their sanity.  Some of their responses are generated by the cultural mores and assumptions of our Western society, by our general lack of knowledge of and sensitivity to spiritual realities.  At the Association of Transpersonal Psychology Conference held in California in 1992, Stan Grof reported that our Western culture is the *only* culture that does not have a place within its fabricate for altered states of consciousness. With no cultural understanding or context to see such experiences as developmental rather than psychotic, the individual fears for his well being.  How will he be able to care for himself?  Will he go crazy?  Will he loose his job?  How can he explain what is happening to his family and friends when he has no context

---

[76] Grof, Stanislav and Christina, *Spiritual Emergency*, Jeremy Tarcher, Los Angeles, 1989.

for it himself? Some postulate that these psychospiritual crises are evolutionary events, part of a natural developmental process. The ramifications of such psychospiritual crises being the phenomena of normal human development (rather than the symptoms of impending mental pathology) are multifaceted. A personal crisis is at hand with few known resources that would facilitate rather than misdiagnosis and mistreat.

Of primary importance, the map of what would be considered "normal" psychological functioning and experience is greatly expanded by such a contention. Prevalent views of pathological mental states are therefore challenged in that these psychospiritual crises often closely resemble mental disturbances. If indeed some people are being diagnosed as mentally ill when in fact they are experiencing a psychospiritual crisis, it follows that inappropriate treatment, care, and perspectives are being applied. The economic ramifications alone of such misappropriation of psychological and mental health resources are staggering.

The contention that pychospiritual crises are a prelude to higher level functioning of an individual implies that there are social and cultural gains to be achieved. These psychospiritual crises tend to effect many core levels of human perception:

> ...the more varied and complex aspects of modern man's per-
> sonality are involved and need to be transmuted and harmonized
> with each other; his fundamental drives, his emotions and feelings,
> his creative imagination, his inquiring mind, his assertive will, and
> also his interpersonal and social relations.[77]

An individual who has integrated these spiritual experiences into his or her everyday life stands to contribute to society from a larger sense of self. From a psychological perspective, such a model of human development serves to greatly expand our understanding of the human psyche, treatment modalities, and insight into related human psychological functioning. On a very personal level the

---

[77] Assagioli, R., "Self-Realization and Psychological Disturbances," in *Revision, The Journal of Consciousness and Change*, Volume 8, Number 2, 1986, p. 21.

implication of being "normal" as opposed to "pathological" strips the effect of cultural bias and prejudices which arise from the label "mentally ill." One note of clarification is in order. As the Grofs have so aptly stated:

> It is important to emphasize that not every experience of unusual states of consciousness and intense perceptual, emotional, cognitive, and psychosomatic changes fall into the category of spiritual emergency. The concept of transpersonal crisis is not oriented against traditional psychiatry: it offers an alternative approach to individuals who can benefit from it and are capable and willing to accept it.[78]

## THROUGH THE THRESHOLDS TO QUIETUDE AND ECSTASY

I had lived a major portion of my life either resisting, denying, or battling this deep-rooted part of my nature. In the years that followed I learned to trust it more and surrender to its inherent process. Now I was in the position of being asked to speak publicly about such things. It was terrifying in the beginning. At the same time there was an enormous sense of liberation and relief. Suddenly, I was walking my talk. When you've been raised with what feels like a large canyon between who you are and who you are supposed to be, living without that split is an adjustment. The image I'm shown to help describe this is of a rubberband that has been stretched out and then somebody lets go and allows it to resume its normal stance. There is a shock effect, a realignment of the energy field.

During my work with SEN I met and came to know some of the pioneers in the transpersonal realms of our Western psyche. Through these contacts, my own synthesis continued and a gradual

---

[78] Grof, Stanislav and Christina, "Spiritual Emergency: The Understanding and Treatment of Transpersonal Crises," in *Revision, The Journal of Consciousness and Change*, Vol. 8, Number 2, p. 7.

reorganization of my persona resulted. What was so refreshing was their total acceptance of reality as I was experiencing it. Their enthusiasm to explore its manifestations encouraged me towards integrating the happenings rather than exploiting them or repressing the material. If enough of us bridge this canyon and heal the split between our "little selves" and our "higher selves," if we integrate and actively include the mystical side of our nature into our culture, what potential might we access? My response drove me toward its healing potential rather than activating its destructive nature, which could have resulted in fragmentation or my own destruction. I certainly have come to appreciate why others have called this part of the path "the razors" edge. It can feel quite narrow and sharp.

I began to learn new techniques to better facilitate the work as it presented itself. The teachers I was led to seemed to be versed in processes that encouraged the healing of the body/mind split. The involvement of the body in any approach was necessary if unity was what I sought. Ken Dychtwald describes what I believe is happening today to thousands of individuals on this planet. He reports the findings of the nineteenth-century Canadian physician, Dr. Richard M. Bucke.

> Bucke felt that at some time in the twentieth century a point would come when the human race would make some sort of quantum leap in its own evolution to a condition of more expansive self-awareness, greater intellectual clarity, improved moral harmony, higher consciousness, and loving unity among all beings of this earth. He felt this change would come about when sufficient information and experience had been generated to enable mankind to emerge from the conflicts, confusions, ignorances, and psychoemotional poverties within which it had become trapped by its own weaknesses and stressful developments.
>
> Bucke suggested that this transformation would be focused upon exploration of the untapped domains of the body and mind, and that these developments would allow for the birth of a new and higher perspective, an elevated way of being, feeling, seeing, knowing, and relating... The outcome of this change process

would be mankind's eventual evolution to a new level of human consciousness which he called "cosmic consciousness"... Bucke believed that human evolution to a state of cosmic consciousness would dramatically accelerate when large numbers of people became interested in exploring the realms and limitations of their own bodymind potentialities. This exploration would begin on a very private, personal level, but would eventually precipitate the development of a massive transformation of all human beliefs and forms.[79]

Bucke describes three levels of consciousness, the third being "cosmic consciousness" as described above. The first of the two preceding levels is what he calls "simple consciousness" which "is involved with food, shelter, self-defense and procreation."[80] In other words, we operate out of a basic instinctual need for survival. In the second level of development, we reach a stage of "self--consciousness" in which we "simultaneously inhabit the worlds of sensation, perceptions, and biological urges as well as the world of language, beliefs, thought, and self-reflection. In other words, we are not only aware, we are also aware of ourselves being aware."[81]

The Kundalini process will take you to each of these three thresholds of consciousness, resolving the wounds that would keep the psyche from reaching its final destination. Your time spent in the looking glass will reveal the grosser wounds, as well as those hidden in the subtle bodies. Harmony within the system cannot exist until all discord from all life cycles has been discovered and transmuted. Recall my dream experience upon departure from Zurich: Day Three signified facing my demons and transmuting them. Transmutation in its final stages is not a partial process, but involves the entire organism. Some additional clearing would present itself before that stage began.

About 2 months after beginning my work with SEN a lovely man who became a dear friend and fellow explorer entered my

[79] Dychtwald, Ken, *Bodymind*, Jove Books, New York, 1984, pp. 257–259.
[80] Ibid, p. 258.
[81] Ibid, p. 258.

life. Joe was the first man I had been with who encouraged and supported allowing the energy to flow dynamically through, finding it's own level of volume rather than imposing a feeling that I had to temper it in any way. He was a wizard in every sense of the word and validated the experiences that continued to flow. Our meeting marked a period in which the memory of past lives would evoke dramatic changes in this one. I began having a lot of past life experiences of Egypt. I was dressing one morning as I prepared to go to work. I had just pulled up my blue jeans when something hit me between the shoulder blades knocking me to the floor. My body went into convulsions, flipping me around the floor much like a fish out of water. I managed to get to the phone and called the office for help. When I described what was happening, they suggested I contact a gentleman named Paul who was on our referral lists. He lived in Montana and had a good reputation for clearing unwanted entities from your energy. I called. He said he would do the work in a day or two and call back with the results. The information I got during meditation was that I had been born carrying the energies of two Egyptian sorcerers, a male and a female. They sat positioned in my subtle body above my pineal gland. My karma with them had been completed and it was time for them to leave. In the meantime, the Shakti energy was assisting their departure and clearing the area. It felt like a war had been waged in and on my back. I called a friend to come over and sit with me. When she rang the doorbell, I couldn't manage to walk with the contortions being experienced by my body. Slowly, I crawled to the door. When she first arrived, she said my face was purple from the neck up. Her presence was very comforting. I am always amazed at the two levels of awareness operating during these experiences. One level thinks it must be going crazy and is scared, while the other is calm and has an all-knowing sense of things. Actually, a third witnesses it all without analyzing it or judging it in any way.

The experience went on for several days. On the second day in the early afternoon, I began to feel a tingling sensation move throughout my body. I entered a very calming altered state. I knew

Paul was working. The energy calmed and I knew they had gone. Sure enough the next day I received a call. He reported that he had done a clearing of two Egyptian sorcerers, one male and one female. He said they had been with me since birth. They had been located in the subtle body above the pineal gland. They were gone now. His validation of the information I had received was confidence-provoking in one sense, and thought-provoking in another. The remarkable thing which seems to have been a lasting result of this experience is a quietude that settled throughout my system. Until this time no matter how vivid the experience or lucid the instruction, a struggle would occur within between that part of me that trusted the guidance and another part that was constantly cynical of everything I did or said. Though discernment is an important part of any process, cynicism is not. The Kundalini process left no stone unturned. Another opening was beginning, the Shakti energy continued to move up the spinal column and eventually over the top of the head splashing down into the throat region and entering the belly (which I will describe in more detail in Chapter Eight).

After this clearing, I also began to observe an image of myself that would appear at night about 6 feet from my bed. Over a 6 week period it appeared regularly. Within the image was another image of myself as a light body. The light body was crouched in a fetal position at the foot of the outlined form of myself. As the weeks evolved, it began to gradually stand up until it completely filled the other figure. Once the form was complete, I never saw it again. Was this more of the realigning I was experiencing? Though it was fascinating, what did it mean? I'm sure there may be a more esoteric meaning given to this phenomenon, but I interpreted it as the new life that was being awakened within me. In fact, I now feel that it foretold of a new body that I would soon conceive and gestate for several years before giving birth to it. Time will bear witness, for I'm still in the gestation period which has lasted over nine years now. With that in mind let me share Dychtwald's remarks on how our bodyminds are the link in the evolutionary process.

The belief that self-development may be the process through which an evolutionary transformation to a higher state of human consciousness is developing can best be appreciated when we realize that we are at present the *end product* of the entire evolution of life on our planet. Having laboriously developed throughout hundreds of millions of years to our present state of being, we are, in a sense, riding on the crest of the evolutionary wave that has been pushing onward throughout history. This development has recorded itself in our bodyminds and, in addition, has molded our bodyminds into the vehicles, the human ships, by which this evolutionary journey is destined to continue.

Therefore, with each passing moment, our bodyminds are in the process of flowing through time, carrying us from yesterday to tomorrow across a flexible bridge that is ourselves. In this way, our physical structure and form at any given instant is simply a slice of the ongoing living/dying process within which we are inextricably immersed. In this way, all of our physical characteristics and shapes are acutely reflective of the physical and emotional activities of our lives, revealing our histories with their scars and uneven terrain, and also suggesting our futures with their potential for development and transformation.[82]

During the period that followed I began to experience moments of ecstasy, particularly while making love. Numerous occasions presented themselves in which I had an experience of what I call "merging with my divine lover" or my Beloved. There are no words to describe the total feeling of completeness and love evoked by these experiences. I began to realize that love is not just an energy, but rather a state of consciousness.

---

[82] Ibid, p. 260.

# CHAPTER EIGHT

# Pregnant with God

## PERU: AN ENIGMA WITHIN A MYSTERY

A S I LOOK BACK UPON THE MANNER in which this story has unfolded, I marvel at the deep process in which we are all involved. Once you remove the veil from over your eyes you again can experience the magic of life—not its predictability, but its unpredictability and surprise. This part of my story is harder to describe because I am still enmeshed in its belly or it is still in mine.

It was not until May, 1989, that I began to meet with other individuals who have experienced this part of the journey. As with each other phase, I was unable to locate information about the process until I found myself deep within it. The Eastern spiritual traditions describe with much more elegance what such a process will reveal. Since my path had never brought me into the East quite so emphatically, I am still learning much about spiritual emergence phenomena and how they relate to the individuation process and union with God. June Singer, in her book *Boundaries of the Soul*, describes the individuation process as follows:

> The individuation process, in the Jungian sense, means the conscious realization and integration of all the possibilities immanent in the individual. It is opposed to any kind of conformity with the collective and, as a therapeutic factor in analytical work, it also demands the rejection of those prefabricated psychic matrices—the conventional attitudes—with which most people would like

to live. It offers the possibility that everyone can have his own direction, his special purpose, and it can attach a sense of value to the lives of those who suffer from the feeling that they are unable to measure up to collective norms and collective ideals.

In "The Relations between the Ego and the Unconscious," an essay in which Jung set forth the fundamentals of the individuation process, we find that "Individuation means becoming a single, homogeneous being," and, in so far as "individuality" embraces our innermost, last, and incomparable uniqueness, it also implies becoming one's own self. We could therefore translate individuation as... "self-realization." It is an easy thing to say "be yourself" but quite another thing to know who you truly are. How can you be yourself if you do not know the self? Therefore, the process of individuation becomes a seeking after self-knowledge.[83]

I was to discover that my individuation process—the task of seeing who (or what) lay beyond the ego personality that I thought of as "me"—would unfold via a series of episodes that stretched beyond the mind's imagining. If you will bear with me, I will once again allow the story to speak for itself—this time in its raw form.

My inner teacher spoke to me while I was still in Switzerland, just as I was entering my "dark night of the soul." I cried that night and said, "When will this be over?" He responded, "All will be resolved on the night of the *blue moon*." I explored this symbol but could find little information about it at the time. It was two years later when a friend called and later sent a book called *The Secret of the Andes* by Brother Philip.[84] In this book I would discover that the Valley of the Blue Moon is located at Lake Titicaca in Peru. She wanted me to go with her to explore what all of this might mean, but the time did not seem right. I put it on the back burner, so to speak, since I was moving to California and a new life.

I had been in California for one year when my intuition began urging me to go to Peru. I "argued" that I didn't have enough

---

[83] Singer, June, *Boundaries of the Soul*, Anchor Books, Garden City, New York, 1973, pp. 158–159.

[84] Brother Philip, *Secret of the Andes*, Leaves of Brass Press, Ca., 1976.

money, much less time, to go on such a journey. But Psyche was relentless. Finally, I accepted the challenge. I had met and was dating a wonderful man named Russ; he has since become my best friend and husband. He decided he would accompany me and so we purchased tickets to Peru. Within the next few days I received a letter from a friend and co-worker in Switzerland who said Spirit had instructed him to wire me some money. Yep, you guessed it, the exact amount for my ticket. So preparations began. We were to fast 13 of the 16 days we would be there. Our intent would be to walk through Peru on a vision quest, allowing Psyche to guide our every step.

The American Indians believe that when you go on a vision quest you marry yourself and Mother Earth. In other words, journeys that invoke deep voyages into the psyche activate new parts of one's "true self" revealing false identities. As we look in the looking glass and realize our truth a time of commitment follows. We must then unite (marry) with ourselves bringing that aspect of our power into our waking lives. As we do so, we break free from our childhood conditioning and merge more with "Mother Earth," the collective feminine. Looking back on this, I seem to have bumbled into that marriage in spite of myself at the Sun Dance. I had experienced a ceremony which formalized my commitment to God and to the "Work." My marriage to God had initiated a process that purged my system of abusive relationships. Something deep within me had said yes; yes to being who I am without apology; yes to a process that would integrate spirit and matter. The Sun Dance had opened an archetypal door leading to a life of service to the Mystery. Peru would be the birthing ground. For we no sooner reach one plateau than it is time to pierce the next. Looking back I felt as if the plateaus were like steps leading me into higher realms of awareness; each disclosing another level of commitment; another set of tests and lessons. Looking back I can see my relationship with God unfolding as if with a mate. The time in Waco as I began to awaken to the teachings of Jung and alternative views of spiritual experience was like the courtship. The first visitation of the "Hooded Ones" before we left for Switzerland was like my engagement. And, the Sun Dance was my marriage to the divine. What would our trip to Peru manifest? Each step in my relationship with the divine seemed to be healing my dysfunctional relationship with myself, creating a deeper understanding of the feminine.

Instructions continued to come during meditation. We only knew we were to go to a certain place at Lake Titicaca and Machu Picchu. Upon our return, we were to stay in isolation for five days and allow the process time to integrate. What process was being activated? Would the journey itself evoke something new in our lives? What could it possibly be and how would we know it?

We arrived in Lima in August of 1988; we were excited and a bit anxious. We would get a hotel room for the next three days until we could make connections by air to Cusco. This gave us time to acclimate to the high altitude; it is important to sleep when your body needs it. Also, a nurse friend of ours suggested we drink Coke if we began to feel any sense of nausea. Though Coke was not a part of our fast, we took the advice to heart. It did seem to work wonders. We did a little sightseeing, but mostly we read, rested, and shared our dreams. Catching a "hopper" to Cusco was the next adventure. Although everyone showed up with their tickets an hour or so before the time of departure, when it was time to board, everyone ran to get their seat—first-come, first-served. What a sight it was: women carrying infants, old ones jabbing with their canes, children hanging to their mother's hands for dear life—all racing for that seat! It reminded me of the musical chairs that I used to play as a child. Once on board, you settle back to take survey of what it was you ran to catch. As I looked out the window, I realized there was a black crow caught between the panes of glass. It was just stuck there. That image alone should give you a sense of the condition of the plane. I had the impression our plane was reaching the end of its journey. We said prayers and up we went.

Cusco is a beautiful place. Its people have wide, round eyes that feel open and warm. The old stone buildings and cobblestoned streets create an ambience that is intriguing. We met a wonderful cabby named Nicholas who acted much like our guardian angel during the whole trip. For $20 a day he would drive us around the countryside as we explored the ancient ruins of a people from long ago, the Incas. One day on such an outing, Nicholas took us to the Pisac ruins. He waited below while we climbed the stone structure. As we began our ascent, I noticed an old Peruvian man dressed in a bright red poncho. He was carrying something in his hands that was covered with a red cloth. I mentioned to Russ that he felt like a medicine man. I can't explain exactly except to say, that I have noticed that such people have a very different energy around them—it is more electrified. We followed him for a while. I was afraid we were being intrusive, so we sat down and waited to see his reaction. He turned looking at us conveying a wish for us to follow. Surprised, we looked at each other and then proceeded on up the mountain. When he reached the top, it was about sunset. He removed the red cloth revealing a mirror inlaid in carved wood. He placed it on the stones facing the sun. He then knelt down and tapped on the stone. He pulled a small box out that seemed to have coins of some sort inside. He turned his body away from us, raising both arms toward the sun. After a few minutes, he again wrapped the mirror in the red cloth and tucking it under his arm, turned and walked away. We walked up to the space where he had stood, the box of coins was gone. What had happened to them? What was the ritual about that we had just witnessed? I looked in the direction the old man had gone and noticed him quickly disappear around the corner. Russ and I continued to follow as he completed the circle he was making through the ruins. I saw him descend the front stairs and disappear down the main street of the village. I hurried, but once I reached the bottom of the stairs I could not see him anywhere. I was about to give up looking when I saw him step out of a cavern just down the street. He was wiping his hands with the red cloth and looking at me, smiling. If I could only speak the language! How frustrating this all felt. We decided to go into the cavern and see what would happen. The cavern was a one room darkly lit area with a few wooden tables and benches.ÌThe old man sat at the table closest to the door. Across from him at another table sat a couple drinking beer. The mirror sat on their table and was turned facing us. There was a vacant table next to them, so we sat down and ordered a bottle of beer. When the beer arrived, we shared it with all there. The old man acknowledged us with a smile. Suddenly, the old woman and man sitting next to us turned and began to speak in Spanish. She came over to me and took my face in her hands. She began to speak with great emotion as she kept pointing to me and then to the heavens. She laid her head on my chest and began to cry. I could not understand exactly what was happening, but I felt as if I was in some way assisting her in a healing. This behavior went on for several minutes, and then she began to thank me and seemed more calm. Our taxi driver came and so we left. As Nicholas drove out of town, I turned and saw the old shaman from the mountain standing in the street with his right hand raised in the air giving a farewell gesture. What had this all been about? I'm not sure I will ever really know, but it certainly helps describe the magic and mystery prevalent in Peru.

Another incident occurred which I now know laid the foundation for what was about to take place upon my return to the States. Shortly before visiting Machu Picchu, we were meditating and doing deep trance work at Lake Titicaca. I received a series of what I call "fracture fritter" visions, a series of seemingly unconnected images.

*In the first image I entered the ground and discovered a spaceship embedded there. A series of pictures followed: a set of large granite steps that had a primitive appearance, a sense of following those steps up followed and finally, a Peruvian woman with a baby tied to her front.*

The last image stood out because it seemed to be more the custom to tie a baby to the mother's back.

Days later we caught a small train going up to Machu Picchu. I purchased a small book containing descriptions of the village. To my surprise when I opened it, one of the first things I noticed was a picture of what was called the "Big Steps." They were identical to the steps in my vision, so I told Russ I thought we had been given a map. We would start at the Big Steps and follow my feet. The body's memory will often take over in a situation where a past life announces itself—so it would be that day. Once the train arrived we boarded a bus for the final leg of the journey. We were waiting in line when I suddenly had the sensation to turn around. Standing directly behind me was an Indian man carrying an eagle feather. I turned to tell Russ and when we again looked, the man was gone. Though we found it interesting, we didn't give it much more thought. We boarded the bus and started a rather exciting ascent to the top of the mountains. The road was narrow and the drivers moved the buses quickly up and down, sliding by each other with uncanny timing. Their room for error was acutely obvious to the passengers as we peered straight down the steep cliff walls which felt a breath away. The ride seemed to awaken the senses and the view encountered when we stepped off the bus took our breath away. I cannot explain the total gestalt effect that occurred. It was like walking through a portal in time. The Andes loomed above and below creating a cradle in the center where the old ruins of Machu Picchu rested. The atmosphere seemed charged with electricity and a sense of wonder permeated everything.

We found the Big Steps and I let my heart and my feet lead the way while my mind watched. As we got to the top, a deep sense of remembering began. Russ and I both seemed to access a place within that had total recall of a lifetime when we both lived here as children. We stood looking out across the ruins. A small-child feeling ran through our bodies and running, as if in play, we described what each room's function had been: where we lived, ceremony rooms, favorite meditation sites, etc. Later we would acquire site information that validated what we had somehow known. As with most past-life memories, the experience seemed to unfold with more detail as time went by. What we remembered was of a life when I was being raised to be a priestess. Though my training was strict, my free time was full of exploration and hours of joy shared with Russ as my brother and closest companion. In the initiation that I was preparing for, the top part of my skull would be removed to allow the Sun God to enter. If I recovered from the ordeal, I became an instrument of the Gods for the people. In any case, my relationship with Russ could not continue. Once the initiation was begun, Russ found the pain of the loss of his companion to be unbearable and went off into the forest to die. Great waves of emotion cascaded through us as we both individually sought out our old meditation sites and privately recalled a long forgotten past.

After some time, we rejoined each other and were about to leave when suddenly we saw the last "fracture fritter" vision—a woman with a baby tied to her front. She seemed somewhat out of context because most of the people in the ruins that day were tourists. We sat down and waited to see what might be revealed. A small inner voice said to turn around. When we did we saw the majestic figure of the Indian who had disappeared from the bus line descending the stairs carrying his eagle feather. I gathered my courage and approached him. I spoke to him and to my surprise he answered me in fluent English. I had heard of a medicine man that traveled into California from Peru, and had tried to reach him before leaving the States, but to no avail. His name flashed into my mind and I asked if he could be that man. When he answered that he was, I was totally taken back. We spoke briefly and exchanged agenda's and agreed to meet later. Several women were traveling with him, one from Oakland, California. We were amazed! We returned to our motel feeling a need to be still and digest the events of the day.

The next day we prepared to leave for Lima where we would be spending two days before our departure to the States. A subtle sadness settled over us for we had come to love the beauty of the land and its people. Before leaving for Lima we had tried to secure reservations at a hotel, but all the phone lines were down. We decided we would take our chances and get a taxi driver who could drive us to a couple that looked appropriate. When we arrived at the airport, a taxi driver ran up and grabbed our bags. His English was poor and our Spanish worse, so we tried to communicate through sign language. He guided us to his cab, put the suitcases in the trunk, and opened the back door gesturing for us to enter. No sooner had we sat down than he closed the door and proceeded to take a thick rope and tie us into the car. He said something quickly and then ran back into the terminal. We couldn't stop laughing. After about 15 or 20 minutes had passed, the joke seemed to be on us. We had begun to climb out of the window so we could get the rope untied when our rather strange guide reappeared with another older woman. Evidently, he had needed another fare to make his trip more profitable and had creatively captured us. He untied the rope allowing the elderly woman into the front seat and sped off. After delivering the lady, we showed him two possible hotels from our travel book. He waved the book aside and insisted he knew just the right place—no problem. When we arrived at the hotel we were surprisingly impressed. Russ stayed with the luggage while I went inside to investigate. Upon entering the lobby I immediately ran into one of the women who had accompanied the Indian shaman at Machu Picchu. I said in astonishment, "What are you doing here?" She replied, "How did you know where we were?" I said, "WE?" She said, "Yes, Inti will be here in the morning." Needless to say we stayed. We spent the following day with Inti listening to his vision of a healing city of all cultures that he would build in the Andes. He had just attended a meeting of medicine people from the North and South Americas, the first in over 500 years. Something was afoot, but what? We returned home inspired but full of questions. What had our trip really been about? Had the Valley of the Blue Moon initiated us in subtle ways we had no knowledge of yet? Many unresolved questions remained. Though our journey seemed complete, something else still stirred.

Our inner guidance had instructed us to stay in "our cave" for five days upon our return. That meant a period of isolation with no telephones, visitors or outside interruptions. We followed through as requested. The days proved uneventful, yet restful. Many wonderful things happened while in Peru, but to our surprise our return home would be the beginning rather than the end.


## THE BUDDHA BELLY

The next chain of events set in motion a clarity of intent that was facilitated by a variety of approaches and teachers that both lubricated and massaged an intensive *implosion* of consciousness.

It was September 7, 1988. I was at home with Russ and Quita, who shared an apartment with me. I had just returned to work after our journey to Peru. I was watching television when a movement similar to a heartbeat started pumping in my right leg. It increased in severity until the leg of my blue jeans started moving. My housemates noticed the movement and asked me what was happening. I didn't know. I had experienced this phenomenon before, but not as exaggerated. The "heartbeat" then moved down into my foot, back up into my thigh and entered my vagina. At that moment a brilliant white Light absorbed me and I seemed to disappear within it for some 10 or 15 minutes. While in this state I had no awareness of anything. I would later understand that I had entered my first states of samadhi. A blissful feeling prevailed as I returned to a more normal state of consciousness. No sooner had I regained a sense of myself than the same process began again except this time the pulsating started in my knees. Though Russ and Quita could not see what I was seeing, they had a deep feeling that something profound was at hand. When the Light again absorbed me, it felt as if my entire auric field[85] expanded and lost all boundaries. I became very dizzy and nauseated. When Russ or Quita spoke to me, it was as if I could experience their words as solid forms. If they spoke too quickly, the words seemed to spin me around causing more nausea. It was the same with their touch. My hypersensitivity required us all to move with a stillness. A great feeling of reverence pervaded the entire incident. Though we had no idea of what was taking place, a sacredness was felt by us all.

Both Russ and Quita are medically oriented people, having spent many years working in hospitals: Russ as a clinical laboratory technologist, and Quita as a paramedic. They continued to watch my biological functioning, looking for anything which might point to a physical ailment. (In fact, throughout the entire process following this experience, they have monitored and tended to my physiological well being.) They put me to bed. There was so much energy running through and around me that both my friends had physical reactions to it and the heater in my waterbed blew out. The flow of energy, needless to say, was strong but we participated as openly as possible. It is important to remember that when a Kundalini episode is in progress it affects all present. In order to facilitate the process most effectively, being receptive as you follow Shakti's lead will support a more positive outcome. I liken it to childbirth. The midwife is not having the baby, but if she follows the process clearly she assists in a way that is most compassionate, both to the mother and the child. Such complete trust and surrender to nature brings remarkable results.

As I lay there in bed, my whole being seemed to be absorbed in bliss. For the next two hours I experienced such a bliss that words are unable to describe the richness. My body became so hot that

---

[85] The *aura* is to the energetic field generated from within and surrounding the physical body.

both Russ and Quita were reluctant to touch me; I, however, felt cool and comfortable. I now know what mystics must mean when they speak of becoming drunk on the divine, for that is exactly how I felt—such intoxicating ecstasy and peace, such harmony! Suddenly, "something" about the size of a small man's fist formed under my skin at my pelvic region and with a twisting movement, extended itself up to the middle of my abdomen, stopping at my heart region. It then dropped back down to its original position and began the same process again. Each time it did, you could hear a popping sound as if my muscles were relaxing outward, releasing their hold in some way. My belly began to expand and "an energy filled it." Russ and Quita became quite alarmed, but neither knew what to do except surrender to the process and observe its happenings. Though the pain was unbearable at times, I had a deep sense of quietude. This went on for two hours until I finally drifted off into sleep, around 3:30 a.m. When I awoke the next morning, my belly was extended to the point that I looked about five months pregnant.

The energy field produced by the experience affected my friends as well. Russ' reaction was immediate. He began experiencing *kriyas* (convulsive movements of prana throughout the body) for the next four hours. Quita had diarrhea for the next few days and on the third day came home saying she wasn't feeling well and immediately passed out. I pulled her onto a cushion and she became very hot and had body convulsions which lasted the next four or five hours. Whatever was happening certainly had impacted all of our lives. The depth of the experience was yet to be revealed.

Initially my belly would be a bit smaller in the morning, but as the sun would go down at night, "the energy" seemed to come into me, my belly enlarging and generating heat. At first, there was a wonderment about it all, but then the fear began to surface. What is happening to me? What is this thing in my belly? Can't anyone tell me what this is? What's the correlation between it and the sun? Have I gone mad? If it's in me, what will happen when it comes out? Who can answer some of my questions?

I sought advice, perspectives, and guidance, but to no avail. In fact, some mirrored my fear by asking if I had seen the movie "Alien." In that movie a grotesque entity emerges from a man's abdomen, destroying him in the process. "Please give me another image," I would respond. "Can't you see my fright?" No, they couldn't.

What was happening was so foreign to Russ, Quita and me that I often was left feeling isolated and alone inside myself. I don't know what I would have done without their support and understanding, though I know this whole affair pushed them to their limits as well. To add to my confusion, my whole body took on the feelings of pregnancy. My sons were grown and childbearing was behind me, yet I looked down each morning and saw the shape of a pregnant woman. Occasionally, the form that appeared that first night moved around in my belly giving the appearance of a child moving in utero. All other physiological signs functioned normally. I had no problems with my digestion or elimination.

I had been in many doctors' offices throughout a six-year period because of other strange phenomena resulting from the Kundalini energy. What would they do with this? Though my persona was screaming loudly at the irrational occurrences, there seemed to be a place of deep knowing that prevailed. My inner teacher assured me that all was as it should be, that I was pregnant with Self. I decided I would wait until Christmas and if no change had taken place by then, I would seek medical advice.

Actually, the process unfolded in stages. In the second month I was given a map of sorts during a meditation.

> *I saw myself sitting in a lotus posture with my shadow spinning around me. All my self-doubts, my fears and limitations screamed at me persistently. A deeper level of trust and surrender was being asked for, as well as a purging like none I had ever experienced. The scene changed and the second stage of the process was revealed.*

*In this stage I would learn the meaning of what I call Zen stillness, a stilling of the mind which I was to realize must be accomplished before the third stage can be entered. I saw myself laying inside of an opened egg witnessing the birth of me; naked, vulnerable, and new.*

*It was in this Zen stillness that my Beloved appeared. It is difficult to describe, for he is more like an energy than an image. When he came and embraced me, wrapping his white cloak around me, I suddenly found myself in a most beautiful world. How do I describe a place that is experienced with all of one's being? All of the saints and sages I held dear to my heart were there. I suddenly realized that Love is an entity and I stood within its heart. Such humility washed through me and peace reigned in every cell. Visions were shown to me about the work for which I was being prepared. Love was what it was all about. Love was the power behind it all.*

*At one point I was told that I was in the Land of the Bodhisattva. I didn't know this word but when it was spoken I watched an etheric, clear fluid pour out of my heart, extending down around my body, encapsulating it. As this culminated, the sound of small bells tingled around my feet and a feeling of completeness prevailed.*

It was shortly after this meditative experience that, through a chain of synchronicities, I would discover a book entitled *How to Grow a Lotus Blossom* by Roshi Jiyu Kennett.[86] Within its pages were illustrations matching in detail the scenes I had just seen in my vision of the Land of the Bodhisattva. For the first time since my "conception," I had something concrete and of this world to relate to. For so long it felt like I had entered a Void where there was no ground left to stand on; all my preconceptions of a reality as I had known it exploded and I was hurled out into space, spinning, constantly spinning. For the first time I caught a glimpse of the Reality being revealed.

Synchronistically, another friend sent me an article entitled "Holy Men and Fat Bellies."[87] It described some of the physiolo-

---

[86] Kennett, Jiyu Roshi, *How to Grow a Lotus Blossum*, Shasta Abbey, Mt. Shasta, Ca., 1977.

[87] "Holy Men and Fat Bellies," *Magical Blend*, Vol. 2, January, 1989.

gical effects that such a process initiates. Again, Kennett Roshi's name appeared among those listed who had undergone a similar process. I had a deep yearning to talk with a woman about this experience. I immediately called her and arranged an appointment. Due to her schedule and mine, we could not meet for several months. She did suggest that I consider celibacy. She said that we should hold it as if it would be for a lifetime and realize that this part of the process usually lasted three to five years. It was comforting to receive validation. Speaking with a woman had also been important to me, for as I have struggled with the understanding of this process I have continually sought out literature, but have found very little about Kundalini by women. Her advise has proved to hold profound clarity, giving me a field of reference during the "groundless stage." Another article by Gopi Krishna arrived and in it he said he did not advocate celibacy except during the part of the Kundalini process when the nervous system and neurological system were being adjusted. Since I was in an intimate relationship with Russ, this would prove to be another challenge.

The next few months were difficult physically. Morning nausea became a ritual. Some mornings I would awake with severe headaches. The top of my head would become so hot it ached. Other mornings, I could hardly walk; my feet, ankles, and hands felt arthritic, but after an hour or so, they would return to normal. Some days my whole body would become so cold that I felt like walking death. The energy would jump sporadically to different areas of my body which had, at one time or another, been ailing. For example, in my early 20's I had had surgery to remove a pineal cyst from around my tailbone. Shortly after the surgery, I fell and broke it. As a result, the tailbone was crooked and had acquired a calcium deposit. The energy seemed to focus on this area creating a great deal of heat and pain which lasted about two days. When I explained the phenomenon to my physician/body therapist, he examined me and said that a lot of correction had occurred which normally would have taken much longer. In addition, marks or swollen areas would appear on varying parts of my body. One in particular (which seemed to reappear) was a raised triangle just above the tailbone. What particular significance all this had, I'm not sure. I was beginning to gain a deep appreciation for the intelligence inherent in the energy, and its apparent plan for healing within my system.

When working with people as a therapist, my belly would grow larger and radiate heat. Many times they would express how badly they had been feeling. They would begin to emote, sharing feelings strongly held about their particular situations. After a short time, they would leave feeling remarkably clearer, but I would go home nauseated and ill and vomit for the next several hours. I had become so psychically sensitive that I had to become more reclusive in my activities. The question that constantly rose in me was, "Can't I do this differently?" All I knew was that I would have to be very conscious of following the energy, and in maintaining a balance between my activities. In order to maintain my own balance, I had to trust the energy completely, following as it dictated. I worked when I could and I surrendered into rest when my body allowed.

Every time I tried to psychically take a peek at this process, I could only view an image of a brilliant light seeping from under a covered space. I was told, "You are pregnant with the Divine and you must be patient. All will unfold in its natural time." I met with several friends who were open psychically; all but one were blocked from "seeing." Gloria, whose work I much admire, was able to confirm through a reading what I had intuited. This again helped me to contain and integrate what was being presented. Gloria speaks in metaphors which seem to capture the essence of the experience at a deep archetypal level. An excerpt from Gloria's reading explained:

> *The first thing that I want to say is that when I attuned to you I found the two of us on some sort of mythic wave of energy. It was like some crazy fountain in the cartoons that takes you up and*

*up. When it burst, it was in other dimensions; nothing physical, nothing to be talked about on this plane.*

*A lot of what is at work here is not easy to describe. It is like being on the inside of something rather than on the outside. On the inside of something there are no words. There is another whole world. If you went to the interior of the earth, there would be another whole universe that doesn't have much to do with what is on the outer skin of the earth. If you turned time inside out, there would be a whole other universe, and therefore another language.*

*It is like merging realities. These merging realities have not coalesced a construct of any kind. There is no scaffolding. There is no mental hardware. We don't have any software in our computer that fits. If we can accept these conditions, we will know that whatever is spoken of here is a pale reflection of what is the reality beyond even what we can conceive of a "reality" to be. We can "sense" it more than know it. It is where universes interface and bend.*

*I am looking into a very contemporary painting. You might have a line of energy that looks hard and seems real. It seems to be black. It then forms a shape like a Mobius strip. As it turns, its color becomes dark purple. Still further out, it becomes a whole other color. Somehow, that is time-space bending.*

*As we speak of the world of spirit and flesh coming together, it brings with it a memory of the unknown. As the veil thins, that memory becomes more pronounced, yet has no name. If one were to force the mind to contemplate beyond the veil, it would blow the computer. There is nothing in here upon which the mind can do a reality check. In order to do that, it would have to cluster memories. It would have to be able to say, "Ah yes, this is like a chair, or God or hate." But to be subjected to a reality that says over and over again this won't compute—no data—is to disorient to the point of fragmenting the whole thing. It is destroying an ego.*

*What I'm seeing is this dense collection of what looks like molecules except it shapes itself into a body, as in yours for example. The processes destroy all that, moving it into a place where it regroups. This reminds me of a principle in physics. When a particle is destroyed, its molecules will go to the furthest extreme of the energy field and then regroup at a higher frequency.*

*Most people don't have the strength of spiritual ego, "spiritual selfhood," to hold together that which is not held anymore. Imagine yourself in a little earth body. Imagine that the boundaries of that form are completely destroyed. Now imagine a mythic picture of yourself as big as the sky. Imagine what kind of psychological, psychic and spiritual ego it takes to make that jump from this one to that, and not loose it. Therefore, the interim period is one of seeming danger. The ego must die carefully. If it dies too abruptly, you would have this sense of self wandering around in about 30 million parts, but not regrouped at the higher state. One of the ways you have chosen to deal with this transition is to birth, even as you die. You will have to sense your way into this because the metaphors are crude.*

*I am shown buttercup flowers. It is their job to grow and make a container. They are beautiful unto themselves, but they also contain emptiness. In their emptiness pours an elixir that is then sought out by the bee and the butterfly. There is a question which arises. Where is life in all this? There is a Mystery that is present even in the most dense forms. What holy force brings forth the elixir in the first place and draws onto it that which transmits the next step? It is a Mystery.*

*When you are into the soul of things, you are into a mystery that cannot be contained by logic. It is a Mystery. On earth now is a time of great dissemination of the Mystery. You are not the mystery, but you can contain it. You are not the Mystery, but you can disseminate it. The flower that lives only to hold the sweetness which we call life, while remaining empty, must love a great deal. Its whole reason to be is to hold that sweetness. That is its role in the scheme of things.*

Christmas came and went. My ego wanted desperately to put a time limit on this experience, but time is an illusion of the physical plane, so I had to surrender that need as well. I contacted a metaphysician and began going to him regularly. He was wonderful in helping me integrate and bring balance both to my mental and physical realms.

The energy was forcing me into a more reclusive posture with the world. We moved into a small house in the redwoods. These surroundings seemed to bath and nurture my body. My shifts in living arrangements seemed to reflect the shifts actually going on in my mind. The house was encompassed by nature and secluded so that a natural stillness surrounded it. My mind also seemed to take on more of these same characteristics.

## NO SELF: THE SILENT MIND

The next phase of the process got a bit scary. I would be having a conversation with someone and the next thing I knew, we were at the end of the conversation. I would have no recall of what had happened in between. There seemed to be no interruption for the other person with whom I was conversing. It was as if something else just swooped in and took over. There seemed to be no pattern to it. Was I disassociating? Was I finally going to lose it, lose my connection to reality? In the midst of my fear, a friend suggested I read *The Experience of No-Self* by Bernadette Roberts. What a gift. Her brilliant description gave grounding and confirmation to my process. In particular, she writes:

> I wish I understood the mechanism of self-consciousness, or how it is possible for the mind to bend back on itself, for if I did, I could more easily convey a better understanding of no-self and its most noticeable effect—the silent mind. But whatever this mechanism is, the state of no-self is the breaking up of a self-conscious system whereby the mind can no longer see itself as an object; and at the same time it loses the ability to find any other object to take its place, because when there is no self there is also no other.
>
> I might add that the mind has never had the ability to see itself as subject—this would be as impossible as the eye seeing itself; yet I think this very impossibility may be the clue to the type of consciousness that remains when consciousness without a knowable subject or object becomes the whole of it. This type of consciousness is not available to our ordinary way of knowing, and because it cannot be experienced or understood by the relative mind, it falls squarely into the realm of the unknown and the unknowable.

When we can no longer verify or check back (reflect) on the subject of awareness, we lose consciousness of there being any subject of awareness at all... The first question to be asked is whether or not self-consciousness is necessary for thinking, or if thinking goes right on without a thinker... Where before, thought had been a product of a reflecting introspective, objectifying mechanism—ever colored with personal feelings and biases—now thought arises spontaneously off the top of the head, and what is more, it arises in the now-moment which is concerned with the immediate present, making it invariably practical...

One way to look at this journey is to see it as a process of acclimation to an unself-conscious mind, or as a transition from a relative to a non-relative way of knowing. But however we care to regard it, the fact remains that the initial, most noteworthy effect of the falling away of the reflexive mechanism is a silent mind. This means that the silent aspect of the mind is actually the absence of self, or as I prefer to call it—the silence of no-self.[88]

When I asked for an image to aid in my understanding of this stage, I was shown a large golden drop moving towards and finally merging with a drop matching its appearance yet smaller in size. After a few seconds, the two would separate again returning to their original positions. I was told that the absorption would happen in stages to allow time for the ego to adjust. Of course, my ego shook in the face of this. What would happen upon final absorption? Would the "I" disappear into nothing? I continued to have a deep feeling that at some point I would go through an actual death process with the possibility of no return. "Death," in any event, was the doorway to a final passage. I kept trying to think of what I could do to help facilitate this process, but there is *no-thing* to do, because the process is like a river flowing towards its goal.

Throughout my awakening I have had the great fortune to be led to many healers and teachers who have shared their own

[88] Roberts, Bernadette, *The Experience of No-Self*, Shambhala, Boston & London, 1984, pp. 85–87.

individual techniques that facilitate awareness. Dreams have always been a powerful guide in my awakening process. *Acting* upon symbols or instructions from my dreams have led me into territory I would never have journeyed on my own. Russ and I have come to call this procedure dream activation, for we are all learning to become reality engineers. One such meeting took place as a result of a dream that had presented itself to me in 1985 while I was still in Zurich.

> *In the dream a group of Indians came to me and made a circle around me. They presented a root to me saying, "You must drink of this in order to assist in your prophesying and healing work."*

I had tried for several years to find the root referred to in the dream, but nothing ever seemed to present itself that rang true. Now here it was several years later and the meaning of the dream was about to be revealed. While having lunch with a new friend, the dream resurfaced in my memory and insisted on being told. After I shared it with her, she immediately said, "I know what that is. It is ibogaine." Chills ran through my body. I had never had such a response. I began to research it and discovered it was a root that had hallucinogenic effects that "elicited vivid dreamlike sequences which may be contemplated while awake with closed eyes, without loss of contact with the environment or alterations of thinking... the quality that makes *it* valuable to psychotherapy is that of facilitating access to otherwise unconscious processes, feelings, or thoughts."[89] All my resistance surfaced. I was certainly having plenty of psychic experiences without the use of such plants, but still the dream persisted. It finally led me to my dear friend, Claudio Naranjo, a spiritual teacher and psychiatrist from Chile, who has been a constant support. His deep knowledge of mythology and elaborate understanding of such archetypal journeys validated the

---

[89] Naranjo, Claudio, *The Healing Journey*, Pantheon Books, New York, 1973, p. 5.

happenings and assisted in my subsequent stages of integration. Upon hearing my dream and listening to the experiences I had been undergoing, he referred me to a wise old man who would later become my teacher. The dream had introduced me to the shamanic healing work of plants. It is through this work that my body began to detoxify and heal. One session taught me about disintegration.

> *I both was the experience and the observer of the experience at the same time. I saw myself dissolve completely. No sooner had the dissolution been completed then I would reintegrate, reforming as before. At first this experience was terrifying. As it continued to cycle from form to formless, something in me began to relax. Finally it began to feel natural, much like breathing. Just at that moment the vision changed dramatically and I felt myself physically land sitting in a lotus position in the center of a round room lined with books from top to bottom. I felt very reverent, as if I had landed in a holy place. I realized upon gazing around the room that there were no doors, only a round hole emitting light just above me. The only way in or out seemed to be from above. I sat very still wondering where I was and how I had gotten in here. Suddenly a voice spoke, "You must become comfortable with your disintegration before you are allowed into the sacred chamber."*

This experience became vitally important to me and provided a sense of comfort as Shakti introduced the next part of the journey; a time in which the visionary experiences would involuntarily present themselves in ever increasing numbers. I was learning how to let God breathe me! In that march I continued to meet many more wonderful healers and sages: a kahuna from Hawaii, an American Indian shaman, a Tibetan monk, and a Zen Buddhist priest. I wasn't necessarily seeking them out; circumstances brought us together, but their presence affirmed my process and encouraged me to endure. Each would share different aspects of their teachings giving me a variety of information to draw from. The kahuna healer at one point in our conversation raised my arm and began laughing as she shouted, "Victory! Victory!"

Around December, 1988, I met Jack Downing, a metaphysician, who was instrumental in helping me to maintain a balance both within my body and my mind. His friendship and support was invaluable to both Russ and me. You know, if we can but only "let go and let God," much grace showers upon our lives.

Jack introduced us to a man who was close to Swami Muktananda for many years. Ironically, I had just picked up a small book by Muktananda called *Kundalini, The Secret of Life*. He informed me that the physical manifestation of the "Buddha belly" as I had described it had a name in Sanskrit—*kumbhaka*. I discovered that the breath was intimately connected to our ability to still the mind. My body seemed to have a working knowledge which was leading me into deeper awareness.

> To control the mind, to make it still and even, yogis try to control the breath. This is why they practice so many different kinds of pranayama, or breath control. During the process of Siddha Yoga purification, natural pranayama begins to take place. The prana and apana (the outgoing and incoming breaths) become even, and eventually the breath begins to be retained within. This is called *kumbhaka*. Shaivism says that to keep controlling your breath is not true kumbhaka. In true kumbhaka, the prana and apana become one. At that point, prana does not go out, nor does apana come in. When the prana stops, the mind becomes still, and you experience supreme tranquillity. Great beings are in the state of inner stillness. If you look at the picture of my Guru Nityananda, you will see that he has a big belly. This is not because he ate too much, but because of the inner kumbhaka.
>
> This inner kumbhaka is extremely valuable. The state of kumbhaka is the state of pure wisdom, pure knowledge. When spontaneous knowledge takes place, you come to know the *hamsa pranayama*. You become aware of the self-born mantra going on within you, of the syllables *ham* and sa flowing in and out with the breath. This is the Siddha mantra, the natural *japa* of perfected beings. It is the awareness of "I am That," the awareness of your identity with the Truth.[90]

---

[90] Muktananda, Swami, *Kundalini, The Secret of Life*, SYDA Bookstore, Box 605, South Fallsburg, N. Y. 12779, p. 35.

My experience of kumbhaka has been a spontaneous occurrence—a boon of grace, one that changes my life daily. Stilling the mind becomes a process. Though Bernadette Roberts' description conveys what the psychological implications of that process entail, Muktananda describes the physiological mechanism involved at this stage of development.

It was shortly after learning of this that an episode with spontaneous breathing occurred. It was around 10:00 p.m. one evening and the three of us were watching television. I decided to lie down on the couch. As I began to do so, it was as if time froze and I went into slow motion. I saw a vision of myself superimposed upon this reality. In the vision I was falling down into a crystal clear pool of water. Once in the water a funnel formed and down through it I fell. Just as I exited through the funnel, I snapped back into this consciousness and my head laid on the pillow beneath it. I had a feeling of pending death. I was very dizzy and disoriented. I tried to ground myself, but to no avail. I became very nauseated, so I went to the bathroom. I vomited profusely, and my body began to shake all over. I felt very weak. I stood over the sink trying to regain my composure. Suddenly an explosion of light went off in my head like none I had ever experienced. It felt like light was pouring in from outside, as well as from inside out. I had the sense that my head would bust at any moment, much like a watermelon in a press. All I knew to do was get on my knees in a fetal position and try to stay centered, breathing into the process. As I did, a calming took over which seemed to permeate my very essence. A part of me moved into a witness position, while another part of my consciousness remained with the body. A heat was being generated from the belly moving up the spine filling the brain. This time the heat was cool in nature. My breath took on an intelligence of its own. It began to breathe me as I watched. The breathing was rapid at first and then slower, until the breath stopped completely for rather long periods of time. My body felt stonelike in nature, and my consciousness seemed to tumble, as if I were being propelled into outer space. The visual sense was of my body moving rapidly through a star-lit space. I was both watching the experience and in the experience at the same time.

Russ and Quita found me and put me to bed. They were very frightened by my erratic breathing. They were afraid I would die when my breathing stopped for so long. I finally was able to speak and tell them I was O.K., but that they had to give me permission to go wherever Spirit planned to take me. I wasn't sure what that might mean, I only knew that it felt like I would break if they tried to will me to stay. I told them it would help if they would meditate, creating an environment of stillness. So, once again, the three of us formed a container allowing the Mystery to dance, revealing still further knowledge.

The breathing would come in waves. Each time the breath would stop, new sets of visions progressively unfolded. I could see myself as a small dot of consciousness, moving quickly through a labyrinth. Other visions came and flew by in rapid succession, as if being released. It didn't seem to matter what the vision was about, but rather that they were part of a process of release. This went on for about two hours.

The next day I called my friend who had lived with Muktananda and described what had happened. He said this was a form of pranayama. Muktananda says, "As the Kundalini rises to the sahasrara (topmost spiritual center or chakra), you begin to see divine effulgence. There are one thousand knots in the sahasrara which shine with the brilliance of a thousand suns, but instead of being scorching like the sun, their light is cooling. This light is so powerful that when it reveals itself to you, you don't have the strength to stand it. When I saw that brilliance within myself, I fell down, because I could not bear its intensity."[91]

A book that has been invaluable to me is, *No Mind, I Am the Self* by David Godman. In it he relates the story of Sri

_____

[91] Ibid, pp. 43–44.

Lakshmana Swami's and Mathru Sri Sarada's quests and attainment of self-realization.  Swami Lakshmana realized the Self through a spontaneous act of self-inquiry. He states:

> In self-inquiry you have to catch hold of the "I"-thought by giving up other thoughts. If other thoughts intrude ask yourself "For whom are these thoughts?" and you will find that the answer is "They are occurring to me." Then question yourself as to who is this "I" that is having these thoughts, or ask yourself, "Where does this »I« come from?" If you are ripe, that is, free from other thoughts, the "I" dives into itself and experiences the bliss of the Self. In the end the "I", which is the mind, must die. The mind won't kill the mind by itself so the grace of the Guru, who is the Self, is most important. The death of the mind is Self-Realization. As there is no mind after realization, the Self remains alone, one without a second.  It is eternal peace and bliss and it is beyond time and death.
>
> Beingness means "I am" and "I am" means the Self. When the mind is quiet the "I"-thought may experience a little of the bliss that is emanating from the Self, but you will not experience pure beingness until the "I"-thought has completely subsided into the Heart.[92]

It was through this stillness in the mind that my Beloved would appear. As described previously, sex had become a tantric dance, a cosmic encounter. Celibacy was still in question. I struggled with what was happening inside me and with my body and with the question of how to handle this and remain in a relationship. While making love my body would become statuesque and a merging with my divine lover ensued.  The energy was so vivid and vital that it was as if each cell exploded into light.  Then, my body started slowing the process down, as if the energy was too much.  I would have the feeling that I could or would explode.  Russ and I tried to adjust to this by going slower,

---

[92] Godman, David, *No Mind, I Am The Self*, Sri Lakshmana Ashram, Nellore Dist, A. P., India, 1988, pp. 90–91.

but my whole body was orgasmic. Other physical signs warned that a shift in such activity was in the air. We struggled with what was being asked: was my process asking me to "take thee to the monastery"? Would my relationship with Russ be strong enough to endure through the inevitable stages ahead? These were just a few of the many questions flowing through my mind. Confusion reigned. Deep inside I knew celibacy was entering my arena. I have a friend who once said, "It's not that we chose celibacy, but rather it chooses us." After meeting with others more experienced in such matters, I learned that this too is a natural part of the transformation. In an article by John White entitled, "Sex and Sublime Awareness," Gopi Krishna addressed this topic:

> What about celibacy? In growing to higher consciousness, is it necessary as some claim, to abstain from sex and to "mortify the flesh"?
>
> From Gopi Krishna's point of view, the answer is a firm no—with one reservation. Since he himself is married and has three children, he strongly disagrees with those who regard sexual contact as detrimental to spiritual evolution. Moreover, he points out that during the Vedic Age thousands of years ago, when many of the great yogic scriptures were first written, several hundred inspired sages were recognized as enlightened men, and in almost every case they were married and had children...
>
> ... Generally speaking, he says, celibacy is contrary to nature, since enlightenment is an evolutionary process, with heredity playing an important role by stamping the genera of the enlightened so that their biological gains through spiritual disciplines can be passed to their progeny. Suppression of sexuality out of contempt or hatred of our "lower nature" is an act of ignorance leading only to atrophy of the sexual system. The biological fact that only the primates, and especially humans, are perennially ready for sex is a clue to linkage between our animal origins and our higher destiny. But there is a critical period during the Kundalini process—lasting possibly as long as a year or two—when celibacy is important. During that time, the fluid essence is needed for remolding the nervous system and brain.

Otherwise the Kundalini awakening will be "aborted" through misuse.[93]

Although coming to a decision to honor the need for celibacy certainly tested our relationship, it has also propelled us into a deeper understanding of one another. Through such changes a new way of being in a relationship evolves. Where this will take us, we are not yet clear, but in our commitment to the learning, we are clear.

As many have stated, when the student is ready, the Teacher will appear. For many years I have been graced by short intervals of teachings from those wiser and more learned, but always the inner teacher had led the way. Suddenly, amidst such change, I was led to Anandi Ma and her husband Dileepji. Anandi Ma is the spiritual heir of a 116-year-old yogic master, Dhyanyogi Madhusudandasji of Ahmedabad, India. As a couple, they presented a wonderful mirror for Russ and me to look into. After describing what had been happening these last few months, they recommended that we both receive Shaktipat.

As described in *Shakti, Hidden Treasure of Power* (Vol. 1) by Dhyanyogi Shri Madhusudandasji:

> The ceremony of Shaktipat is a very significant initiation. In the entire world, few gurus are capable of performing it. Through Shaktipat, Divine Energy is transferred from Guruji to the disciple for the purpose of hastening the awakening of Kundalini (Life Force) in order to increase the spiritual development of the initiate. The energy acts whether or not it is immediately felt by the disciple during the ceremony. This initiation will awaken the Kundalini if it is dormant and will hasten its upward progress if it is already active.
>
> By the Shaktipat, Guruji takes personal responsibility for the spiritual welfare of the disciple. Just as soap washes a cloth, the bad karma of several lifetimes is erased by his/her touch. He

---

[93] White, John, "Sex and Sublime Awareness," *Journal of Human Behavior*, Aug., 1977.

takes this karma on himself and disposes of it through the use of his accumulated powers. Only after that can the doors of self-realization open for the disciple.[94]

Due to scheduling problems Russ and I received our initiations at different times. He found it to be pleasant with no particular reactions. I went alone expecting something similar, yet unsure what might be stirred. Immediately after receiving the Shaktipat initiation, I experienced a hard pushing pain that ran up my right leg focusing particularly in the hip. It was as if I was paralyzed for a time and therefore had to surrender into the pain. Paradoxically, a great joy seemed to fill me, tears falling uncontrollably. As I drove home, the energy pushed up the spine stiffening my body, resulting in a severe headache. For the next week I became very ill with headaches, nausea, and vomiting. Since that time, nausea has completely disappeared for me. My times of waking every morning to vomit were gone. Many of my physical symptoms were greatly relieved. It has also been a special treat for Russ and me to have a couple to discuss things with. Anandi Ma says, "The infinite is in the form of pure love." Pure love is certainly experienced as one sits with them, soothing the sharp edges that such transformation brings with it.

Anandi Ma shares a story which seems to capture the essence of initiatory experiences performed by a teacher. "The scriptures give an analogy of the Guru as being like the insect—the bumblebee—and disciples being like a caterpillar. It is said that the bee bites the caterpillar and takes it to its nest and traps it there. The caterpillar, with the intensity of the pain, is constantly thinking and meditating on the form of the bee. The concentration is so intense that the caterpillar eventually takes up the form of the bee itself."

In another wonderful book, *The Cloud of Unknowing*, edited by William Johnston, there are statements which seem to sum up this process nicely:

---

[94] Dhyanyogi Shri Madhusudandasji, *Shakti, Hidden Treasure of Power*, Vol. 1, Dhyanyoga Centers, Pasadena, Ca., 1979, pp. 75–76.

The incomplete self must die in order that the true self may rise. Unless the grain of wheat falling into the ground dies, itself alone remains; but if it dies it brings forth much fruit...

The thought and feeling of self must be annihilated. Yet this annihilation is less terrible because it is the work of love: "For this is the way of all real love. The lover will utterly and completely despoil himself of everything, even his very self, because of the one he loves. He cannot bear to be clothed in anything save the thought of his beloved. And this is not a passing fancy. No, he desires always and forever to remain unclothed in full and final self-forgetting." If we love, death will inevitably follow and self will be forgotten with terrible finality. But it will be a joyous death.[95]

Death and birth—the flip side of the same coin. Although much is dying and passing away, there is definitely something stirring in my belly. Something is gestating and waiting to be born.

As I look back over these last few years, I marvel at the Mystery which continues to awaken the new dream; a dream of what will be. Looking back over the evolution of mankind, each major shift in consciousness was accompanied by a biological change as well. Many are experiencing such alterations now, and as time passes, they will speak more freely about them. The truest test will be believing in the process, in spite of the objections of the "consensus" reality, and letting it take us to our wholeness. In trusting in these processes, we must learn to let go of old ideas, old identities, old habits, and in so doing, return to the true source of our essence.

Each of us has our path. We must avoid the historical error of distraction from the goal. We so often forget that it's not that work is our life, but rather that *life is our work*. When that type of shift in attitude occurs, we experience the world in a much different way. We can no longer wait for someone else to discover and shape our reality. We must all realize that the answer to what

---

[95] Johnston, William, *The Cloud of Unknowing*, Image Books, Garden City, N. Y., 1973, p. 13.

we seek lies within ourselves. All knowledge is there if we only choose to look for it. As stated in C. A. Meier's book, *Ancient Incubation and Modern Psychotherapy*, "The forbidden thing is at the same time the remedy. The taboo must be broken before a cure might be affected. The paradox is the highest thing in God's cure."

# CHAPTER NINE

# Circles Closing

Self-knowledge was the key
Self-understanding was the desire
Self-discipline was the way
Self-realization was the goal.

"Entering into the Silence"
Twylah Nitsch[96]

## A DEEPER STAGE OF SURRENDER

ALTHOUGH MY NAUSEA SUBSIDED after receiving Shaktipat, the energy continued to work throughout my system. The spontaneous trancelike states of samadhi increased. At times the energy flowed with such force up my spine that my backbone would become stiff and lean me forward, locking my hips in a posture that proved to be uncomfortable after a time. If the energy ran for an extended period of time (an hour or more) I would have difficulty walking and had to be assisted. At one point I began to experience what I call "shape-shifting." An example of this phenomena happened one evening while at home. I was sitting down when suddenly I felt a cool movement of energy shimmering around the lower parts of my legs. I thought it quite quizzical and began to observe. At the same time I noticed that I was unable to move or direct my legs in any way. It was as if my connection to them had been severed. The energy continued

---

[96] Nitsch, Twylah, "Entering into the Silence," in Bancroft, Anne, *Weavers of Wisdom, Women Mystics of the Twentieth Century*, Penguin Books, New York, 1989, p. 38.

to move subtly in a swirling motion around each leg. My feet began to slowly move bringing the toes to cross each other while the heels remained in their original position, pointing forward. I actually had the impression that my body was recalling a time when it had been crucified on a cross and the bones broken in the lower legs. My bones then seemed to dematerialize and reshape themselves bowing outward as if they had been deformed for years. I called Quita. When she walked into the room, she gasped at the sight. "Does it hurt!?" "No," I replied, "but is it going to stay this way?" We both were dumbfounded. After a few minutes the cool swirling energy began to move again, the bones straightened and all seemed to return to normal. Then the whole experience would immediately repeat itself sometimes for several hours.

No sooner had I made the psychological shift to accommodate these happenings than a still deeper stage of surrender was called for. The loss of body consciousness that I had experienced in my lower legs extended itself up my whole body. One day as I was at home meditating and doing some deep trance work, a similar feeling as I have just described surrounded my body. An energy whose intelligence I could actually "hear" thinking entered my body through my feet and began to roll my body around on the floor placing it in various yogic postures and then freezing it there. At that point a brilliant light would totally absorb me for several minutes at a time. During these periords of absorption I had no awareness of the external world. A complete state of bliss consumed me. When I returned to a more normal waking consciousness, I would feel the energy shimmer, gently shaking my body allowing it to release from the frozen posture and rest for a moment. Then the whole experience would repeat itself placing me in still another posture. Many times in the immediate moments following these sessions, moisture would form and a tear would drip from my third eye, that point known as the sixth chakra located between the eyebrows. I called it "God's tear." It gave me a feeling of closeness I cannot express in words. This process would go on for various lengths of time—half an hour or sometimes several hours. It was as if I could hear Shakti thinking: "This posture will release the blocked energy here. We must restructure her footing there. And so on." This was a bit much for my western mind to grasp. It was as if my consciousness was present but sat about three or four feet above my head. While in these states it was very hard to communicate. I would have to visualize the word in its form and bring it manually with my mind through my brain and into the mechanisms of speech. When the words came out they felt forced and they were few and spoken very slowly. It took so much energy that I avoided it and tried to stay with the experience at hand. When I talked to Anandi Ma and described what was happening, she said in a rather matter-of-fact fashion, "Do not worry. This is a stage called *jada samadhi*. It too will pass." She went on to give instructions to Russ which would assist my return to normalcy if I did not revert to a more normal state after a period of time.

Another phenomena that seemed to reoccur would happen during meditation with Anandi Ma. A soft rose smelling oil would form all over my body. When I asked her about this she described it as the divine nectar cooling the form. In my meditations I was told that each of us has our own unique smell and that we will all evolve to a state of wholeness opening to our divine birthright inherent in that uniqueness—budding and flowering on the Tree of Life, unique and like no other.

Somewhere in the midst of all this I had a lucid dream.

> *I saw a tall evergreen tree that stretched up into the sky far above me. As I stood looking at it, I noticed a small blue dot that grew into a large blue oval. It looked like a blue tinted yet translucent egg. Divine Mother suddenly appeared inside the oval. She also was all blue. She grew in size until she filled the egg. Then she leaned down and spoke directly into my face. She took her finger and poked my heart saying, "Be who you are now! Be who you are now! BE WHO YOU ARE NOW!!!"*

I awoke with the sensation of awe. I could still feel where she had pushed my heart.

The frequency of the experiences of samadhi increased until I was forced to discontinue the workshops we annually presented in Europe and cut back on all outside activity except at a minimal level. What I found most difficult was again finding a way to trust the process as it unfolded in a culture that had no context for such happenings. I remember when the impact of my situation profoundly "hit home." Russ and I were going to visit his family in Missouri so I could meet them for the first time. Would my belly swell? Would the samadhi occur while there? And if it did, what would we say? How would we explain what was happening to me? What I have come to understand is that the Divine has a wisdom and wants us to reach our true source, so when the samadhi happens when others are present, it is as much for their good as for mine. If I can but remain empty, my vessel then becomes an instrument.

I would like to share an experience that happened in our workshop on my last trip to Europe before I went into solitude for two years. I had been having dreams warning me that something was about to happen and that I must trust the process. Well, as you might imagine, that made me a bit nervous. But prepare I did by trying to stay centered and remaining receptive. We were doing a three-day intensive entitled "Relationship: The Doorway to the Divine." The workshop went very well. In our closing session Russ led a Sufi meditation called a Zikr of the Ultimate Communion of Love (as presented by Jean Houston in her wonderful book, *The Search for the Beloved*).[97]   Just as we were completing the experience I saw Anandi Ma descend into the room in her etheric form and then move across the room and merge with me. Then immediately what I identified as Divine Mother energy descended totally filling the room with a soft pink cloud of light. My body went into samadhi, becoming rigid. I heard a loud swishing sound that seemed to roar through me and out into the room. Suddenly

---

[97] Houston, Jean, *The Search for The Beloved*, Jeremy P. Tarcher, Inc., Los Angeles, 1987, pp. 212–213.

one of the participants fell to the floor experiencing Kundalini *kriyas*—that flow of energy that can shake one's body. Russ and a couple of other people went to her aid assisting the process as it naturally unfolded. The rest of the group started to spontaneously chant. Just as our friend completed her process and returned to a normal state of consciousness, I again experienced the loud swishing sound roar through me and out into the room. Another person fell to the floor and went into deep trance. This continued for almost two hours and at least six people experienced a deep cleansing by Spirit directed by the Divine Mother. Finally, my body began to regain itself. I was able to lie down on the floor as my body returned to a normal state of awareness. In closing we stood in a circle holding the moment in silence before departing. A deep bond had been experienced between the participants that no words could capture. Days later as I sat reflecting on this experience I was overwhelmed by the gratitude of witnessing such direct divine intervention in others' lives.

Upon my return home to California another incident happened that seemed to amplify Divine Mothers' presence still further. It related to a dream I'd had while in Europe.

*I found myself in a fenced in area with a gang of people. I was frightened for my safety, so I headed for a corner of the yard, knelled down and began to place a protective shield around me that would make me invisible. Before I had time to finish, the gang and its leader approached me. He motioned for me to come to them and gave me the impression that I would be raped. I grabbed my belly and said, "But you can't. You don't understand, you just can't." My pleas went unheard and still he persisted with his plan. Just at that moment, the gang became quiet and began to move apart as a rather tall Mexican woman approached me. I could tell from her power with the group she must be their medicine woman. She said emphatically, "She is an angel with the seed of God within. Do not touch her!" At that the gang backed away. I was so grateful that I kneeled before her clutching her knees and, looking up into her eyes, spoke nothing but said much. She sang a short chant to me and I answered her with another chant.*

I awoke with the combination of those chants running through me like a song. I felt warm and peaceful all over. Since I had no way of recording the tune, I hummed it all day trying to capture it, but to no avail, after a few days it had escaped me. I felt that the melody was a healing song and hoped I would again discover it. Several weeks went by as we finished our tour in Europe, and headed home. Russ and I were determined to become couch potatoes. The first day back around 3 o'clock I heard a sound like wings make as a bird lands. The sound drew my attention to the front sliding glass door. Three rather large white birds were descending. They landed forming a triangle and appeared to be moving in slow motion. I motioned for Russ to look and walked slowly to the door. I looked up and in the redwoods surrounding our front porch a flock of the same birds sat quietly in the tops of the trees. When I walked outside they all flew away again making that same wing-stirring sound. I thought it quite intriguing, but gave it little more thought. The next day at the exact same time I again heard the same sound, except this time my attention was brought to our sliding glass doors at the back of the house. Again, three rather large white birds were descending in a triangle formation in slow motion. Russ and I looked at each other and wondered what all of this could be about. I said, "If this happens again tomorrow something's definitely up." Sure enough on the third day the experience again repeated itself. I grabbed my poncho and Russ and I went out onto the front porch walking slowly beneath the birds nestled in the tops of the great redwoods. I said quietly, "My angels are here. They are trying to tell me something. I wonder what it is." We continued our walk. It was a cool day with very little breeze. Suddenly out of the blue a set of wind chimes began to play. To my surprise it was the tune from my dream. I thought, "I must be making this up" when suddenly Russ stopped and looking startled said, "That's the tune from your dream!" We couldn't believe it. The Earth and her subtle magic is awe-inspiring. We began to hum the tune so we could remember it long enough to get home and record it. As soon as we had it down, the wind chimes stopped, leaving only the stillness. The song is still with me and I share its beauty when I can. The verbal phrasing that accompanies the tune is "Ananda" (a-nan-na--a-nan-na-ane-nane-nan-nan-da). Shortly after this experience I was reading and discovered that there is a meaning for the word. Ajit Mookerjee describes it in the following way:

> Asana (posture) is meant for the control of the body and mind, to permit the free flow of psychic forces through the physiological mechanisms. It is a unitive, contemplative way, an altered state, through which a new reality evolves, a new unit comes into existence in which the old two are lost. "Sexuality and spirituality become two ends of one energy." As Rajneesh remarks: "Tantric sexual union is falling in love with the Whole Cosmos, it is a total surrender to the Whole Cosmos." In surrendering we become feminine, the feminine depths of our psyche then dissolving, transcending—a total experience of oneness—and a tremendous energy is released. From the tantric point of view, the consummated human being is man and woman fused into a single unit. When the idea of basic unity, that the two are inseparable, emerges, the state of *ananda*, of infinite joy or perpetual bliss, is reached. This state of bliss is the closest approximation one may experience to the state of liberation. The inner life-force is aroused to its full potential through the mystic process of awakening the Kundalini Shakti.[98]

The "angels" had brought me a key to help me understand some of the spontaneous posturing that had been occurring. Though I had dipped into this wonderful state of bliss through the jada samadhi experiences, I had not been able to maintain it. My mind seemed less troubled, my compulsions releasing, yet still the yearning for unity relentlessly prevailed.

In this journey Shakti was now guiding me through a process that seemed to be totally rewiring my nervous and neurological systems. The process was so complete that I felt it in the very

---

[98] Mookerjee, Ajit, *Kundalini, The Arousal of the Inner Energy*, Thames and Hudson, London, 1989, pp. 62–63.

marrow of my bones. In the appendix of a most profound book entitled *Unknown Man, The Mysterious Birth of a New Species,* this phase of my journey was described as follows:

> Here we cross the threshold from the realm of Energy-Power into the realm of Mind, the domain of the Mental World. And so begins the real mystical experience. Attention shifts to the braincore with its mystical ascent through the entire nervous system. The peak experience of this level is the first satori of the void, "but remaining as both the knower and the known." In India it is recognized as Nirvikalpa Samadhi, the "formless ecstasy." The seed of self-consciousness remains and this samadhi is only temporary, as it remains both the subject and the object of contemplation. However, the traveler cannot de-volve, he cannot fall back now. One subtle sense is now available, being a heightened sense of "seeing." It is marked by the opening of the third eye.
>
> The seeker now has control over the mind, whereas before this point he was a slave to it. His or her control can even extend to others while the physical body now surrenders to a semi-conscious control from the mental level.[99]

As this process unfolded a deep cleansing occurred. In meditation I was told to contact Peter, a chiropractor who was a homeopathy practitioner, and would be instrumental in my rebirthing stages. I'll never forget how I felt when, after his hour-long examination was concluded, he rolled his chair up close to me and gently looked into my eyes and said, "I doubt many know the severe pain you have been enduring." I began to cry, surprised that such emotion was there.

One of my last severe episodes happened in January of 1991 during the Middle East crisis. It lasted for several weeks in which I ran a fever and fell in and out of deep states. Visions would appear detailing the progress of the war and highlighting the young men involved. The next day I would see the same images

---

[99] Yatri, *Unknown Man, The Mysterious Birth of a New Species,* Simon & Schuster, Inc., New York, p. 283.

on television as the news reporters shared the current happenings. For the first time, I could feel the pain of all the mothers that have come before me, experiencing this same dilemma—the possible death of their child. I weeped for my sons and for all our young innocent men who have been sacrificed. The pain seemed centered in the marrow of the bone and was inescapable. For days at a time I could not walk and had to be assisted. Finally, it passed and with it a new level of regeneration began. Peter was God-sent. Some of the paradox he discovered was that I was diagnosed with Epstein-Barr Virus. The irony was that the Epstein-Barr syndrome demands a quiet interior while the fire created by the Kundalini was far from quiet. The Kundalini was again creating a purge of the biological system. Strict dieting and an education on the energy surrounding me were initiated. I discovered that the heater in my waterbed affected me as did other electrical systems in the house. He suggested that I set up my bedroom and call it sacred space allowing no one else's energy in it but mine and Russ's. The television and stereo were removed from the room because they created magnetic fields. My body was so hypersensitive that all my thinking had to go toward creating a stillness in the atmosphere around it. To my surprise all these changes made a remarkable difference. My rest was quieter and my body continued to feel better.

## TO INDIA IN SEARCH OF MORE ANSWERS

Plans began to formulate as Anandi Ma and Dileepji prepared a small group of us for a short trip to India. The group consisted of disciples that were from all over the United States. There were about thirty in all with a general mix of men and women ranging in ages from early thirty to sixty. Some had been to India before, but most of us were there for the first time. Anandi Ma would be taking our group from Gaumukh in the north of India to Rameswaram in the South. Hindu prophesy states that your soul will be set free from the wheel of life if you retrieve water from the Ganges in Gangotri and pour it over the shiva lingam (symbol of universal creativity) in the temple in Rameswaram. She was planning to leave mid-September, 1991. Since I had committed to helping Tigre with the medicine eagle gathering, I asked if I could join them during the trip. She assured me that would be fine. My plans were made. I would be joining them the first of October in Madras. We would travel for several weeks doing practices and participating in Hindu rituals throughout India in their most sacred temples. We would then return to Ahmedabad to stay with Guruji, the 115-year old guru to whom Anandi Ma was a devotee. The majority of the group would then return to the U. S. leaving only three of us to stay on. I would remain in India until the end of December. My time there would prove to be a time of circles closing; a time when new levels of meaning would be introduced to situations and symbols presented many years before.

In the month preceding the trip I had a major car accident. I was going to work taking a route down the mountain that I normally don't travel. It was very curvy, and as I came around a severe curve I was met with the reality that a large truck completely stretched itself across the road as it made the curve itself, leaving me with two options: I could either go over the side of the mountain or into the truck—I chose the truck. As happens during such incidents, time seemed to go into slow motion and my observer self took over watching as if in a dream. I realized that I had been set up and wondered what this was going to be about. I then watched as my car crunched into the side of the truck. At one point I felt as if someone shoved me, pushing me over sideways into the passenger seat. At that very moment the truck pushing past hit my sideview mirror exploding it in through my opened window. If I had been sitting up in my normal posture, it would have all blown into my face. When all movement stopped people rushed to help. At first they thought that I may have broken my neck so I was not allowed to move. In fact, they later taped me down to a board to transport me to the hospital. To make a long story short, all turned out well. I received a whiplash to the neck, minor cuts and bruises, and an overall body stiffness which took some time to heal. All and all I felt quite lucky. Looking back at the events that would unfold, I feel this was the beginning of a passage related to a final release in the head and neck regions. I'll explain more as we go along.

And so the journey to India began! I arrived in Madras around 2:00 a.m. on the morning of October 1. Inwardly I was anxious and excited. It was like walking into another world. To go through customs you had to descend a set of stairs and enter a very primitive-looking room. It was dimly lit and filled with lines of people waiting to be processed. I was tired from such a long trip (some 26 hours) and wondering if I would find Dileepji in the sea of faces waiting at the front gate. There are very few Westerners in India so you immediately feel your height and color—your differences. The smells and subtle nuances of the culture impact immediately and bring all of your senses into an alert posture. My intrigue of the adventure was mixed with a strong sense of vulnerability, yet something deep inside felt a great relief as if I had in some way come home.

I met my roommate that morning at 3 o'clock and the rest of the group the next morning around 6:00 a.m. as we departed for the next temple. My dreams began to flow as did intense waves of ecstasy as we entered this surrealistic world. Anandi Ma guided us deep into the temples where non-Hindus are usually not allowed. It is hard to describe because the scene was one imbedded in time. Long corridors of stone surrounded us lit only by the ghee (clarified butter) in the lamps. Deep low tones of chanting echoed through the chambers ushering me into an altered state. The energy felt so pure inviting my heart to open until I thought at times it would burst from the joy released. The energy of thousands of years of worship flowed through me with each breath. My whole body yelled, "YES!"

When we entered the divine temple in Rameswaram the energy ignited within opening me to deep samadhi experiences. A deep peace began to breathe me releasing a genuine sense of knowing. My vision of the Land of the Bodhisattvas swallowed me leaving me in a state of ecstatic bliss. Anandi Ma encouraged me to remain present in consciousness as we poured the water that had been carried from the Ganges over the shiva lingam while priests chanted and repeated a ritual that had marked this doorway into the inner sanctum for thousands of years.

As we continued the journey a struggle began. The hardness of the culture hit as did the difficulties stirred by doing such deep initiatory processes in a group. You meet your edges. You can either take the opportunity to smooth them out or project them onto others and play the victim. It is certainly easier to opt for victimhood, but then you miss your opportunity to heal your vessel. It has been my experience that during times of initiation you are presented with the opportunity to confront all of your fears and complaints head-on, for the dragon (your shadow self) guards the door.

One of the last temples we traveled to before returning to Guruji was the Tirupati Balaji's temple. Thousands of people flowed into the labyrinth leading into the main chamber where the golden image of the God was held. It was considered a great auspicious act to sacrifice your hair, so hundreds walked by with cleanly shaved scalps. Men, women, and children lined up as a continuous flow of hair fell to the ground with the assistance of a sharp blade. Thousands of people had pilgrimaged to this site at great personal cost for this annual celebration. It was believed that if you completed the pilgrimage and received darshan (blessings) from the God much wealth would come into your life, both on a spiritual and physical level. Entering the labyrinth tested your stamina as well as your patience. People pushed and shoved and tempers flared. If you had any fantasy of stoic reverence, you met the first face of the dragon. The challenge was to find the quiet reverent space within, while the testing from the loud, sometimes hostile, environment around you challenged your ego-felt expectation. As this river of humanity roared past the door that announced the chamber of the God within, for just one moment time was suspended, sound seemed to still, and then the river pushed you on. After emerging from the inner sanctum we sat in a group and chanted. The opposites in India collide with every moment and any prior illusion you might have had are smashed.

We had traveled six hours by taxi that day away from our hotel on the beach in Mahabali Puram. The roads were full of potholes and filled with everything from large trucks with faces painted on them to carts drawn by water oxen. Though the heat was mild for this time of the year (90 degrees), the air was full of dust mixed with a black smog which poured from the exhausts of the vehicles. Driving in India is a risk and an adventure. It takes a rare talent to navigate through the constant flow of objects. At times it appears that one driver is playing "chicken" with the other, and just as the truck with the white-toothed grin is about to eat you, the driver dodges to one side just missing the lady on the bicycle on the other side. For someone who had just been in a head-on collision with a truck, the sensation of the constant confrontation was challenging to say the least. In the back of my mind I suppose I kept thinking of repeating that ride to get back home. I know I did as the energy began to mount pushing up into my head creating a pressure at the base of the skull. The energy of this temple and the practices had ignited something. I thought if I returned to the cab and rested for a while, it would be all right. Premonitions of the Sun Dance began to swirl around me, and a voice warned that I would need to call on my Sun Dance self. The pain continued to mount. Try as I might, I could not escape the night's taxi ride or the unbearable pain that was to follow. At one point they moved me into the car with Anandi Ma. It was only then with her help that the process became more bearable. I wrote in my journal the next day a description of the journey:

## OCTOBER 14, 1991

We are off in the car. The road is bumpy with deep pits in the pavement bouncing the body with no mercy. Each shock sends pain up the spine through the neck and adds to the mounting crescendo of pain emanating from the migraine (shakti headache). The vision blurs and waves of nausea flood the system leaving in its trail beads of sweat across the face. I cannot bare it. I must. God would not give me more than I can bear. Tears flow endlessly while heat radiates from my body. It feels like an ice fire running through my veins. What is causing this? Why is it happening here with all these people? I watch two parts of myself do battle. One yells, "You exhibitionist!" The other yells, "Painful silence no longer serves." Oh, to lay down; to be still. My whole system is over sensitized to all around it. Lights, sounds and smells seem to amplify the nerves. Can I endure?

Once in the car with Anandi Ma, the pain seems to quiet, become more bearable. A pillow placed around my neck seems to brace it against the road jarrings. Endure, breathe into it. Once we arrive at the hotel, I lay down falling quickly into sleep. In my dream I am fussing about what's happened. My teacher (unseen) tells me my path is one of austerities. "But it is so intense," I argue. "Intense it must be," he answers. I awake. I feel strange, light-headed and sad, yet resigned. Resigned to what? What is this all about—Anandi Ma, India? The dream had ended leaving an impression of 14 days. Fourteen days have passed since I left San Francisco or is it fourteen days to come? So many questions surface. It seems all I had been so sure about melts so quickly away.

My spine aches. My head and neck feel like they were just released from the claws of a great bird. I have this deep sense that he may return at any moment. In every sacred place on the journey I have prayed for union. I'm not surprised by the cleansing, but wonder why all my doubts attack again. The disciples each talk of the large number of mantras (650,000) they wish to complete, plan to complete or have completed. Is this practice truly part of my new learning? Is my resistance my laziness? How do I find the answers? My path up until now forms itself as it goes, allowing me to learn from the traditions, yet not allowing me to identify with only one. Is that to change?

Who am I? Who asks that question? What happens when the teachings of the Sun Dancer from the west meet the teachings of the yogi from the east? The alchemy of it all is fascinating. I observe as the river catches me in its current and flows toward...

A few days later we all traveled to Bhandwahr, an ashram where Guruji lived for over 60 years. As we pulled up to its gates, the surrounding villagers rallied around our van to welcome us. A magical ambience encompassed the space as we were led by Anandi Ma to a small room. A group of elders from the ashram met with us. As I sat in this circle watching these figures clothed only in loin cloth, I seemed to enter a feeling of dream time. Adults and small children pushed through the crowd struggling to get a glimpse of the foreigners through the small windows of the building. Had I been part of a small group of disciples like this before? Certainly a feeling of *of dèja vu* was prevalent.

We traveled on to Ahmedabad where Guruji resides. Due to his age he was living in a small apartment and cared for by an older couple, a doctor and his wife. We stayed in his ashram (Hansol) located just outside of town near the airport. The women were assigned to rooms in one part of the complex and the men to rooms in a separate section. The facility itself was very small but, though primitive, very comfortable. The swami who monitored the daily operation of the ashram was 86. He was a rather tall and robust gentleman with a white beard. His white hair was pulled back in a twist on the back of his head and he wore an orange dhoti (a piece of cloth wrapped around the waist) leaving his chest bared except for an orange shawl tossed over his shoulders. He had a stern gentleness about him with a smile that would melt your heart.

As I sat in my room I contemplated my forthcoming meeting with Guruji. I looked around at my surroundings. It was so peaceful and the people so kind. The language seemed not to create a barrier, but rather presented a challenge. With open hearts and a bit of sign language, we muttled through. There was a lush green courtyard directly in front of our rooms with small bungalows lining each side of it. Each bungalow was the same. Each had a bedroom with one or two cots. A room to bathe in consisted of a bucket and a water faucet with a hook on the wall to hold your change of clothing. Just around the corner from the washroom was a toilet which normally in India would be a basin set in the ground with a place to put your feet on each side. Due to the number of Westerners visiting they had installed Western toilets with a small bucket sitting next to a water faucet which you filled and poured into the toilet in order to flush. A small area used for preparing food was on the back section with a door opening out onto a Muslim cemetery with the river running beside it. In the front was a narrow stairway leading down into a small room used for meditation and prayer. As I looked out of my back door across the cemetery a sense of stillness settled around me. A cluster of small animals scurried around. A small squirrel that looked like a chipmunk skittered here and there. Two dogs ran playing together as a peacock strutted by. Looking across the cemetery the sun moved through the dust suspended in the air highlighting the haze at dawn. I was to meet Guruji the next day. I had so many questions. Where would I start? Part of me felt like a small child, vulnerable and naive. Another part felt foolish and unworthy. Questions seemed to have no place, yet another part pushed on wanting to understand, wanting to reach the place where the parts that questioned would dissolve.

Guruji lived in such a simple way. He was 115 years old and in rather good health except that one of his legs made it difficult for him to walk, so he was lifted and carried in a chair from place to place. He seldom went anywhere anymore. The world came to him. He laid in his bed in the back of the apartment with one window opened for ventilation. Above him was a picture of Hanuman, an incarnation of Lord Shiva, who represents unquestionable service. Just above that was a small opening where two pigeons had made their nest. They flew under the constantly stirring ceiling fan and in and out of the opened window adding a feeling of benevolence to the atmosphere.

Along one wall as you entered the room was a long table with an alter. Gifts of fruit and donations to the work were mixed with flowers of all colors that were given in devotion to this teacher and living saint in exchange for his darshan (the gaze of the master) or blessings. Guruji was dressed in a white dhoti. A stillness encompassed him like no other I had ever experienced. His eyes had a piercing quality and at times he spoke as if "God possessed" giving knowledge of a very personal nature to those that came. Watching him work left me in awe. The apartment was full of busy sounds—cooking in the kitchen, building shelves in the living room and people going and coming constantly for darshan. As I observed the in-and-out flow of people through the apartment, I likened it much to the movement of breath—steady and constant. His presence was much the same. As we sat in the living room later I listened as stories were shared of the healings that occurred through Guruji from cancer to life-threatening conditions.

It's fascinating to step outside of your life's drama at times and see the wonder of how fate weaves such meetings. Before I left for India Russ and I had decided to marry and hoped that Anandi Ma and Guruji would perform the ceremony. They had both agreed, and the ceremony had been set for December 15. I would stay on in India after the group left and Russ would join me on December 9. Little did I know that much would unfold in the meantime that would make us both re-examine the deep commitment we had voiced. It brought to mind an excerpt from an article in *Weavers of Wisdom*:

> The price of being able to find the "other" as a living wisdom within myself had been that I must want nothing from it, I must turn to it with complete acceptance of what is, expecting nothing, wanting to change nothing; and it was only then that I received those illuminating flashes which had been most important in shaping my life.[100]

---

[100] Milner, Marion, "An Experiment in Leisure," in Bancroft, Anne, *Weavers of Wisdom, Women Mystics of the Twentieth Century*, Penguin Books, New York, 1989, p. 35.

And so the next three weeks would provide an understanding of the full meaning of this excerpt and "the price" of finding "the other." After visiting with Guruji I arranged for a train ticket to Delhi where I was to meet a friend. Something inside knew that this meeting would probably not happen, and the thought of going on my own brought feelings of fear and insecurity. Traveling in India by yourself, especially for women, is a challenging experience to say the least. It requires that you stay intuitively alert and, if at all possible, sit with the women and children. A friend of mine who is a Tibetan lama and travels to India a lot gave me some advice that proved very helpful a few times. He said that if at any time I felt that I had gotten myself into an unsafe position I should "chunk" my ladylike manners and make a scene. When I did have to use this tactic, whole families would graciously come to my aid. Please don't get me wrong. All in all the people of India are generous and kind, but our cultures are so different that things can be misunderstood quickly and you can find yourself in rather precarious situations. Trying to figure out the train system proved to be intriguing as well as frustrating. You cannot purchase one ticket from your first station to multiple destinations in other parts of India, which means you must go through the ordeal of long lines and confusing train tables at each stop along the way. The system has no center and no connecting links. The rickshaw drivers say, "As you like," which means "as they like." Off you go into a direction unknown to you, and about the time you realize this, they are trying to manipulate you for more money. I began to read my experiences as lessons allowing the whole gestalt of the trip to teach me. My first lesson: I must stay clear about my direction, not allowing myself to be swayed off my mark, otherwise it will cost me. My naive child self was becoming tempered. I didn't want to become a loud American or a soft piece of putty, fear-ridden and skittish. The middle path would have to be found. The question of owning my own authority once again surfaced. If my friend didn't come, I would be on my own. If I didn't exercise my inner muscles, the trip would become very difficult.

Another friend took me to the train. I found my way to my seat which had been filled by a whole family. The crowded situation only amplified the discomfort inside. I finally found a seat on the aisle occupied by a small girl who spoke very good English. What a comfort she was! I arrived in Delhi before dawn and made my way to the hotel where I was to meet my friend. After two days and no word, I decided to go on to Rishikesh, a small village located in the lap of the Himalayas on the banks of the Ganges River. My destination was to be a trek into the Valley of the Flowers. I thought I would rest a day at an ashram in Rishikesh and then take the bus another few hours further up into the Himalayas where I would then have a days-long hike before reaching the Valley.

Years before during a holotropic breathwork session[101] I had experienced a vision through my body.

> *During the experience my body had begun to simulate a birth process. At one point I seemed to float above myself and as I looked down I saw a large pink and very clean wound that started at my throat and extended down the front of my body to my vulva. Just at that moment I watched as the wound turned into a vulva and birthed a new world. The world was round like a mandala and inside a living vision moved. A scene appeared of a beautiful mountainous landscape. On top of the mountain stood an old Indian man with large white wings, holding a staff up to the heavens. As he raised the staff you could hear women and children in the valley below shouting cheers of joy and throwing flowers.*

It was years later as I was preparing for my trip to India that I discovered that there was indeed a Valley of Flowers. Upon hearing the name the memory of that vision reappeared in my mind—the circles were beginning to close.

---

[101] "This method, combining simple means, such as faster breathing, music and sound technology, and a certain form of body work, can induce the entire spectrum of experiences that we used to see in psychedelic sessions. This is a process of purging and clearing old traumas; it often opens the way to very pleasant or even ecstatic and transcendental experiences and feelings." Grof, Christina and Stanislav, *The Stormy Search for the Self*, Jeremy P. Tarcher, Los Angeles, 1990, p. 144.

My trip to Rishikesh presented some tests, but all in all I fared the journey well. I found my way to the Ved Niketan ashram located on the shores of the Ganges. The Ganges is spoken of as a river with great spiritual significance. It is said that if you bathe in the Ganges that all of your sins will be washed away and a great healing will occur. It had a magical feeling to it as I looked upon it. It flowed wildly with large white stones lining its banks of silver and gold sparkling sand. It flowed through the quiet quaint village of Rishikesh. A hanging walk bridge extended over it connecting both sides of the village. The ashram I was to stay in was on the side that had no vehicles and so life felt slower and the noise much less. People were constantly arriving in large and small groups to bathe and do rituals in the river. The sounds of people chanting God's name mingled with the many odors of food and animals as the streets opened to the day's activity. As I crossed the bridge people began to act excited and hurried to one side peering down. Much to my surprise as I looked down into the moving waters I saw a large white snake swimming to the shore. A sense of right timing filled me.

I checked into the ashram and breathed a sigh of relief. I had finished the first part of my trip successfully and had found a safe place to stay in a beautiful spot. My room consisted of a concrete-looking walled area with a cot. A bathing room and toilet were adjoining.  On the wall facing my bed was painted a mural showing a man meditating with visions flowing out of his head and encircling the space around him. Over the door was painted a large eye. My doubts and fears continued to consume me. I missed Russ and the comforts of my lifestyle. My attachments screamed at me wanting attention.

A major earthquake had hit the Himalayas killing thousands. Large aftershocks brought landslides and more destruction. The weather was bad and travelers' warnings were being announced. I was confused about whether I should continue. My confusion only seemed to add fuel to the self-doubts that consumed me. Finally, I decided it was not safe and therefore I would stay in the ashram for about a week allowing myself to meditate and face the barking dogs within. The vision of the Valley of Flowers had depicted the birth of a new world through the healing and evolution of a wound. Would my stay in India evoke such outcome? The vision had led me to my first stop on my pilgrimage. The earth had moved and marked my spot for contemplation. With this decision to stay in Rishikesh another part of the process was initiated. My dreams became instructive and reading material and books would miraculously present itself to me providing the answers to some of my questions. My journal entries read:

## OCTOBER 27, 1991

Each time I've done a vision quest, I am struck by the constant struggle I find myself in with myself. I know that if I persevere I usually reach a stage of deep surrender and then acceptance occurs. The mind gets quiet and a feeling of harmony pervades my system. It is in that place that God speaks. I've started fasting in preparation for Shaktipat which Guruji will perform upon my return. I've been here almost a month and still the inner struggle continues. Breathe into it. Relax and let go. Let go and let God. This has become my chant.

Shadows of figures gather for prayer and move in the courtyard outside my room. Bells sound, filling the air with a clearness. Chanting can be heard throughout the village as all celebrate the rising sun, the dawn of a new day.

## OCTOBER 28, 1991

I found several books today that speak to some of the ways my path have both taught and initiated me into deeper aspects of self. In one entitled *Kundalini Tantra* I found the word *tapasya* which was described as the practice of austerity. It was described as a very powerful method of awakening which not everyone can handle. I wonder if understanding more about this practice will give me a deeper understanding of the dream experience that occurred after that difficult taxi trip? The text states, "Tapasya is a means of purification, a burning or setting on fire so that a process of elimination is created, not in the physical body, but in the mental and emotional bodies. Through this process the mind, the emotions and the whole personality are cleansed of all the dirt, complexes and patterns of behavior that cause pain and suffering. Tapasya is an act of purification."[102] The last three years have been such a process, though my process seemed to include the physical as well.

Another process called *aushadhi* is described as the awakening through herbs. "It should not be interpreted as meaning drugs like marijuana, LSD, etc. Aushadhi is the most powerful and rapid method of awakening but it is not for all and very few people know about it. There are herbs which can transform the nature of the body and its elements and bring about either partial or full awakening, but they should never be used without a guru or qualified guide. With the help of the correct herbs, purified aspirants were able to visualize divine beings, holy rivers, mountains, sacred places, holy men and so on. When the effects of the herbs were more concentrated, they could separate the self from the body and travel astrally. People were able to enter a state of samadhi and awaken their Kundalini. In this particular field of awakening, the sexual instinct was completely eliminated. However, the aushadhi method of awakening is no longer practiced because it was misused by the ordinary people who were neither prepared, competent nor qualified. As a result, knowledge of the herbs was withdrawn and today it is a closely guarded secret."[103]

My process had introduced the use of herbs as a means of invoking healing states (See Chapter Eight). It had entered through my study of the shamanic path and the teachings of indigenous people around the world (North American Indians, tribal peoples of the Amazon, etc.). Now here I sit in India reading about a process that has been invoked for thousands of years with the results manifesting much like mine. More circles closing. A synthesis is afoot!

---

[102] Swami Satyananda Saraswati, *Kundalini Tantra*, Sri Keyriwal, Bihar School of Yoga, Bihar, India, 1984, p. 35.

[103] Ibid., pp. 36–37.

In another book entitled *The Centre of the Cyclone* Osho writes on the subject of enlightenment. A dear friend once asked me, "Just what is enlightenment anyway?" Osho describes it in this way:

"Two schools have always existed. One school is of sudden enlightenment which says enlightenment happens suddenly, it is non-temporal. Another school, just contradicting the first, which is of gradual enlightenment says enlightenment comes gradually, nothing happens suddenly.

"And both are right, because both have chosen one part of the phenomenon... But I tell you both are right. Enlightenment happens suddenly. It has always happened suddenly. But understanding takes time."[104]

At one point he says, "Ego cannot exist without time. Ego breathes in time."[105] When I study these two concepts I see the paradox "I" have been placed in. My ego keeps clocking my time here in India while my mind keeps chatting about "missing Russ," "missing my routine," "missing my comforts." "I" keep wishing for what isn't here so I won't be here—present in the moment. The more I ponder the question of enlightenment the more aggressive my mind gets. The question then becomes how to step into that objective viewer place so as not to polarize these two poles. I must follow the tension as it appears rather than allowing myself to be distracted. The ego is uncomfortable because it is in unfamiliar surroundings. Through its loss of control I can again see my attachments and my attachments are what cause the discomfort.

We saw a film tonight on the last years of Christ by Richard Boch. The closing line of the film seemed to summarize my days work well, "The power was in Christ; the pattern was in Jesus."

## OCTOBER 29, 1991

I continue to work through the issues as they surface. I am confronted by the extreme differences of our culture when like magic Osho in his book *The Centre of the Cyclone* again speaks.

---

[104] Osho, *The Centre of the Cyclone*, Diamond Pocket Books, New Delhi, India, 1989, pp. 56–57.

[105] Ibid, p. 42.

He says that wholeness is a still point with a moving periphery. In the east the focus has been on the still point, and in the west, the moving periphery. Our challenge in today's times is to bring those two separate focuses into one, creating wholeness. If those in the east refuse to extend their focus to include the moving periphery, they will die in their own filth. Likewise, if we in the west do not extend our focus to include the still point, we will go mad. One only has to look around to see the profundity of his words. It certainly brings understanding to my current situation. Stay in my center while moving through the sometimes chaotic feeling environment of so many people with not enough space.

I contemplate my upcoming marriage and wonder if in taking my vows that means the celibacy we have been experiencing will shift. Osho writes, "Only then some day in love the witnessing will happen. And when it happens, ecstasy has happened to you— the first glimpse of the divine has descended upon you. From that moment onwards sex will not be sex at all. And sooner or later sex will disappear. This disappearance gives you brahmacharya[106]— then you become a celibate."[107]

The longing and the yearning are so deep, and the tenacity of the ego so strong. When I follow the tension, I find it is like a knot in my solar plexus. Does some of the fear, some of the resistance come from our memory of having the umbilical cord cut—that separation made permanent from a world that was? Is it a primal energy faced or one created by the mind?

One last insight swirled around me as I laid in my bed contemplating that last week. I laid looking at the eye painted over the door to my room. Suddenly, as if in a flash, the realization hit me. In 1982 when my process had begun with such vivid visions, one particular image that continued to reappear was what I came to call "the eye of God." An eye would appear above me and then clear in its center forming other images which later proved prophetic in nature, foretelling of events that would come into my life. Each time the God's eye would appear, it would eventually move closer to me until I could see clearly through it as if looking

---

[106] Brahmacharya means the way the divine behaves.
[107] Ibid, p. 84.

through a portal into another world, one much more alive with color than this one. It was as if I was under a microscope and someone was looking down upon me. An old man with a white beard would appear each time just before the prophetic visions would form. The last time I saw this image the old man appeared as usual, but this time he stepped aside and a young woman with dark hair looked down upon me. Suddenly, I realized that that old man and young woman were Guruji and Anandi Ma. They had entered my life in 1982 and some nine years later I was in their homeland learning from their culture. Another circle closed; another mystery explained. I wondered if it was time to step through that portal into that other world? Spirit's interweaving in one's life is amazing. Somehow just realizing once again the intricate way in which one's life's plan reveals itself calmed me.

The time in Rishikesh had been one of inner confrontation. Through that work my mind had quieted and the fears stilled themselves. My next part of the journey was to be to Lucknow to receive darshan from an 82-year-old sage that people called Papaji. I had no idea how I might find him except I had been told that if I went to the Carlton Hotel in Lucknow and inquired there, they would be able to direct me. The Carlton Hotel was a large colonial-looking estate with beautiful grounds and very comfortable accommodations. When I inquired I was told that taxis would be gathering in the morning which would be taking a group of us over. To my surprise the hotel was almost full of people from the West seeking an audience with Papaji.

The next morning I caught a cab and was brought to a very modest house. We stood in line outside the gate until it was time to enter. There was probably around 60 or 70 of us. We squeezed into a regular-size living room sitting in various positions on the floor. Those who could not fit into the room sat on the veranda outside listening through speakers. Papaji entered and moved through us to a small platform at the front of the room. He was very lively, warm, and full of humor. He teaches the pathless way and says that to reach enlightenment you must give up all maps and release all intentions, allowing the river to flow into the ocean naturally. As he began to speak the shakti began to move through my system, kriyas gently causing a sensation of shaking to move up my spine and into my head. I struggled to keep my system quiet so as not to disturb the group. After 30 or 40 minutes, he concluded and left the room. The group dispersed and stood or sat informally around the house as tea was served. I tried to stand in a less conspicuous space allowing the energy to move gently. I inquired if it was possible to get a private audience with Papaji and to my surprise was shortly thereafter ushered into his private room. Several people sat around him. One of his disciples motioned for me to come and sit on the bed between he and Papaji. The energy continued to mount causing some discomfort in my shoulders and neck. After 10 minutes or so Papaji asked me where I was from. I took that opportunity to explain to him that I had been going through an intense Kundalini awakening process for nine years. I explained that at times it brought me inconceivable bliss and at other times it was quite painful. He looked into my eyes and said, "Yes, I can see by looking at your face there is a center blocked. If you'll come tomorrow I'll work with you. O.K.?" Suddenly, he slapped me hard between the shoulder blades and said, "Very good!"

I had to make arrangements to change my train tickets extending my stay. It felt like an important part of the process was about to open. It was important to take my time with it. Little did I know what that would eventually mean. By the time I returned to my hotel the pain in my neck and shoulders was increasing. I decided to sit out on the grass and watch the sunset while visiting with some visitors from Europe. The pain increased until I had to excuse myself. As I began to walk away one of them started laughing and remarked that I had a ball of mosquitoes gathered just above my head. As I walked away they remained centered over my head. Seems the energy must be intensifying. My resulting journal entries speak for themselves:

## NOVEMBER 1, 1991

The pain in my shoulders and neck increases. I can't seem to get relief unless I'm lying down. That deep yearning gnaws at me. My prayers ring through me like a song, "Oh Lord, please bring this pilgrim home!"

The pain endured throughout the night. It seems to originate in my neck and run down the muscles and through the nerves of my left arm. Nothing seems to be able to relieve it. Will I be able to endure my session at Papaji's this morning? Will his "work on me" bring relief? Or, has that work begun and this is some part of that process? My belly is smaller than its' been in three years. Some shift is occurring, but what?

## NOVEMBER 2, 1991

I sit at my hotel today reflecting back over yesterday and still trying to synthesize its meaning. I had had a dream during the night leading into this "nightmarish" day. In the dream Papaji was there and I appeared in front of him. I was watching the dream and experiencing it at the same time. I had an outfit on which had small cellophane compartments all over it with things filling each pocket. As Papaji initiated what was called in the dream "an enlightening process," I began to twist like a pretzel. I awoke. This dream proved to be prophetic, announcing a process soon to follow. I struggled to ready myself for Papaji's, but the pain in my neck and shoulder were becoming more difficult to contend with. If I can just manage to get there! Maybe I can see him early and return to the hotel shortly after. No such luck. When I told one of his helpers I was in severe pain, he said, "That's wonderful. Have a seat." I laid down and waited for two hours until the tea break. Another student asked if I wanted to see the Master. I said yes definitely if it was the right time. He led me to his door, but it was closed. I braced my head and left arm upon the door frame, twisting until I could find a position where the pain was bearable. A few more people were brought in for tea, so I knew it would still be many more minutes. When the unconscious is working nothing makes logical sense and you at times have a feeling that you can't be heard. It feels like a definite plan is in motion and the best one can do is surrender to it knowing Shakti is moving something through. With time the process will make profound sense. And so I struggled to maintain such an attitude, rather than call on my old victim self.

Finally, another one of Papaji's students recognized my pain and took the actions that got me in to see Papaji. He said, "What happened to you?" I explained the pain had started yesterday and continued to mount. I reminded him of our conversation and wondered if this was the blockage going or the energy causing difficulties with the neck injuries acquired in my car wreck several weeks prior. He sent for a doctor who works with him and asked him to take a look. To make a long story shorter, we did do some process work around the pain and its causes, but still the pain was increasing. The doctor's departing words as I left were, "This is an intuition, but I feel that you are about to take another step deeper into the unknown. Your old birth patterns are resurfacing expressing the fear of the aloneness such a step implies. Remember stepping into the emptiness is where all form falls away."

With these words, I made my way slowly to the front of the house. There two angels in skin awaited. One lovely gentleman offered to see me to the hotel safely and the other offered his services as a naturopath physician.

Once in bed I thought the pain would subside, but instead it increased shooting burning sensations down the muscles of my left shoulder and arm. A cold fiery sensation ran up my spine enlivening each nerve along the way. There was no way to get relief. Finally, in early evening the doctor arrived. His compassion and sensitivity to my situation was like a salve. My worst fear of becoming ill in India while all alone had come to pass, but as I have mentioned many times Grace provides. The doctor had had a girlfriend who also had gone through a difficult Kundalini awakening demonstrating so many of the same characteristics as mine. He, therefore, had an intimate understanding about *how to follow the process*. And following the process is the key. If one tries to make the process adhere to a certain tool, rather than using the tool to facilitate the process, the results and outcome can become quite different. About an hour into the session, a huge knot which felt like twisted muscle rolled down from my neck across my shoulder and finally released. Though the situation wasn't resolved, it had shifted.    He continued to administer homeopathy treatment and acupuncture. The night was long and arduous, sleeping very little.   Outside music and chanting went on all night, celebrating the New Year.   For three days rituals and ceremony are offered to the Goddess as the New Year is ushered in.

## NOVEMBER 3, 1991

When I arose this morning, the pain was becoming more bearable. The homeopathy cure was to assist in the repair of the traumatized spine and nerve endings. It seems to be working. I must, however, lay flat.  I slept better last night, although my neck and spine are still quite sore.  The intensity of the pain has become more generalized into the shoulder and arm. At times the heat in my head and body become unbearable. Sitting with my feet in cold water and doing pranayama breathing exercises (breath control) brings down the heat. My belly has been flat, but now is beginning to expand again. The room boy just came in. He has been worried about me.  He said, "Don't worry.  God says it will be alright tomorrow."

I must try to remain sitting up and learn how to cope in preparation for my 16 hour train ride tomorrow. I think I'll once again have to call on my Sun Dancer to make this voyage. The young doctor had to leave, so I'm on my own again. The paradox is that as each day passes, my inner strength keeps growing. It's interesting how pain brings us immediately into the moment. I wonder if joy doesn't do the same thing. What transpires when they both share the same moment?

(Note & Observation) I realized this morning that in the first episode with Anandi Ma the pain was on the right side extending up into the brain. The pain this time is on the left side extending down through the arm. I wonder what is the significance of the pathways?

The last leg of my trip was to be to Mt. Abu located about 8 hours north of Ahmedabad.  It was here in a place called the Elephant Cave that Guruji attained self-realization. My hope had been to stay a few days visiting the many holy sites located there and meditate at the Elephant Cave before returning to Ahmedabad. I wasn't sure my neck and arm would allow the additional travel. I decided that I would wait and decide when the train pulled into the Mt. Abu station.

Though the pain still persisted and had begun to manifest as a burning sensation running through the muscles, I had spells when it became quiet. Traveling in general was becoming easier as I adjusted. I noticed how much something in me had shifted. I was much more relaxed, quiet, and free-flowing. I decided that I would get off at the Mt. Abu station to complete my pilgrimage. Luckily I met an English-speaking family and shared the cost of a taxi up the mountain to the quaint village of Mt. Abu. I checked into my hotel. The town itself was very picturesque. The people were more relaxed and open than other places I had been. I took my time visiting some of the local temples and enjoying the beauty. I asked around until I was able to acquire correct directions to the cave. It was located near town overlooking a small lake that was to have been created by God's thumbprint. My next journal entry summarized my feelings:

## NOVEMBER 7, 1991

I went to Guruji's cave today. It sits up on the side of the mountain overlooking a lake. The path leading to the cave consisted of stone steps leading past many small cave areas where sadhus (saintly renunciates) lived year round. Once I arrived I sat in meditation and sang prayers absorbing the ambience of my surroundings. Later I continued to chant prayers as I circumambulated the lake. A feeling of completion descended over me. As I sit and reflect back over these last days, a deep sense of knowing peeks its head into my vision. I have made friends with India. In Stephen Donaldson's book, *The First Chronicles of Thomas Covenant, The Unbeliever*, he describes culture shock as follows: "Culture shock is what happens when you take a man *[or a woman]* out of his own world and put him down in a place where the assumptions, the standards of being a person—are so different that he can't possibly understand them. He isn't built that way. If he's facile—he can pretend to be someone else until he gets back to his own world. Or he can just collapse and let himself be rebuilt—however. There's no other way."

My solo journey had not only unveiled new meaning to old parts of my puzzle (i.e. the god's eye), but it had helped me face myself. As I embraced India in all of her paradoxes, I began to embrace me. The cave had marked a part of the trip that brought completion—an emptying of my cup. My return to Hansol would begin to fill it.

## GURUJI AND A NEW POINT OF FOCUS

When I arrived at Guruji's ashram in Hansol complete joy filled me. I just wanted to bend down and kiss the ground. So much had happened during those past three weeks. My shoulder had become bearable, but was certainly still very present. I would later learn from Guruji that the series of head/neck/shoulder experiences was burning up old karma in the nadis (those channels in or along which the life force circulates) in my head. He said that although this was very painful, all would be well shortly; a circle closes. I would be staying at Hansol for the next month. During that time my body became very strict with me, particularly with regards to diet. The only food I ate was fruit blessed by Guruji, one potato at lunch, and water buffalo milk. Once I tried to eat some other food, but the moment it touched my lips my face went white, broke out in a cold sweat, and my body went into convulsions. I was later told that mine was a purification diet, so obviously a deep cleansing was taking place.

On November 10th I went with two other disciples to sit in meditation with Guruji. Much to my surprise this would prove to be one of the most auspicious days of my life. The irony was that my father had died 17 years ago to the day and through that experience I had embarked upon a journey which now had brought me to my "spiritual father." His pronouncement would affirm what Spirit had already shown me. The American Indians say that when your vision is spoken publicly it then begins to manifest in this realm. Was that what was happening? The 17 year-journey had peeled layers of pain off of me, it had revealed a reality that was bringing healing and peace into my life. I would like to share my journal entry because it reveals still more circles closing.

## NOVEMBER 10, 1991

I visited Guruji today and shared with him my journey. A lovely gentleman was present who helped with the translation.

Question [to Guruji]: As the river (soul) nears the ocean, it begins to dip into it. What can one do to relax those last holds of the ego and accomplish the final surrender?

Answer: Do you want to leave the body? If not, then you must know you will go in and out of samadhi, but the ego is necessary to keep you present in this reality.

Question: The more I've traveled and talked with swamis and yogis and listened to their experiences, the more I realize I've been seeking something I already have.

Answer: There once was a great saint who realized that all that one wants is already inside. Another great saint had to do a mantra to come out of samadhi, so he could do the service for which he came. You must do sankalpa [thoughts and imagination, the act of willing].

Question: As I approach my wedding date, I have a question. I have been celibate for two and a half years. Does this mean that those sexual feelings will return?

Answer (He sat up in bed animating with his movement the statement he was about to make.): "You are a highly developed soul. In the next few years a state of pure love will come to reside with you and work through you serving many." I said, "But can't you live a celibate life and be married." He said, "No, it will only create conflict and throw you back into hell [a lower level of consciousness where dualities reside]. The energy has destroyed your womb moving you into the pure state of a brahmachari yogi. This is a great blessing. It is not necessary for you to marry. It is important to understand why you have come! Continue to do your sannyas (perfect dedication)."

Later in a letter to Russ I went on to explain further:

It felt as if God had just plucked me. A very deep surreal sense of being was left. I sat quietly for the next half hour and then we left. Others in the room suggested I wait and talk to Anandi Ma. I went to bed in a daze. Guruji was with me all night long and though I couldn't remember the details, I could feel the parts of myself expressing—a sense of total paradox was involved. The Shakti heat is running like crazy throughout my system, particularly through my spine, neck and shoulders.

The next day I meditated and sat still contemplating the situation. Again, we returned to Guruji. We go every night from five to seven. I hadn't even sat down when he had the interpreter ask me, "Jyoti, are you still confused?" He went on to explain what I was being prepared for. [His description matched the many visions that had come in the last few years. I am not prepared to speak of such matters yet. It is important to hold to oneself material that comes in such profound ways honoring it and allowing it to grow into a more integrative space.] What a paradox! To be in the moment when a great sage and saint speak your visions aloud and in the same blow question the container forming—the upcoming vows of marriage.

What can I say. I love you and together we have walked into the middle of a great mystery. I have to follow, not because I don't love you, BUT BECAUSE I DO! Take some time to digest this and see what is right for you. I want to support you in whatever it is you decide.

During this discussion, three pigeons which live in his room kept flying around in circles over our heads. Quite a commotion and exclamation point. Afterwards, the interpreter told me he had been coming to Guruji's for over ten years. He had never seen Guruji take such a firm stand. When you sit with Guruji, it is like sitting with God.

I know how hard this must be for you. Guruji's timing of this proclamation (the anniversary of Dad's death) and the detail of the experience as he spoke was like having the whispers of my heart shout out. I went to the temple last night and asked for guidance. The irony of it is that it's almost like the feelings we had after visiting with Kennett Roshi. I don't think the information has changed, but we now stand at yet another doorway. Did you think coming to India wouldn't activate the next stage of our process? Yes, *our* process. I kept thinking of the movie "Brother Sun, Sister Moon" last night and of what a deep unconditional love those two shared. They formed a vessel for the divine to dance through. You are my best friend—one who has been beside me when "my Beloved" comes. Now, I'm told he will come to stay and you will get to share in that atmosphere. I know you are also at a different stage of life, and that puts a pressure on you that you must face and be honest with. I don't know what the answer is to be, but please know I want to work with you until we come to a place inside that meets the situation honestly. The Self is marching through our lives again, so what's new. Isn't that why we came together—not to hold ourselves back from that happening, but for a comradeship in the dance. There is just so much more here at stake than you or me or dinner at five.

I don't want to convince you or argue for a position. I'm just trying to candidly share my feelings. Excitement, awe, amazement meet puzzlement and letting go. Letting go doesn't have to mean going away, it can mean going in.

Last night I awoke remembering when Divine Mother appeared to me and said, "Be who you are now!" I think that's what wholeness is all about. Being myself in its entirety. That doesn't mean it's a process that excludes but rather includes. The ego struggles, argues, doubts and, in spite of it all, the process continues to unfold naturally. Look back over the last years and see if you can see that. There hasn't been a pushing. There's been a following of process. The process may have pushed my buttons, pushed my edges, stretched my envelope, but the results were always more health, more depth and more expansion. At least that's been my experience. I've got to be me and you've got to be you!! You are wonderful. It's not that we've done it wrong, we've done it right else why did the door to heaven open. A life of service as Guruji is describing it reminds me of what Cornelia said, "Remember, once you choose to merge with the archetype your life is not your own." I made that choice several years ago—now guess what, it's your turn.

I posted the letter to Russ, but it would be three more weeks before I would talk to him again. I went to the temple of the Divine Mother and prostrated myself on the floor before her asking for strength and clarity. There were no doubts about what Guruji had said, only a desire for understanding about the situation between Russ and I as it was evolving. Was I being selfish to think I could have a life of service and spend that life with Russ as well? Why did the men in my life react so strongly each time I stepped closer to the Source? Was this my karma or my own blindness to an unconscious pattern?

I continued to pray and struggle with the issues surfacing from the events I have described. In my readings I came across a discussion on the role of the guru:

> Question: What is the role of the Guru?
> Answer: The Guru is the Self in the Heart of each devotee. When the devotee makes an effort to be without thoughts or to surrender to the Self, the Guru within responds. He watches the efforts made by the devotee and transmits the grace of the Self. This grace purifies the devotee's mind and pulls it towards the Self. Eventually, if the devotee is ripe, the Self pulls the mind into the Heart and destroys it.[108]

In the preceding days I had several dreams which seemed to add to the gestalt of the experience.

> *I was sitting on the couch in my home about to talk with some clients when I felt myself slipping away. I tried to get Russ's attention, but it was too difficult to speak. My body went rigid as it does when I enter samadhi states. I entered a deep trance. A voice said, "When the mirrors of your mind break, you can't speak for a while."*

When I asked Guruji about the dream, he said that it was foretelling the stage I was about to enter. He said, "Now you use

---

[108] Godman, David, *No Mind, I Am The Self*, Sri Lakshmana Ashram, Nellore Dist., A. P., India, 1988, p. 73.

your mind to speak, but there will come a time when you will speak without using your mind."

Still I continued to wrestle with my inner doubts and demons. Demons that resulted from being born into a culture that had no place for those of us whose perception of the world included angels, spirits, and that "other" dimension. Feelings resurfaced of wanting to belong but never quite fitting in. Memories of faking it to play the game, yet aching inside and never quite knowing why. Still more heads appeared on the snake. My fear of failure screamed at me. Would I come all this way, see the doorway, touch it eventually, only to have it snatched away at that final moment? Do these fears arise out of a primal fear experienced by the ego at birth? Does a past life hold part of the understanding for these feelings that persist? Maybe it's not even important to know why, for the power may be in the recognition of the pattern. My journal entry read:

## NOVEMBER 20, 1991

Still trying to process what's going on inside. I tried to talk to someone about it, but it's so difficult to communicate such complex feelings with the language barrier and all. I keep remembering the story about an aspirant who went to his Master and said, "Please Master, help me to realize God." The Master suddenly grabbed his head and pushed it down under the water in a basin sitting in front of them. The aspirant struggled, but could not get free. Just before drowning the Master let him go. The aspirant gasped for air. The Master said, "And that's how bad you must want it, before the Self can be realized."

The ego and the mind are tricksters, both can create the illusion of separateness. I talked with another friend and was able to process through some of the things that were surfacing. It is so important to discriminate, choosing those who can hold your process without contaminating it. Such holding brings clarity and healing. That has been reaffirmed on this trip so many times. Some along the way have certain techniques or helping skills which they have been trained in (bodywork, guided imagery techniques, nutritional modes, psychotherapeutic models, shamanic methods, etc.) and are encouraged to use them as tools. Unfortunately, the technique or the tool sometimes becomes the process insisting that the client's process fit the tool, rather than the tool being used to facilitate and assist the process of the client. With Kundalini particularly, or any individuating process, the process itself can have a universal expression through presenting symptoms, but the process itself is individually different. When someone is in a full blown episode, they are usually hypersensitive. All your senses have expanded. Many times they are able to read thoughts and are certainly affected by the atmosphere around them. In other words, if they are making you angry, they not only know it, but they feel it run throughout their body. If the practitioner is unable to let go of all preconceived ideas of what is happening, he/she can complicate rather than facilitate the process. If, however he/she is able to follow the process, Shakti does the work and the helper compliments the process as needed. Such sensitivity results in the crisis ending in a shorter period of time revealing informative outcomes. Such wisdom in facilitating is validating and enriching to all involved.

During the midst of my inner struggle I was directed to participate in my first *anusthan* (spiritual meditative practice). Though I was apprehensive, I found that each day revealed new understandings of the work of prayer. I noticed subtle vibrations, sounds generated both internally and externally, and changes in breathing patterns fluctuated as the repetition of the mantra grew throughout the 11 days of practice. The following excerpt from *Satsang with Baba* by Muktananda captured my experience and emphasized its importance:

> The mantra, after mingling with the breath, begins to mingle with the mind, and then it spreads through the blood and bodily fluids and begins to affect them also. If you practice japa[109] for a short while, you will find it very difficult to do without it.

---

[109] *Japa* as described in *Pragya-Yog*, a phamphlet from India, is regarded as a cleansing process. The object of japa is to insistently invite God to assimilate in one's inner self and in all the activities of life by constantly calling on one of the names of God.

Through japa you achieve the stages of Maha Yoga effortlessly. In the initial stage, you may not be able to take any interest in it, and it may make you restless. But soon it balances the prana. One great seer says that you may or may not perform other good actions, but if you perform japa, you can obtain the fruits of all good actions with great ease. All the body fluids, all the different constituents of the body should become permeated with japa. Only then will you realize its true meaning. Tukaran Maharaj used to say that through chanting or japa it's not only your heart and mind which become transformed, which become divine, even the body becomes divine.[110]

As I sat in meditation an emptying process unfolded and with it revelations that seemed to bring a quietude within. Within this silence I have continually been brought back to the words "bridal mysticism." I realized that the first time such words surfaced was in the experience during my vision quest in the Alps of Switzerland when my spirit visitor shouted the words, "And now you are the ravished bride!" Since that time it has been validated by three of the elder wise men of my culture who spoke of bridal mysticism as my path and my destiny. What exactly does that mean? The best description of the stages of bridal mysticism are given by Richard of St. Victor.

The great Richard of St. Victor, in one of his most splendid mystical treatises, has given us perhaps the most daring and detailed application of the symbolism of marriage to the adventures of the spirit of man. He divides the "steep stairway of love," by which the contemplative ascends to union with the Absolute, into four stages. These he calls the betrothal, the marriage, the wedlock, and the fruitfulness of the soul. In the betrothal, he says, the soul "thirsts for the Beloved"; that is to say, it longs to experience the delights of Reality... Then the Soul with pertinacity demands more: and because of her burning desire she attains to pure contemplation, and so passes to the second degree of love. In this she is "led in bridal" by the Beloved. Ascending "above

---

Muktananda, *Satsang with Baba*, Shree Gurudev Ashram, Ganeshpuri, 1974.

herself" in contemplation, she "sees the Sun of Righteousness." She is now confirmed in the mystic life; the irrevocable marriage vows are made between her spirit and her God. At this point she can "see the Beloved," but "cannot yet come into Him," says Richard... In Richard's "third stage," however, that of union, or wedlock, it is clear that the soul enters upon the "Unitive Way." She has passed the stages of ecstatic and significnant events, and is initiated into the Life. She is "deified," "passes utterly into God, and is glorified in Him": is transfigured, he says, by immediate contact with the Divine Substance, into an utterly different quality of being... In the fourth degree, the Bride who has been so greatly honoured, caught up to such unspeakable delight, sinks her own will and "is humiliated below herself." She accepts the pains and duties in the place of the raptures of love; and becomes a source, a "parent" of fresh spiritual life.[111]

Another insight flashed through. One of my patterns viewed vividly. As God called me forth at each new stage of development in my life, the men in it said no, they couldn't go any further. I had to go on. Each time the death of the old form of our relationship naturally occurred due to our own growth, my masculine side broke away, rather than transcend it. Once again the challenge appeared. Could Russ and I meet this split head on and transcend it? An image was shown reminding me of the last moments of my father's death. I once again saw him saying no to the change that was coming until those last moments before his physical death. Then in the final stage I saw a quieting as if the struggle had ceased and in that moment the Light came and absorbed my father. In order to transcend this old pattern, we would have to stay focused on God—then and only then would everything fall into place. If we loose our focus, it will scramble and we will feel the struggle. If we maintain that focus, a radiant light will appear and we will be absorbed into it.

As I examined the pattern by following thoughts as they arose, I could readily see my false self pop out and flit around trying

---

[111] Underhill, Evelyn, *Mysticism*, E. P. Dutton & Co., New York, 1961, pp. 139–140.

to say all the right things, trying to follow the action back to its source. A Voice said, "You get caught in the doing of it, instead of the being of it. The doing of it creates the split—the experience, the experiencer—the subject, the object. The being of it removes that split. The subject and object become one in all its varied expressions."

Just before receiving Shaktipat from Guruji, my eyes found this quote by Swami Vivekananda that seemed to leap out at me reminding me of the events at hand:

> You have now to build your life on this great ideal of personal service. Through that, all the other ideals will gradually manifest in life. Obedience to the Guru without questioning, and strict observance of Brahmacharya—that is the secret of success.[112]

Was that just a coincidence? Sometimes when God talks to you it's not a whisper! And so the whisper would grow louder still in the days that followed with Russ's arrival. The next few days were paradoxical in many ways spinning us deep into issues collectively held by men and women and profound in their final result. I guess you could say that we were invited into the rose garden and discovered our thorns. If we were to enter a spiritual marriage we must do it consciously. The following passages from my journal capture the struggle and allude to the magic afoot.

## DECEMBER 15, 1991

I've been to Bombay to meet Russ and returned. We've been talking and processing our feelings since the first moment. We've tried to stay open and honest in that expression not wanting to suppress them or deny them. Some days have been harder than others, but in all we persevere. I've discovered another pit of rage and anger that was hiding deep inside. The catalyst is the feeling tone and the response of the group to *our* situation. When

---

[112] Vivekananda, *Hanuman Chalisa*, Sri Ramakrishna Math, Madras, India.

celibacy is discussed it seems to generate feelings that focus on rescuing Russ in a sympathetic fashion. Statements like "He looks like he's hurting so much." "He's going through so much change all at once." I know all that is true, but what about the other side of the equation. Then when I have those feelings, I feel guilt. When I follow the feelings back, I run into a collective imbalance in our culture in which women are *expected* to hold the suffering, so we have babies and tend to families many times all alone. Yet, in the old paradigm of my parent's generation, men were cared for and served. I remember reading a statement by Vicki Noble in which she reviewed a study she had run which showed that men's greatest fear was being consumed by a woman and women's greatest fear was that they might be raped or killed trying to get to their cars in the parking lot. What a huge gap in the way we experience the world. No wonder there is so much trouble in our ability to communicate with one another. My anger stirs from experiencing the denial in our culture about such a dangerous imbalance. The thing I am struggling with now is finding it at the spiritual level. Somehow Russ and I have to find a way to hold what is happening to us understanding that spirit is bringing that which will stimulate our own development each individually. If we allow ourselves to fall into old victim spaces, we will loose our focus and fall into confusion. When once you begin to step outside of consensus reality the challenges are the same. We must make this step with integrity. Today I'm just going to accept the rage, anger and sadness wanting to wash through. I want to try to stay in my witness self so that I can observe when I project those feelings rather than own them. I must also use discrimination when those projections come at me from others, weighing their validity and giving them back if they don't belong. In my dream last night, I had a baby, but I was confused in the dream about whether I had fed it or not. I must honor the new piece growing in me and protect and nurture it so it can grow in a healthy manner. After all, honoring the feminine wherever she resides is our quest for planetary healing. Our focus on the masculine has developed that side of our nature, but in order to have balance, we must focus equally on the feminine. It is not necessary to place these dynamics in polarized positions. The need to compete should be neutralized. How can we do that? By listening to Rumi:

Out beyond ideas of wrongdoing and rightdoing, there is
a field. I'll meet you there.[113]

## DECEMBER 15, 1991
## (LATER IN THE AFTERNOON)

When we arrived at Guruji's we discovered he had fallen out of
bed during the night, hurting his neck and shoulders. He was
in considerable pain. Ironically, the area affected was the same
area that I had been struggling with for over a month, so I knew
intimately the pain he had to endure. My heart opened to him
as I watched this evening as this incredibly compassionate man,
sick and in pain, gave darshan to people as they continued to
come. His level of selflessness was so obvious I could do nothing
but weep, not in sadness, but in gratitude and appreciation for
learning from one such as he. After a while we all left the room
and went into the living room to wait. An orthopedic surgeon
was coming to examine him and determine if there had been
a fracture. To our relief the doctor didn't seem to think there
was one, but insisted we keep him still and quiet for several days
before taking him to the hospital for an X-ray. It was time for us
to leave so each disciple went in to receive darshan. As I came
up, Guruji turned his face toward me and said, "Jyoti, do you
want to get married?" A shock wave seemed to rush through me.
Emotions seemed to stir, yet go numb all at the same time. My
mind couldn't think. It was like the world had stopped. I said,
"But Guruji, Russ and I don't want to do anything to interfere
with our spiritual progress or the Work." He said, "You must pray
all the time and say sankalpa. The difficulties will be removed.
Don't worry, be happy. If you want, we can get a priest. It is
up to you." I said, "If we marry, it won't take us away from our
Work?" He said, "No, other saints have married and produced
beautiful works." He went on to name them. Waves of energy
seemed to flood throughout my whole system. The thing which
seemed to emphasize the process even more was experiencing this
lovely man speaking to me of such things as he lay so ill. It seemed

---

[113] Moyne, John and Coleman, Barks, *Open Secret, Versions of Rumi*, Threshold
Books, Putney, Vermont, 1984. p. 3, section 158.

to set a paradoxical state in action. I asked him if he was going to be allright. He said, "Don't worry, all is for the best. I will be fine." I said, "I love you." He said, "I know." With that a stillness seemed to penetrate the room.

Russ and I left and sat in the living room. His action had pierced my heart, waves of gratitude welled up and over. I could feel HIS presence near. Suddenly, someone turned on the television and there on the screen was Michael Jackson singing about God's presence always being with you no matter where you walk. As he sang I watched an angel circling the periphery. As the last part of the song ended, the angel descended and wrapped its wings around him until the image of two became one. The image enacted the experience of visits from my Beloved piercing my heart even deeper. It was too significant and synchronistic, shaking my system to its very core. The television was turned off and silence fell loudly over the room. When God is speaking the entire gestalt becomes animated and is used as a vehicle for communication. I couldn't speak. Neither could Russ. We just looked at each other, but we could not speak. Russ had been working on his question about all this for several days. Obviously, he had gotten his answer. The state of Brahmachari was not going to change, so our marriage vows would be a spiritual commitment to the Work. We both said goodnight in a state of shock. Guruji's impeccable timing continues to amaze me.

## DECEMBER 16, 1991

We awoke and after breakfast talked and processed what was coming up for each of us. So many feelings had been touched. Our fears and our heartfelt commitments seemed locked in battle. At lunch we discovered that a Brahman priest had just happened by Guruji's that morning and arrangements had been made for him to come back at four to perform the ceremony if we wanted. In the old tradition a couple was married by the priest in the temples in front of the icon (visual representation of God). Vows were spoken and flowers were placed around the necks of each of the couple and the deity. Dileepji suggested this as the form for our ceremony. The ceremony was to be performed in front of Guruji at his bedside with Anandi Ma assisting. When I voiced my concern for Guruji's health, I was told that he had reached a state where all can change around him, but his state of consciousness remains the same.

We agreed and preparations were hastily started. One of the Indian women went with us to buy the traditional clothing. The right jewelry and accessories were either bought or borrowed. By four o'clock a complete transformation had taken place. I was amazed. When we were brought to Guruji, he looked at us and said, "You look like a princess and a prince."

Anandi Ma and Guruji sat on either side of us with the priest in the front. A small group of people gathered in the small bedroom and the ceremony was performed. Afterwards, Anandi Ma took us to each elder in the room. We bowed to their feet, as they both gave us their blessings and a present of money to represent the prosperity to come. She then gave us her blessings saying, "Remember this is a spiritual marriage. You have much work to do." The kitchen then got busy serving food and drinks. What a joyous day!

Afterwards we returned to the ashram. Russ went to his quarters and me to mine. The love of God we shared transcended all else. This certainly was a different way to spend a honeymoon. A great peace resided.

At breakfast the next morning, we were told that one of the staff from the ashram had died. He had been ill for a couple of weeks. I was struck by how close birth and death always work. Our marriage had represented a birth of a new phase of our life and our work. In addition, I had started my period, which made me "an untouchable" for the next three days. Russ could not sit next to me or even touch me, amplifying the vows we had taken the day before and reminding us we had entered terrain not traveled by us before. The impeccable timing of the wedding ceremony re-emphasized and accentuated the hand of fate involved in our lives. For you see, either one of the events just described would not have allowed a wedding to take place for several weeks. Since our stay in India was coming to a close, Guruji had selected the only window prior to our departure.

Heyoehkah energy is an energy used by Native Americans as a great teacher and healer. It is an energy that uses opposites to stimulate awareness. It is a trickster that serves like a slap on the back to realign your point of focus. In this way the Heyoehkah energy had actively spun us 'round requiring us to look more closely at all the dynamics at work. God had shaken us both, so we could more consciously walk through this portal in time. We had had to confront not only our hidden agendas and personality fears, but affirm our intention and focus. A deep surrender had pierced our hearts and opened us to new beginnings. What all this would mean, we did not know. Our commitment to the journey had been tested and a new gratitude to service of the Mystery forged.

## CONCLUSION

My stay in India had been a time of synthesis, a time of viewing old patterns as they had been tested and transcended, and a time of animating the new patterns resulting from such deep introspective work. Obviously, the cognitive understanding of the events of India would be far reaching in my life. I would come to see that my return to the States would also bring a period of regeneration for my body. There were times when I would have visions in which I would see a large shimmering etheric image of Guruji standing in front of an image of me. I would step into Guruji and as I did an etheric fluid clear in color would pour out of myself from the area midway between the solar plexus and the heart. It would continue to flow until the space between Guruji and me had completely filled up, forming a new body around me. Was this a view of what was to come? I had come to understand while in India that although the process I was in was intense at times, it was but the preparation for the Work that was to follow.

Guruji's predictions about my health would come to pass. Instead of watching the life force leave, the ability to feel the strength of that life force filling my body brings much joy. I had learned a lot about our culture and its bias toward illness: now we would learn in a similar fashion about celibacy and the subtle ways our culture impregnates each of us with regard to our sexual identities and roles. His predictions of my preparations for my life's work would further challenge me to share the deep mystical states that have brought health and well being back into my life. I truly believe it is time for the sharing. I recall an incident that happened in June, 1992, at a medicine gathering I was assisting with in Arizona. Prior to the four-day ritual I arranged to meet with a Cherokee elder who is well known among the indigenous people for her work in the world for peace. Her teachings are universal and therefore highly regarded by many other esteemed spiritual leaders. When we met I told her I had received in meditation a message that I was to meet with her and share the story of my belly. I was also to convey what I had been told by Spirit—that there was a tribe of us and that it was time for us to begin to meet. To my surprise she smiled and said, "Do you need me to validate your story? If so, yes, it is true what you say and I too have such a belly. I have already begun to meet the women of our tribe as I travel around the world. The energy we hold is that of peace. There will come a time when a small group of us will be called to meet in Central America. We will form a small circle and sit with our bellies turned out, our backs forming the inner circle. We will begin to chant and pray moving the energy from our bellies down into the earth and back again through our bellies.  For in so doing, we will awaken that same energy of peace held in the belly of the earth, allowing it to be birthed." I responded, "But I'm never quite sure how to speak of such things with others. What should I say?" She said, "Come we shall call the gathering together and tell the story!" To my surprise she walked right outside and after all had gathered she began to tell the story of a time that is upon us in which a tribe of women have come to earth carrying the energy of peace. She reminded us that it is a time to honor them for the gift they help birth. Another circles closes!

What I've come to realize is that each of us is awakening with our own individual role in the divine plan. A great shift is in the making and each of us is being offered a chance to participate— some will do so consciously and others will do so unconsciously. Needless to say, evolution will march on. Though the crisis may feel overwhelming, the opportunities are as equally prevalent. I'm reminded of a story told by Muktananda:

Is it possible to develop will power and is this a useful thing to do?

To develop your will power, you must first learn to completely still your mind, to empty it of all thoughts. If your mind is distracted by all sorts of things, what will you be able to do? Your will must be exercised in the pursuit of good things, as well. You must have full faith in your own Self. You should put all the energy of all your being towards the particular aim which you have in mind. I will illustrate this with a story from the *Naradiya Purana*. You know, the sparrow is a peculiar bird. It will do whatever it wants to. Once a couple of sparrows were wandering along the seashore. She was expecting, and she laid her egg right on the beach. They were very happy and started dancing with joy, leaving the egg there. A wave came and washed the egg away. The sparrows became very angry. First, they politely requested the sea to return their egg. "You are very great, O Sea, and we are very ordinary birds. This was our first child and we had it after a long time. Please return that egg to us."

But the sea did not respond, so they began cursing. That, too, was in vain. So they got very angry and decided to empty the entire sea, and began emptying it on the shore. How much water could they possibly remove? But it was their firm decision to empty the sea.

Other birds tried to make them understand that it was impossible. They would not understand. On the contrary, they became more determined. They said, "We don't want to hear anything like that." The couple got angry. "Go away, you useless creatures. You don't understand us," they told them. And they continued working, dipping their wings and beaks, removing water.

Then Narada, the divine seer, happened to pass by and saw this. He also tried to make them understand that millions of sparrows wouldn't be able to empty the sea. They told Narada also, "We don't want to hear anything. If you want to help us, come and help make the sea dry."

Seeing their decision, Narada decided to help them. He thought. "They will die if they persist like this, poor things." He was a very intelligent and wise saint. He said, "I'll help you. After some time you'll get your egg back."

He blessed them and went straight to Garuda, the king of birds. Garuda was Lord Vishnu's vehicle and he was very strong. If he collided with a mountain, the mountain would crumble. Narada said, "You are the great king of birds. You should go and see how unhappy your subjects are."

Garuda said, "What has happened?"

Narada said, "The sea has taken away the egg of the sparrows. The sea is so proud he will not listen to them. But you are so powerful—next to your beak the power of the sea is nothing. All three worlds are scared of you. You are the servant of Lord Vishnu. Go and tell the sea to return the egg to them."

Garuda understood the matter and went straight to the sea. The sea opened up at the touch of his powerful wings. All the sea animals became terrified. The sea became frightened and wondered why Garuda was so angry. The Lord of the sea folded his hands and came to Garuda and asked him what was the matter. Garuda said, "Why have you taken the egg of my subjects? Where is it? Return it at once!"

So the sea was searched and the egg was found and returned to the sparrows. This is the result of strong will power, of resolute effort. If you want to reach the highest, you must work hard.[114]


## REFLECTIONS


Looking back I realize that Russ and I have been like the two sparrows. We have gone to the sea of unconsciousness and continued to dive into it looking for our originality. We have had to go up against our culture's bias and judgements, but our deep desire for wholeness created such a deep yearning that it propelled us on even when our personas screamed in protest. Clarissa Pinkola Estes explains in her book *Women Who Run With the Wolves* that those men that were called into the feminine initations at Eleusis had taken on the tasks and travails of female learning in order to find their psychic queens and psychic offspring.[115] She goes on to explain that the animus enters its own seven-year initiation so that

---

[114] Muktananda, *Satsang with Baba*, Shree Gurudev Ashram, Ganeshpuri, 1974, pp. 50–52.

[115] Estes, Clarissa Pinkola, *Women Who Run with the Wolves*, Ballantine Books, New York, 1992, p. 452.

what the woman has learned will be reflected not only in her inner soul but will also be written upon her and acted upon outwardly as well. So it seems to have been these last few years with Russ in our relationship. We have both come to know that our lives have been dedicated to the service of the feminine face of God, for it is through her that a new world will be birthed. For wasn't it through Mary that Jesus came among us?

I once read that the most unselfish act an individual can perform is to reach a state of self-realization, for in that act seven generations before you and seven generations behind you reap the healing. Why then does our western culture resist the living word of Christ? Why does it demand we only read about such happenings, rather than incorporate the teachings into our lives in such a way that self-realization is seen as the ultimate expression of our wholeness, not an inflated idea that is unattainable but to a very few? Why do most of the stories shared come to us only through the eyes of our male disciples? If we are to walk in the beauty way, the path of balance, don't we need to encourage the spiritual development of our feminine side as well? Don't we need to understand more about creation as Matthew Fox professes? For it is out of that side of God's nature that we are all born.

Though the material I have shared may prove challenging, I know I share what many others today are experiencing. We live in a time when new myths are to be born; a time of expanding the envelope of reality to include new possibilities; a time when if we refuse to evole into the next state of awareness our physical reality as we know it will not survive. Evolution will march on, so we are left with the option of choice. As in the individual process, we can choose to resist what the unconscious is presenting and meet the destructive side of its nature, or we can embrace the change that is happening and celebrate it's birth.

In an article entitled *Coyote's Eyes: Native Cognition Styles* Terry Tafoya quotes Christopher Fry: "We have wasted Paradox and Mystery on you, when all you wanted was Cause and Effect." He goes on to say, "If one checks on the origins of the terms

»Paradox« and »Mystery,« one discovers that paradox means
beyond or contrary to opinion, and that mystery means to close
(the lips or eyes). And this is very much a part of Native American
teaching: that one's knowledge must be obtained by the individual,
regardless of what current beliefs may be, and the gaining of that
knowledge does not come from only listening to elders, or seeing
what others have done."[116]

My guidance has encouraged me to enter the mandala traveling
to each of the four directions to obtain the teachings inherent there.
Reflecting back on my journey, I have done just that; not out of
a conscious intention to do so, but out of a surrendering to Shakti.
In that surrendering I healed the relationship with myself. In order
for the healing to be well balanced, I have discovered that I must
be willing to not only clear the psychological patterns, but develop
discipline through spiritual practice. In order for integration to be
complete both included the body as each step was revealed and
integrated. As I entered the inner labyrinth I found myself in the
North, the place of the teachers; all those that have been and all
those who are to come. Guided by the teachings of Carl Jung
I studied the way of the dream and discovered a rich world of
mythology and the spiritual teachings of various cultures. I began
to realize that if I allowed my own inner authority to take the lead
my education became more meaningful with a depth increasingly
revealed. In the West,the place of dreams; my teacher was found
in the Sun Dancer called Tigre who amplified my need to reconnect
to my Cherokee roots and remember the teachings of my people.
It was in this place that I began to understand the importance
of ritual. For through ritual we create container so that Spirit
can dance. Shakti continued to call me 'round the hoop to the
direction of the South, the place of childhood innocence. It was
here that I would learn from the medicine plants another level
of surrender. Their teachings would enliven an ancient way of

---

[116] Tafoya, Terry, "Coyote's Eyes: Native Cognition Styles," in the *Journal of
American Indian Education*, Special Issue, Aug. 1989, p. 36.

healing and prepare my body for deep levels of purification For in the closing gate of the mandala, that in the East, the teachings would be about death; death of preconceived ideas; death of existing patterns that had ruled my life; death as birth. For this is the place of illumination—the doorway into the Mystery. She had called me to her bosom to drink of her wisdom but the stilling of the mind into the heart was required before such emptiness allowed for the filling. I came to realize that anything is possible if only we can suspend our thinking long enough to see what the Mystery will present. It is in such stillness that God speaks. My initiation here would be by a man and a woman, Dhyanyogi and Anandi Ma. They gave me a new name, Jyoti, and sent me toward the core. Once one has visited each of the four directions, it is then time to enter the core, standing in your center being who you are. I remember once when Spirit spoke saying, "You don't have to do anymore, Jyoti, you just have to Be." My immediate response was, "Yea, but how do you do that?" I have come to learn that in the states of samadhi, one is in a state of Being. It is in that state that we begin to reclaim our originality.

Joseph Campbell said that if you follow your bliss, your bliss will follow. I have found that to be true, for when I look back it was that following that led me to a life that is healing daily; a life that is not dead in old form, but alive in the moment. A deep faith is forged in the individual's inherent ability to heal one's self. In that quest I have come full circle to reclaim something I had lost—my soul. If enough of us acknowledge that yearning and reconnect with what Clarissa Estes calls the Wild Woman and Robert Blye calls the Wild Man our instincts will lead us home into the center of the mandala, to our original state of wholeness. In that state we can again manifest balance on the planet and love can become a state of consciousness shared by all rather than hate, fear and violence. It's up to us to choose!

### ❀ DharmaGaia

→ is a small Publishing House specializing in Oriental cultures, Philosophy, Psychology, Ecology and New Science.
→ Among our Czech authors are well-known specialists from Philosophical Faculty of the Charles University, and the Oriental Institute of the Czech Academy of Sciences.
→ Recent authors and publications include among others Vedic Hymns, Upanishads, Buddha's Suttas and Jatakas from Pali Canon, The Diamond Sutra, Shantideva, Lao-tse, Jiddu Krishnamurti, H. H. The Dalai Lama, Indian, Chinese, Korean, and Japanese poetry, Aldous Huxley, Timothy Leary, Peter Furst, Terence McKenna.
→ We publish in all European languages.


### ❀ DharmaGaia

Uhelný trh 1, 110 00 Prague 1
Czech Republic
phone/fax: +420-2-2423 8551
e-mail: dharmagaia@post.cz
icq#: 13368926